Telling the Story in the Data

Telling the Story in the Data

Narrative Writing for Doctoral Students and Qualitative Researchers

EDITED BY

Caroline Heller

Foreword by David T. Hansen

TEACHERS COLLEGE PRESS
TEACHERS COLLEGE | COLUMBIA UNIVERSITY
NEW YORK AND LONDON

Published by Teachers College Press,® 1234 Amsterdam Avenue, New York, NY 10027

Copyright © 2023 by Teachers College, Columbia University

Front cover design by Edwin Kuo. Illustration by Omelchenko / Shutterstock.

All rights reserved. No part of this publication may be reproduced or transmitted in any form or by any means, electronic or mechanical, including photocopy, or any information storage and retrieval system, without permission from the publisher. For reprint permission and other subsidiary rights requests, please contact Teachers College Press, Rights Dept.: tcpressrights @tc.columbia.edu

Library of Congress Cataloging-in-Publication Data is available at loc.gov

ISBN 978-0-8077-6734-4 (paper)
ISBN 978-0-8077-6735-1 (hardcover)
ISBN 978-0-8077-8122-7 (ebook)

Printed on acid-free paper
Manufactured in the United States of America

Contents

Foreword *David T. Hansen*   vii

Acknowledgments   xi

Introduction: The Seminar That Inspired This Book *Caroline Heller*   1

Seminar Syllabus: Narrative Writing for Qualitative Researchers, Spring, 2019   7

1. **Invitations and Permissions: Consider the Meatball**   19
   Krysta Betit

2. **Before, Between, and Beyond: Communicating Meaning**   24
   Garo Saraydarian (followed by drafts of paper by Garo)

3. **Finding the Story in the Data**   39
   Denise Mytko (followed by drafts of papers by Denise and Thelma Goldberg)

4. **The River Is Wide**   51
   Rebecca Redlon (followed by drafts of paper by Rebecca)

5. **Meaning Through Journeying**   65
   Krysta Betit (followed by art work and drafts of chapter by Krysta)

6. **Representational Adequacy: Bringing My Scene to Life**   78
   Jeanne Lima

7. **Finding Narrative Gifts in Film**   89
   Allison Horváth-Tucker

8. Number Our Days: A Study of Community — 95
   Thelma Goldberg (followed by drafts of paper by Garo Saraydarian)

9. Sweetgrass: A Chance to Feel — 112
   Avigail Shimshoni

10. Envisioning and Embracing — 124
    Kat Marsh (followed by drafts of paper by Kat)

11. Wrong Question and Finding and Writing the Angle of an Interview — 145
    Kat Marsh (followed by drafts of paper by Kat)

12. Circle of Trust: Vulnerabilities Carefully Rendered — 160
    Rebecca Redlon and Garo Saraydarian

APPENDIXES OF SEMINAR HANDOUTS

Appendix A: Revision Worksheet — 171

Appendix B: Taming the Chaos of Your Data — 173

Appendix C: Thoughts on Characterization — 177

Appendix D: Sentiment and Sentimentality — 179

Appendix E: Objective Correlative: T. S. Eliot — 181

Index — 183

About the Contributors — 187

Foreword

This one-of-a-kind book tells the story of a writing seminar for doctoral students taught by Caroline Heller. Readers familiar with Caroline's work know she is a gifted and wondrous writer. Readers will now learn that the same can be said about her pedagogy. I have facilitated many a doctoral seminar on writing and have studied numerous texts on writing up one's data. But I have never encountered a scholarly book that both portrays and enacts the nitty-gritty of narrative composition in such a comprehensive manner. The book invites us into a dynamic writers' studio, where we witness Caroline's doctoral students transforming before our very eyes as they slowly, unevenly, yet progressively develop their writing prowess. It is as if we become silent participants ourselves, engaging secondhand in each of the 12 seminar sessions recounted, chapter by chapter, in the text. I believe every qualitative researcher, whether novice or veteran, who follows this account to its end will be powerfully motivated to reimagine their own approaches to writing.

The seminar at the center of the book is entitled Narrative Writing for Qualitative Researchers. Caroline conceived the course as a response, in part, to her own doctoral experience. While appreciating what she learned from her faculty about the nuts and bolts of research, as well as about the value of theory, she found herself turning to writers such as John Berger, Annie Dillard, Barry Lopez, E. B. White, and others in order to come to grips with two time-honored questions of representation: (1) How does the researcher do justice in their prose to the reality of the people whose lives they seek to understand? and (2) How does the researcher do justice to the reality of their own deepest sense of the truth of things? Caroline wanted her own doctoral students to be able to engage both of these questions systematically. As she remarks, the seminar reflects "the belief that it's high time we find a place in doctoral education to tell stories about how *hard* it can be to tell stories and to help our students find pathways to their own sense of representational success" (emphasis in original).

Caroline brings to the seminar her own extensive writer's experience, including in her superb books *Until We Are Strong Together: Women Writers in the Tenderloin* (Teachers College Press, 1997) and *Reading Claudius* (Random House, 2015), where she encountered questions of representation firsthand. Her syllabus, which is included at the start of the book, features a wide array of highly regarded writers and qualitative researchers, as well as some documentary films (along the lines of visual anthropology). In addition to these assigned readings, the syllabus details the specific writing assignments with which her doctoral students engage, each intended to develop technical skill while motivating imaginal vision. The 12 chapters in the book, all composed by Caroline's doctoral students, then take up, consecutively, the 12 sessions of the seminar. The authors address writerly concepts such as "front story/backstory" and "wide lens/narrow lens." They examine questions of timing, structure, organization, and flow, as well as what to include and what to exclude. They wrestle with the differences between expressing sentiment and sentimental writing—the former a truly artful challenge; the latter an indulgence all too easy to stumble into. They wonder about the meaning of restraint, of why less can be more, and about why every sentence must matter and *how* to make it matter.

These chapters are marked by a compelling sense of honesty and frankness. The writers blow no smoke and hide behind no veils. They share their fallibility and vulnerability—which, of course, every serious writer confronts—but they are not self-abnegating. They evince a seriousness that is never heavy-handed but recalls the wonderful charge the writer Italo Calvino (1978) gave to his peers—to seek "lightness" in their writing, not to be confused with light-heartedness, but a kind of prose that does not weigh on the reader but buoys them through the movement of reading and contemplating. A quiet sense of confidence slowly grows as the authors share their writing from session to session, as they refine the arts of criticism and of receiving criticism, and as they parse the seminar readings and documentary films for truths about the writing craft.

As mentioned, a distinctive feature of the book is how readers are brought in as witnesses to the authors' growth as writers. "If I am to draw a conclusion about narrative writing from our first class," one contributor, Krysta Betit, writes, "it might be this: to write is to love something enough that you want it to live on." (p. 46) Before our eyes, she and her peers make the turn from a clinical to an ethical orientation. They experience why writing about others can lead to *caring*, not just for those particular others but for the human condition we all share. To consider a second example, in Chapter 12, Rebecca Redlon and Garo Saraydarian, referring to the indispensable work of revision, remark, "What was before, at best, a task we were better at preaching to our own students than following ourselves, at worst, an excuse for procrastination that blocked further growth, became an act of re*visioning*" (emphasis in original; p. 256). We see the authors coming to grips with why refined perception and to-the-point prose can mutually inform one another.

No reader of contemporary qualitative research can fail to notice how thin a line it can be between engaging substantively with reality and getting caught up in a labyrinth of words. The authors illuminate this state of affairs by examining in fine-grained detail the relationship between description and what is described.

Echoing their teacher's remark noted above, the authors demonstrate how truly difficult it can be to get things right—or as right as possible. They show us the oil-and-water difference between "moving words around" and actually *saying something*, and how terribly easy it is to be seduced into the former exercise. The authors echo the summons to the writer to foreground reality and to look for words in that disciplined spirit. For the qualitative researcher, this reality encompasses people and what they do and say, wherein *their* words—unlike the writer's—ipso facto take on a material, substantive quality. The writer must earn their words' substance by putting them in the service of reality.

Michel de Montaigne, the 16th-century French essayist, sheds still-timely light on the difference between "words, just words" and expressing the actual stuff of the world. Montaigne is often credited with inventing the now-familiar form of writing known as the essay. *Essay* derives from the French *essayer*, meaning "to try," "to attempt," "to endeavor." For Montaigne, the essay is a trial of ideas, thoughts, and questions. It is an ever-unfinished experiment in gaining the maximum precision and clarity possible while featuring a lively and fresh narrative voice. Time and again, Montaigne finds himself writing about his writing. Often in the same breath, he comments on the styles of writing in his era, and identifies what he regards as major and frustratingly repetitive flaws: mistaking words for things and eloquence for truth. He urges writers to heed reality, which he summarizes with the French term *choses*, denoting "things," yet in a decidedly un-thing-like manner. For Montaigne, the concept of things (*choses*) encompasses what people say and do, events and interactions, and objects of all sorts. He argues, while also demonstrating in his own prose, that if the writer learns to attend tenaciously to things, the right words for expressing their meaning are more likely to come.

His essays (1994/1575) are rich with aphorisms to this effect: "Provided that our student be well furnished with *things*, words will follow only too easily: if they do not come easily, then he can drag them out slowly" [from his essay on educating children]"; "Once you have mastered the things the words will come freely" [from the Roman writer Horace], which does not mean they will emerge straightforwardly but at least will not be blocked by the writer's lack of scrupulous attention to things; "When things have taken hold of the mind, the words come crowding forth" [from the Roman writer Seneca]; "There are authors who are led by the beauty of some attractive word to write what they never intended" [also Seneca]. Montaigne's own conclusion is: "I myself am more ready to distort a fine saying in order to patch it on to me than to distort the thread of my argument to go in search of one. It is, on the contrary, for words to serve and to follow. . . . I want *things* to dominate, so filling the thoughts of the hearer that he does not even remember the words." It is fascinating to observe Heller's doctoral students come to grips, in their own idioms and styles, with what it is to write of things—that is, of reality.

In the final chapter of the book, Redlon and Saraydarian also note: "The truth of the matter is that good instruction takes as much thoughtful planning and tinkering as the strongest piece of writing" (p. 256). Upon reading this, the reader is likely to realize, perhaps for the first time, that Caroline's presence as teacher has been both on- and off-stage. The authors refer to her directly, though very briefly, at a number of telling moments, making clear how personally engaged she was with each student's evolving writing over the course of the semester. Indeed, one contributor describes her as "an approachable juggernaut," a splendid term of art that rings true to my own experience of Caroline as one of the most enthusiastic teachers and admirers of good prose I have ever known. But there are long stretches where the teacher seems in the background as the authors foreground their struggles, confusions, insights, and accomplishments as writers.

It seems to me the doctoral students' increasingly intense and focused interaction with one another's writing speaks volumes about the trust Caroline helped establish in the setting. As several authors remind us, to share one's writing with others can be an anxiety-provoking, vulnerable experience. It requires real delicacy to learn to comment critically on another's writing: to be both honest yet also respectful of dignity. It is moving to see how over the course of the seminar, the authors learned not only to trust one another but to become that much more eager for one another's frankest criticism. The reader detects Caroline's steady presence, and becomes that much more aware of how much work for the teacher goes into structuring and implementing a course like this. Yet every dedicated teacher knows in their bones how profoundly rewarding such an investment of self can be.

At several places in this most unusual of texts, the writers refer to Barbara Myerhoff's beautiful ethnographic book and film about an elderly Jewish community in Los Angeles, California, entitled *Number Our Days*. Those words from the Bible evoke the value of cherishing the limited time people have together. The authors of *Telling the Story in the Data* seem to be moved by the dictum "number our words"; that is, bring to the act of qualitative research writing all the seriousness, grace, and gratitude the writer can muster. I thank Caroline and her students for making their singular tale available to us all.

—David T. Hansen
Teachers College, Columbia University
June 28, 2022

REFERENCES

Calvino, I. (1978). *Invisible cities* (W. Weaver, Trans.). Harcourt Brace Jovanovich.
Montaigne, M. M. (1994). On educating children. In M. A. Screech (Ed. & Trans.), *The essays: A selection* (pp. 37–73). Penguin. (Original work published 1575)

Acknowledgments

Krysta Betit: Thank you to Ed and Zel, Laura and Zelia for their love and encouragement.
Thelma Goldberg: Thank you to my classmates and Caroline for their support and encouragement.
Caroline Heller: I thank my family, particularly Eileen Ball, for their love and encouragement.
Kat Marsh: I thank my family and the Lesley Community for their support.
Denise Mytko: In recognition of my Manni, Professor Heller, and our community of coauthors.
Rebecca Redlon: In gratitude to my mother and all my grandmothers.
Garo Saraydarian: Thanks to Jen, Ben, and Emmy, and my classmates who became friends through the writing of this book.
Avigail Shimshoni: I thank Nitzan, Lior, my parents, close family and friends, for joining me in this journey in curiosity.

We thank Kristy Donnelly, Che Madyun, and Jessica Minahan, valued members of the class, but whose schedules precluded their working on this book; we have missed their insightful contributions.

The contributors wish to express their abiding gratitude to Caroline Heller for inviting them to be at the center of this project and guiding them to discover meaning as "the fruit of this intimacy."

Telling the Story in the Data

Introduction: The Seminar That Inspired This Book

Caroline Heller

In the summer of 1986, just a few weeks before I began my journey as a doctoral student in education at the University of California, Berkeley, I read an essay by the art critic/novelist John Berger that aimed to explain the process of making a small wooden bird that seemed to be flying.

". . . Looking at it," Berger (1985a) wrote:

> one is surprised by how well wood becomes bird . . . this man-made object provokes a kind of astonishment: how on earth was it made? . . . anyone unfamiliar with the technique wants to take the dove in one's hands and examine it closely to discover the secret which lies behind its making . . . a piece of wood that has *become* a bird. (p. 6)

As invariably happens in the lives of doctoral students, I soon had little time to read anything that wasn't required for my courses; Berger's charming essay soon gathered dust on my nightstand atop other predoctoral readings that I labeled *get back to*.

Fast forward a couple of years to an evening out to dinner in San Francisco. There, I spotted a flyer stapled to a telephone pole announcing a women's writing workshop that was to begin meeting in San Francisco's Tenderloin neighborhood. My doctoral interests focused on language, literacy, and culture, and a community writing program in a neighborhood I knew only for its high crime rate and poverty excited me. I attended the first workshop meeting, and for the next 3 years rarely missed one. Soon, my "scholarly" aim was to understand the lives of the women who attended, the levels of education and support the writing group offered them, and ultimately tell the story of the Tenderloin Women Writers Workshop for my dissertation (Heller, 1992, 1997). To my happiness, I was welcomed as the group's ethnographer, and for those years, I took voluminous field notes, interviewed participants and community members, and drafted preliminary portraits of the writers and the workshop meetings. I was filled with new questions that had never been addressed by my doctoral courses. How would I transform the living people I met each week in the Tenderloin into written words? How would I describe the complexity and humanity of the women, the workshop, and the Tenderloin itself in language that resisted reductions and clichés? How would I develop a narrative voice that could engage the public and the disciplines that inform education in the crucial questions that my research evoked?

My doctoral courses, successful at teaching me formal methods of educational research and the expository and conceptual skills required of literature reviews, had never focused on the challenges of narrative writing that researchers, particularly those pursuing qualitative methods, also face: Once one has analyzed and interpreted data and come to care deeply about the people "living" in that data, how does one transform what one has witnessed in the field into an authentic representation of life being lived? How does one tell the story one's data evokes?

At some point during my dissertation writing, I rediscovered the Berger essay in my long-ignored pile of "extracurricular" readings gathering dust. I realized that Berger's words, ostensibly about the secrets involved in making a wooden bird appear to fly, were about all representational challenges, including the ones I faced. While I'd deeply valued my research professors and those who had taught me the theories that framed my field, it was now Berger and writers like him, devoted to questions of representation and storytelling, who became my essential new teachers.

During the time I spent writing my dissertation, in addition to learning from well-known writers like Berger (Annie Dillard, Robert Caro, Walter Benjamin, E. B. White, and Barry Lopez also became my writerly advisors and later on from amazing writing teachers like Carol Spindel, Sven Birkerts, and Martha Cooley), I learned about writing from the Tenderloin women participating in my research. When I shared my portraits of the workshop *in* the workshop, they critiqued my work with the same tender directness with which they critiqued each other's. Mary TallMountain, whose experience and talent made her the natural leader of the workshop, always cut to the chase. "Caroline, you use smells too much," she told me when I shared a scene I'd written that mentioned a workshop member baking lasagna for the group's lunch. "Take out every third smell!" And in response to another piece I shared, workshop member Salima Rashida told me in no uncertain terms, "Your descriptions are too pretty. Don't tie a bow! Ask if rather than the bow something else might like to be there." Here were teachers from the wider world and from right here in the neighborhood I was "studying" who opened me to the secrets Berger alluded to when he asked how a piece of wood transformed into a living bird. As Berger (1985) also wrote in that essay, "To make a fine bird takes considerable skill" (p. 5). There was craft I had to (and wanted to) learn. Writing well was hard. In addition to uncovering craft secrets, I needed to practice (and practice and practice and practice) my new craft before I would even begin to feel successful.

By the time I defended my dissertation and my doctoral committee asked me questions about validity, reliability, and the analytic procedures I'd used, I'd become even more fascinated by the questions Berger asked of the wooden bird—how successfully, via the clarity, rhythm, arrangement of my words, had I brought the Tenderloin Women Writers Workshop and its members to life? As intimidated as I felt defending my research to my professors, I didn't let the meeting end without bringing up the writing itself. To their startled (and, luckily, affectionate) glances, I asked my own questions of them: "What do you think of this paragraph on page 41? Isn't it a good description of Mary TallMountain? Don't you think that paragraph totally gets to the heart of what Mary is all about?" I'd worked my prose to the point where I felt a kind of shimmer of my mind when I believed I'd written a successful sentence, a successful page—when I felt I'd written a representational story that could affect readers as profoundly as the real people in the Tenderloin had affected me. I continued to care about the aspects of research my doctoral program emphasized, all legitimately high on my dissertation committee's criteria for excellence. But more than anything, I cared about how well my writing conveyed what I wanted to say, how well my own little piece of wood had come to life.

Now a professor in the PhD program in the Graduate School of Education at Lesley University, I want my students to have access *within* their doctoral program to the writing secrets I learned outside of formal doctoral education. I want them to experience the shimmer I felt writing my dissertation and have longed to feel in my writing efforts ever since.

This book, coauthored with nine doctoral students, two of whom received their PhDs during the time it took us to complete our book—Krysta Betit, Dr. Thelma Goldberg, Jeanne Lima, Dr. Kat Marsh, Denise Mytko, Rebecca Redlon, Garo Saraydarian, Avigail Shimshoni, and Allison Horváth-Tucker—who enrolled in my Narrative Writing for Qualitative Researchers Seminar in spring 2019, represents a culmination of that desire. Each student was at a different place in their doctoral work. Avigail, for instance, was in her very first year while Thelma and Kat were already hard at work on their dissertations. This book is the story of our time together in a seminar premised in part on what I learned in my own writing life. It is also premised on the belief that it's high time we find a place in doctoral education to tell stories about how *hard* it can be to tell stories and to help our students find pathways to their own sense of representational success.

That's what this book aims to offer. By examining the inner workings and goals of the seminar as well as the writings that emerged from it, we ask and try to answer Berger's question about successful representation: How on earth is it made?

Our belief that it is the right time to share the story of our writing seminar is influenced by other factors as well. We conduct our work in a period of rapidly changing thinking about the goals of doctoral education, particularly in applied fields like education. Many believe that doctoral students' work, including work that is qualitative in nature, should reach wide audiences. Most doctoral students in education, certainly those I know at Lesley University and in my previous faculty position at the University of Illinois, have worked on the front lines for years, arriving to doctoral study with sophisticated knowledge of educational settings. By the time they finish their dissertation research, bolstered by theoretical grounding and time in the field, they are in a unique position to offer insights that should be heard in the public arena, not just in their dissertation defense. For this to happen, doctoral students need to know how to achieve their writerly goals, which often extend well beyond that all-too-vague term "academic writing." The traditional five-chapter dissertation is being reconsidered, with many faculty encouraging students to engage in less traditional compositional forms that emphasize the thick description that anthropologist Clifford Geertz (2000) long advocated for ethnographic studies and that Park (1921), founder of the Chicago School of Sociology, encouraged in young sociologists—writing that complicatedly *describes*. The historian Barbara Tuchman (1981) described the complexities of social science writing (in her case, historical writing, which many consider part of the social sciences) particularly beautifully:

> So much for research. I would rather talk about the problems of writing, not only because they interest me more but because the average layman underrates writing and is overimpressed by research. People are always saying to me in awed tones, 'Think of all the research you must have done!' as if this were the hard part. It is not; writing, being a creative process, is much harder and takes twice as long. (p. 69)

But in spite of a long literary tradition in the social sciences, 21st-century academics are often discouraged from deeply considering and teaching the craft techniques involved in writing a compelling dissertation and, as sociologist Howard Becker (2007) writes, from creating "an academic culture that recognizes the appeal of such desire" (p. 122). Late in his career, Geertz (1988) himself, discouraged by the modern academic mandate *not* to think about writing craft, grew troubled that too many believed that "concern with how texts are constructed seems like an unhealthy self-absorption—time-wasting at best, hypochondriacal at worst" (p. 1), adding his conviction that *not* "exposing how the thing is done is to suggest that like the lady sawed in half, it isn't done at all" (p. 2). Geertz traced this omission to social scientists' longstanding emphasis on theory building and length of time in the field. If there are problems with representing qualitative data, Geertz wrote, "they have traced their difficulties in constructing such descriptions to the problematics of field work rather than to those of discourse" (p. 10).

Introduction: The Seminar That Inspired This Book

No approach to qualitative research can be compared to in-depth scholarship full with the methodological heft typically taught in doctoral programs. If we add strong narrative writing to what doctoral students (again, particularly those studying applied fields like education) accomplish in their work, they could make a huge difference in public understanding of the challenges of 21st-century educational and social issues and infuse policy decisions with the complexity such decisions deserve. But we can't only *invite* doctoral students to think more fully about writing craft; we must *teach* each other how to do it. In our era of "truthiness," when well-informed beat journalists specializing in reporting on education are a dying breed and news that is superficial and ill-informed dominates our public understandings of education, while "traditional" dissertations are often too turgid and poorly written to have far-reaching readership, this kind of writing matters more than ever.

In a sense this book is a *qualitative narrative* study of our seminar, each chapter written by a student in the class. Our aim is to highlight themes *of* the class, giving readers narrative writing advice (and companionship/comradery), as well as offering them a blueprint for teaching such a class themselves should they choose. And so, we've organized our book according to the trajectory/arc of the semester-long course—taking you to the topics we studied week by week, evoked through each chapter author's experience and introduced by a brief statement about what I hoped to accomplish for each seminar session. In this way readers can learn what individual students made of the seminar as the connections unfolded and our own intimacy, not just with the material of narrative writing but with each other, grew. We had considered naming our book *Meaning is the Fruit of This Intimacy,* a line from Berger's (1985b) "The Storyteller," one of our first readings (from the same Berger volume as "The White Bird"), as an homage to the intimacy we experienced and that was amplified and fortified during our time—in person and on Zoom during the months of the COVID pandemic—drafting, sharing, rewriting, and editing the chapters. But *Telling the Story in the Data,* a title that our Teachers College Press editor, Brian Ellerbeck, suggested, felt like an even stronger invitation into our seminar and the learning that occurred for each of us.

Many of the coming chapters include drafts of individual students' writings that emerged from the seminar assignments, as well as resources and writerly questions that each chapter author hopes will help carry readers into their own writerly futures. This introduction is followed by the seminar syllabus and description of the seminar assignments. You will find the course handouts (I still use that term!) in the appendixes. As mentioned, we include the course syllabus and assignments up front so that those readers who plan to teach a similar course have a bit of a road map to follow, though of course they'll choose readings and films that may be quite different from those that I chose. We include the syllabus, too, because the book chapters conform to the trajectory of the syllabus and in that way, the syllabus itself reveals the arc of the course as well as the arc of our book. Having a look at the syllabus before turning to the chapters will allow each chapter's content and the book as a whole to make even more logical sense.

As you'll discover from my coauthors' self-descriptions at the end of our book, as professionals, as writers, as people in the world, we came together from very different backgrounds. What we shared and continue to share as qualitative researchers is our desire to write well enough so that readers of our research—present and future—will truly *meet* the settings and the people in them as we have, just as years ago I longed for my dissertation committee to meet the members of the Tenderloin Women Writers Workshop as fully as I had met them. This desire is beautifully expressed by the novelist Jhumpa Lahiri (2012) in an essay about writing that I almost included in my course syllabus, had it not already been so packed! "Surely it is a magical thing," she wrote, "for a handful of words, artfully arranged, to stop time, to conjure a place, a person, a situation, in all its specificity and dimension. To affect us and alter us, as profoundly as real people and things do." It is our aim to offer you a few tools to allow you to do just that.

REFERENCES

Becker, H. (2007). *Telling about society*. University of Chicago Press.
Berger, J. (1985a). The White Bird. In L. Spencer (Ed.), *A sense of sight: A collection of essays by John Berger* (pp. 3–12). Vintage International.
Berger, J. (1985b). The Storyteller. In L. Spencer (Ed.), *A sense of sight: A collection of essays by John Berger* (pp. 13–19). Vintage International.
Geertz, C. (1988). *Works and lives: The anthropologist as author*. Stanford University Press.
Geertz, C. (2000). *Local knowledge*. Basic Books.
Heller, C. (1992). *The multiple functions of the Tenderloin women writers workshop: Community-in-the-making* (Unpublished doctoral dissertation). University of California, Berkeley.
Heller, C. (1997). *Until we are strong together*. Teachers College Press.
Lahiri, J. (2012, March 18). My life's sentences. *New York Times*. https://archive.nytimes.com/query.nytimes.com/gst/fullpage-9D05E3DE123AF93BA25750C0A9649D8B63.html
Park, R. E. (1921). *The science of sociology*. Panticanos Classics.
Tuchman, B. (1981). *Selected essays: Practicing history*. Ballantine Books.

Seminar Syllabus
Narrative Writing for Qualitative Researchers, Spring, 2019

Professor: Caroline Heller
Wednesdays, 6:45–9:15 p.m. UH3-100, Office Hours: Wed. the hour before class and by appt.

SEMINAR DESCRIPTION

Qualitative research has the potential to bring out the meanings of human, cultural, community (e.g. school and classroom life-worlds, therapeutic and medical settings) in ways and forms that bring added humanity and relevance to the enterprise of research. This humanity and relevance can only be accomplished, however, if studies are read by audiences beyond academic settings. Most of us choose our dissertation focus (and any other research into which we put long hours) because we feel passionate interest and curiosity toward some question, setting, situation, people, person, social problem—we understand a sense of urgency and import related to our chosen areas of interest. Yet it's always challenging to find the best words and structure to hold the meaning of our inquiries—in research terms, to "translate," to "represent," the "data" to an audience. We are only beginning to understand how much the quality of our work is linked to our capacity to adequately tell the "story" we uncover.

Climbing into a stranger's experience, coming to optimally understand it, and then to appropriately represent that experience is perhaps the fundamental trait a qualitative researcher must cultivate. Investigative journalists, documentary filmmakers, journalistic dramatists, and others who work from information gleaned from inquiring into the human condition are plumbing the same depths of insight and humanity that qualitative researchers within academia explore. While the methodological avenues, public mandates, disciplinary histories, and targeted audiences might be (though are not necessarily) different, all these inquirers must cultivate methods of approach and capacities to "see" inside the surface of situations and convey that seeing to others. All, to a certain extent, have to find the artist within, as well as the researcher within.

In this seminar, we will look at deeply ethnographic (in spirit) narrative journalism, documentary film, and finely honed academic research studies, as well as pieces focused on writing craft, as venues for opening ourselves to representational issues and challenges in our chosen areas of inquiry (even if many in the seminar haven't yet actually chosen them). Each reading and viewing experience, as well as visits from guest researcher/writers and a filmmaker, I hope, points to the question of what it means in method of inquiry and form of telling to understand another human being, another setting, and to translate (aka: represent) that complex understanding to an audience.

In the seminar we'll also address methodological issues because in qualitative research, journalism, and documentary, method and representation are interwoven traits. This interwovenness of storytelling and data is often overlooked in qualitative methodological texts that presume that knowing "method" is all that matters in qualitative work. The result is that worthy academic studies remain unread and underutilized.

Molecular biologist Barbara McClintock said that "the ultimate descriptive task for both artists and scientists is to *ensoul* what one sees" (Keller, 1983, p. 204). Journalist/novelist Leah Hager Cohen wrote, "To the extent that we choose research topics based on a sense of passion and urgency, it is a reasonable assumption that communicating our findings effectively is paramount—not as an academic exercise but as a way of furthering discussion, disseminating ideas and information, and promoting vital dialogue" (personal communication, 2007).

A few who register for this class may be well along in thinking about their dissertation research; others won't yet have homed in on a setting or topic, but simply know that when they do, they want to write about it well. Others may be quite new to formal research altogether. I hope this seminar will be useful to all who register, wherever they are in their work.

SEMINAR OVERVIEW

We will read whole works of narrative journalistic and ethnographic research to give us common ground for discussing choices writers make in their work, including focus, style, and structure of representation. We will read essays and sections from larger works to get at writing craft issues. We will hear guest speakers talk about their research, including the challenges and triumphs of putting words to paper. And we will write (several optional assignments, and four required ones) to help us hone our capacities to think about research and writing and get down what we want to say about our data.

Seminar Syllabus

CRAFT TOPICS WE'LL EXPLORE

- links between qualitative academic work and other genres of inquiry
- the practice of gathering information
- the process of conceptualizing how to shape raw material into narrative form
- writing about people in complex ways
- writing with backstory and front story; wide-lens and focused-lens
- understanding the difference between explicit and implicit analysis
- bridging the emblematic episode to the larger universe of meaning
- finding the story within the situation (figuring out what to leave out and what to leave in)
- evoking themes without shouting them
- using dialogue and quotes effectively
- writing about dramatic moments
- thinking about what the notion of "objective correlative" teaches us
- writing with sentiment rather than sentimentality
- reading studies as both researchers and writers
- watching film as both researchers and writers

COMMON READINGS

All are available from "online" book purchasing sites of your choice (if you choose Amazon, please consider going through the WBUR/NPR website), or (encouraged!) your favorite independent bookstore.

REQUIRED BOOKS

- *At Home in the World* by Michael Jackson, Duke University Press, Chapel Hill, NC, 1995.
- *Pregnant Bodies, Fertile Minds* by Wendy Luttrell, Routledge, NY, 2003.
- *Number Our Days* by Barbara Myerhoff, Simon & Schuster, NY, 1980.

REQUIRED ARTICLES AND ESSAYS

- Shorter Readings (marked with * in syllabus) will be posted under "Resources" or sent to you as an email attachment.

SEMINAR PARTICIPATION REQUIREMENTS

Each seminar member is expected to attend every seminar meeting except in the event of sickness or emergency, to exhibit thorough reading of all the works assigned, and to contribute meaningfully to class discussions, including online (mylesley) conversations (50% of grade).

Each seminar member is expected to complete four writing assignments that integrate elements of the readings and discussions into 4–6 pp. papers that I hope might one day grow into useful components of your future work (each 10% of grade = 40% of grade).

Each seminar member is expected to make an oral presentation of one of their papers, to be shared the last night of class, during which each seminar member will share, too, the process and decisions involved in composing the paper (10% of grade).

TENTATIVE SCHEDULE

In preparation for Meeting One on January 23rd, please have read

- "Dancing with Professors: The Trouble with Academic Prose" by Patricia Nelson Limerick.
- "E. B. White at Work: The Creation of a Paragraph." From Scott Elledge's biography of E. B. White.
- "The Historian as Artist" by Barbara Tuchman.

MEETING ONE: WEDNESDAY, JANUARY 23

Topics: Introduction to the seminar, its meaning, and rationale. Discussion of Limerick, White, and Tuchman writings and their bearing on the seminar.

MEETING TWO: WEDNESDAY, JANUARY 30

Topics: Bridging specifics to the larger universe of meaning, wide angle/focused angle, backstory/front story. Please have read for today:

- "The Storyteller" by John Berger (from *Selected Essays: John Berger*, edited by Geoff Dyer, Random House, 2001, pp. 365–369).
- "After Welfare" by Katherine Boo (from *New Yorker*, April 2, 2001, pp. 93–107).
- "Optilenz" by Caroline Heller (from the *American Scholar*, Spring 2002, pp. 53–58).

MEETING THREE: WEDNESDAY, FEBRUARY 6

Topics: Continuation of topics from last week, plus taming the chaos of data when constructing a narrative, what to leave out and what to put in. Please have read for today:

- "To Fashion a Text" by Annie Dillard (from *Inventing the Truth* edited by William Zinsser, Random House, 1987, pp. 55–76).
- "Difficult Journalism That's Slap-Up Fun" by Katherine Boo (from *Telling True Stories* edited by Mark Kramer and Wendy Call, NY: Plume Books, 2007, pp. 14–19).

For those of you who worked on optional writing assignment(s), we will make time this evening to share them in class.

MEETING FOUR: WEDNESDAY, FEBRUARY 13

Topics: What are the mandates of journalism and documentary work? What questions might we pitch next week for our meeting with anthropologist Michael Jackson under the light of work by documentarian Robert Coles and journalist Samuel Freedman? Please have read for today:

- "Children Out of Bounds: The Power of Case Studies in Expanding Visions of Literacy Development" by Anne Haas Dyson, National Center for the Study of Writing and Literacy, 1995, Berkeley, CA.

The following reading is highly recommended but not required:

- "Introduction," "Reporting," and "Writing" (from *Letters to a Young Journalist* by S. Freedman, 2006, Perseus Books, pp. 1–20; 47–87; 87–133).
- "Introduction" and "The Person as Documentarian: Moral and Psychological Tensions" (from *Doing Documentary Work* by R. Coles, 1997, Oxford University Press, pp. 1–18; 49–87).

For those of you who worked on optional writing assignment(s), we will make time this evening to share them in class.

MEETING FIVE: WEDNESDAY, FEBRUARY 20

Topics: Continuation of topics from first weeks, where appropriate, plus the conduct of ethnographic research for an anthropologist, trying to understand the meaning(s) of home, and then making decisions about structure, words, telling, and representational fit; what it means to research and write a study such as the one Michael "found"? How to deal with "the self" when undertaking a study? How is ethnographic research related to storytelling? Other topics with which to engage Michael and his work: being able to "see "the emblematic (or eloquent) episode" when it occurs in the field, carrying themes through a large piece of writing. Questions to ask yourself: What are the identifiable themes in Michael's book? How does Michael bridge the "emblematic episode" to the larger universe of meaning? In other words, how did the emblematic episodes Michael writes illuminate larger issues? Please have read for today:

- *At Home in the World* by Michael Jackson

The following reading is highly recommended, but not required:

- "An Explanation" (from *Pig Earth* by John Berger, 1979, NY: Pantheon, pp. 5–12).

Distinguished Professor of World Religions at Harvard Divinity School, Michael Jackson, will be visiting the seminar.

MEETING SIX: WEDNESDAY, FEBRUARY 27

Topics: Continuation of previous topics, where appropriate, plus discussion of characterization. Please have read for today:

- "Between Literature and Science: Chicago Sociology and the Urban Literary Tradition" (from *Writing Chicago: Modernism, Ethnography, and the Novel* by C. Cappetti, 1993, NY: Columbia University Press, pp. 20–33.
- "Writing: A Method of Inquiry" by Laurel Richardson (from *Handbook of Qualitative Research*, 2000, SAGE.

First required paper, "Scene," is due today. We will spend time this evening sharing our scenes.

MEETING SEVEN: WEDNESDAY, MARCH 6

Topics: We will watch together *I Am Not Your Negro* directed by Raoul Peck from texts by James Baldwin. Depending on time in class afterwards, we will likely conduct some of our discussion about the film online in the week to follow. (You are also invited to read the book that accompanies the film; comparing the two would be so interesting, but reading the book is not required.)

We will not meet March 13, during Spring Break.

MEETING EIGHT: WEDNESDAY, MARCH 20

Topics: What can film bring forth that text can't? What can text bring forth that film can't? How does the reader/viewer immerse differently in each form?

We will watch the Lynne Littman/Barbara Myerhoff ethnographic film, *Number Our Days*. Please have read for today the text related to the film:

- *Number Our Days,* by Barbara Myerhoff.

MEETING NINE: WEDNESDAY, APRIL 3

Topics: We will watch documentary/ethnographic film, *Sweetgrass*, by Harvard's Peabody Museum curator of visual anthropology Ilisa Barbash and documentary filmmaker Lucien Castaing-Taylor, about the vanishing cowboy in the American West.

Harvard curator of visual anthropology Ilisa Barbash will visit our seminar this evening to answer questions about her film. (Second paper, "Craft," is due today.)

MEETING TEN: WEDNESDAY, APRIL 10

Topics: Continuation of topics from first weeks, where appropriate, particularly those questions we posed to Professor Jackson: plus, the conduct of ethnographic research for a researcher in a literacy program for teen mothers, making decisions about structure, words, telling, and representational fit; what it means to research and write a study such as the one Wendy Luttrell "found"? How to deal with "the self" when undertaking a study? How is ethnographic research related to storytelling? Other topics with which to engage Wendy and her work: being able to see "the emblematic (or eloquent) episode" when it occurs in the field, carrying themes forward through a large piece of writing. Questions to think about: What are the identifiable themes in Wendy's book? How does Wendy bridge the "emblematic episode" to the larger universe of meaning? In other words, how did the emblematic episodes Wendy wrote about illuminate larger issues?

Professor of Urban Education, Critical Psychology, and Sociology in the PhD Program in Urban Education, Graduate Program, CUNY, NY, Wendy Luttrell will be visiting the seminar from NY, via Skype or Facetime. Please have read for today:

- *Pregnant Bodies, Fertile Minds* by Wendy Luttrell

MEETING ELEVEN: WEDNESDAY, APRIL 17

Please have read for today:

- "Wrong Answer" By Rachel Aviv, *The New Yorker*, July 21, 2014, pp. 54–65.

Third required paper, "The Portrait of a Stranger," is due today. We will spend the evening sharing your thoughts on this assignment as well as discussing the Aviv piece.

MEETING TWELVE: WEDNESDAY, MAY 1

Writing meetings with Caroline; there will be a sign-up process.

Celebration! (Pot luck? Someone's home?) Oral Presentations of chosen paper and contemplation of moral dilemma paper, final thoughts, parting words.

Fourth required paper, "Moral Dilemma," is due tonight. Please bring hard copy.

Assignments for Advanced Topics in Qualitative Research: Narrative Writing for Qualitative Researchers, Spring, 2019 (thanks to my writer friends Carol Spindel and Leah Hager Cohen for helping me to think through these assignments).

Informal, Optional Assignment

Prompts:

1. What do you really care about in terms of the research you want to do that brought you into the program? and/or What is it that moves you in a book that you love?
2. Write about yourself as a child telling stories. (Just a few ideas that might get you started: How were stories told in your family? Were stories expected to be the pure truth? Were you expected to have your facts completely right at all times? Were stories "supposed" to be happy? Were you encouraged to tell your stories?)

We will provide time on 2/6 and 2/13 for you to share your optional assignments.

REQUIRED ASSIGNMENTS

Each of the following papers should be 4–6 pp. long. The due dates listed below (and on the syllabus) are the dates when a strong draft is expected. By strong draft, I do not mean "rough draft," but rather a strong paper that incorporates craft elements discussed in the seminar as far as the seminar has proceeded, that is well-edited, but that you realize (like almost any paper, unless you're mighty lucky with that first draft!) can, with time, probably be made even stronger. You are encouraged to form your own writing pairs or groups to respond to each other's drafts before handing in your papers, and you are encouraged to revise in response to comments and your own new ideas. If you decide to continue to work on the papers after their first due dates and want the new draft responded to, these "final drafts" will be expected the last seminar meeting.

1. SCENE. For those of you who are already involved in your research setting, bring to life a scene from that setting or a slice of its "life" that captures the excitement of what you are studying. It needn't (and shouldn't) attempt to be comprehensive—it will consist of a slice, a glimpse, but one that in some way evokes a larger truth about your setting and the people within it. The "scene" should include action, dialogue, and a space in which you suggest the importance of this scene, what it illuminates that is important *about* your setting and the people who occupy it. This paper does not require additional research beyond the your field notes (if you are keeping them), audio recordings (if you are keeping them), and/or memories and impressions, but it might be enriched by incorporating additional research (e.g. calling someone who is/was part of the setting and/or witnessed the scene with you for help reconstructing it, referring to research documents or photographs, etc.). Don't forget to include backstory, front story, wide lens, focused lens, and think about characterization, sentiment vs sentimentality, and other elements of narrative.

OR, if you'd prefer (and/or if you are far from choosing your field site for doctoral research): Write a sketch of your family—or any slice of life of your family. Try to bring to life a sense of your family's culture. Again, it shouldn't attempt to be comprehensive—it will consist of a glimpse, but one that in some way evokes a larger truth about the character of your family. The "scene" should include action, dialogue, and a space in which you suggest what it illuminates that is important about your family culture. As above, this paper does not require research or reporting beyond your memories and impressions, but it might be enriched by incorporating some (e.g., calling a relative for help reconstructing a scene, referring to old letters or photographs, etc.). **Due in class February 27th.**

2. **CRAFT.** A close reading of any of the texts or essay/articles we have read as a class, or a section of these texts, essays, or articles (or you may certainly choose another text that we haven't read together) in which you focus on a single element of writing craft. Just three examples of elements of craft are TEMPO (how quickly or slowly does it read; how long or short the sentences, the paragraphs; how long or short the words themselves; literally the pace and rhythm of the piece as created through word choice and assembly); TONE (what is the emotional tone of the piece; what do you imagine the writer's affect was; what kinds of feelings are being created in the reader; on the basis of the language being used; i.e., sentiment vs sentimentality, talismanic moments/elements, narrative tension); STRUCTURE (how was the piece organized (i.e. How is Michael Jackson's work organized?). **Due in class April 3rd.**

3. **THE PORTAIT OF A STRANGER.** This paper is about reporting, all about the interview. The goal is to create a portrait as vivid and intimate in feeling as you possibly can. You may choose anyone to be the subject of this paper—but it *must* be a stranger, and preferably, someone from a different walk of life. You should interview the person at least twice. The second interview could take the form of a follow-up phone call or email. The expectation is not that the portrait will be comprehensive, but that you succeed in illustrating an aspect of this person in such a textured way that your readers feel it is a real person, someone we can visualize, imagine meeting, have a chat with. **Due in class, April 17th.**

Start this one early. Remember that it takes 5 hours to transcribe 1 hour of audiotape.

4. **REFLEXIVITY/THE MORAL DILEMMA/THE OPEN QUESTION.** Qualitative research and documentary and narrative journalism are linked traditions. One of the things that links them is the implicit dilemma in attempting to tell another person's story. Doing so may create moral dilemmas, including the danger of misunderstanding, misrepresenting. In order to write a narrative that we hope will "represent" a person's experience, we almost always have to infer or even imagine what people are thinking or feeling. This is the most basic moral dilemma we face, but there are certainly others. Write a paper reflecting on a dilemma you have faced or might face related to your work and/or future work, and please relate it to our seminar readings, viewings, and discussions. **Due in class May 8th.**

For this last paper, you will not have an opportunity to revise within the time framework of the seminar, but please take it through as many drafts as possible before handing it in.

My Hopes for Class One, by Caroline

Days before I was to begin teaching my seminar in spring 2019, I reread an article about Svetlana Alexievich, the first oral historian to win the Nobel Prize for Literature. She was inspired by her mentor, oral historian Alex Adamovich, but had little patience for his tendency to theorize within his oral histories. One such project, she noted, was the story of a boy who shared an apartment in Russia with a woman who steals. The boy notices that among her stolen items is half a meatball. The boy is starving and struggles with whether or not to take it. "Suddenly," Svetlana says, "there are three theoretical pages of ruminations on the nature of the Russian intelligentsia. It was a total distraction from what was important! The story! Now I always say, 'Don't put yourself and your theories next to a meatball. You'll lose!'" (Gessen, 2015). I loved that line! And so we begin! To open our first class, I planned to tell that story. To affirm this focus, I assigned three readings about narrative that I love almost as much as I love the meatball story: Barbara Tuchman's "The Historian as Artist," Patricia Limerick's "Dancing with Professors: The Trouble with Academic Prose," and the last chapter from Scott Elledge's biography of E.B. White, "E.B. White at Work: The Creation of a 'Paragraph'." Each focuses on narrative writing in fascinating ways.

REFERENCES

Gessen, M. (2015, October 19). The memory keeper. *The New Yorker.* https://www.newyorker.com/magazine/2015/10/26/the-memory-keeper

Keller, E. F. (1983). *A feeling for the organism: The life and work of Barbara McClintock.* W. H. Freeman.

CHAPTER 1

Invitations and Permissions
Consider the Meatball

Krysta Betit

Our seminar *Narrative Writing for Doctoral Students* was different from my previous doctoral courses. I felt it almost immediately as Caroline began her recounting of the meatball story—a story that would become a touchstone and talisman first for our class, and then throughout our collective work over the next 3 years writing this book. This class was not about the mechanics of scholarship as we had come to understand scholarship, but about written language and how it is deployed in service of the stories we seek to tell through qualitative data. Little did we know then that the class would become the basis of a book. Perhaps we would have paid closer attention to what was happening to each of us beginning in the first five minutes of entering our shared space. But then, perhaps this would have become a different book altogether if we had, for we've come to understand *from* the opportunity to write this book together. It is an enormous opportunity to have gone back into the experience of our class to make meaning of it even more fully. Writing this book with Caroline and my classmates has given each of us that deeper encounter with ourselves and our work.

In my life outside of doctoral work, I'm a high school English teacher. I teach young people to read and write, and yet, when faced with the prospect of writing for an academic audience, I do not rise up as one might expect, tall and ready in full teacher stance. Instead, I become more like my teenaged students—vulnerable, even frightened. Written language is the currency of doctoral work and of the communication of qualitative research, and for those of us intending to engage in qualitative research studies for our dissertations, to engage in language on behalf of others *is* a daunting (if exhilarating) responsibility. What I write as a qualitative researcher not only says something about me, it says much about the people I hope to represent in my research, people I will no doubt come to love. To ignore how readers may receive my representational words is to swerve away from this love.

Usually the first class in a learning setting is dedicated to expectations—here are the things you must do, here are the things you must not do.

This class, however, opened with a welcomed series of permissions and invitations—here are the things you might want to consider doing, and in fact it would be great if you did, even when they might feel antithetical to the things you've been told to do in the past, tacitly or otherwise. That was the beauty of the readings, discussions, and individual and group processes that kicked us off—permission to let go of academic jargon, let go of the mantle of "expected" expertise. Instead, we were asked to recognize that as qualitative researchers our scholarship must be shown not just in our knowledge of theories in our discipline or field, but in our capacity to do right by the people we are fortunate to represent through clear, thoughtful, and engaging writing. We were reminded that good writers are not experts, for good writers are forever beginning again. As a matter of fact, on this first evening together Caroline brought in a framed calligraphy of a quote from poet Rainer Maria Rilke's (1923) "Duino Elegies" that has hung on her wall for many years: "If the angel deigns to come it will be because you have convinced her, not by tears but by your humble resolve to be always beginning: to be a beginner."

We discussed the fact that we honor readers, research participants, and *ourselves* as authors of our research when we convey the stories that emerge from our undertakings not just with accuracy, but with clarity. We further honor all participants when we try to do what the historian Tuchman (1981), the author of our first reading for our first class, invites all writers to do: convey stories not just accurately, but to the extent that our skills allow at any given moment, beautifully. Tuchman alludes to the joy of finding and offering the story that emerges from research, but also the immense difficulty of producing prose that represents well the lives and times of the real people who live in our research. To help me write this chapter, Caroline shared with me notes that guided our first class. Her first sentence mirrored the challenge Tuchman suggested: "We have all experienced this struggle with language—to do justice to our love for the people and situations we research" (Heller, 2019).

Like Tuchman, the sociologist Limerick (1993), author of our second class reading, sees writing not as a sacred ritual for the specially ordained academic, but as a real world craft. As she puts it, "I began to look at carpenters and other artisans as the emotional model for writers" (p. 24).

Limerick believes that many academics tend to write unintelligible prose because we fear rejection and attack. And so, Limerick asserted, we participate in what she called "the cult of obscurity" (p. 22). She offered Lewis Carroll's Tweedledee and Tweedledum as proxies for academics who are afraid to lose their heads and therefore all too often choose to shroud their ideas in prose that no one can argue with because no one can quite figure out what the author is trying to say. And yet we nod dutifully, afraid that our lack of understanding is our own fault.

What was stressed in our first class session was that our best hope is not to defeat our writerly self-doubts, but to recognize them as understandable,

Invitations and Permissions

even necessary, aspects of our care for the people we long to represent well—our research participants.

Being given the opportunity to write this opening chapter taught me that we all display and defeat our self-doubt differently. In my previous "final" draft of this book chapter, I shared in my opening that it was drafted only hours before I was due to walk into our shared space at Lesley University and present it to my coauthors, and that I was devastatingly insecure about my writing, even as I scrawled it. Here I am, a few drafts later and a bit more secure, but even now, as I scan the last few sentences, I wonder how many of them will survive the revisions that might still be necessary. This brings me to E. B. White, the subject of the third reading assigned for our first class.

In *E.B. White: A Biography*, Elledge (1985) presents seven drafts of one paragraph White wrote for *The New Yorker* to mark the 1969 Apollo lunar landing. Each draft reveals an editorial precision that seems grounded in White's reflective stance toward his efforts to convey the enormous meaning of this event. As White put it, "I always write a thing first and think about it afterward, which is not a bad procedure, because the easiest way to have consequential thoughts is to start putting them down" (Elledge, p. 359). In conceptualizing this chapter, I aspired to do what White did: draft, move words around, take words out, put words in, take words out again, put words in again, rearrange, repunctuate, until I had a piece of writing that seemed to adequately represents what I want to say. "Oh, I'll just E. B. White it down now!" I said about the first draft of this chapter when my classmates and Caroline gave me feedback during one of our book-writing meetings. But that's not how things turned out, not just because I'm not E. B. White, but because that's not how I most naturally revise. For instance, White's paragraph got smaller and smaller, while this chapter (though still quite short) got longer and longer. And this brings me to another permission of our class—reflecting about our writing in order to make it stronger is necessary, but we all write and revise our work in different ways. We all have different voices, and what we most need to do is to cultivate our own, understand our own. As wonderful as it was to study E. B. White's writing and to reflect on the wisdom of his revisions, I am not E. B. White. Caroline and my classmates urged *my* voice forward, not his.

If I am to draw a conclusion about narrative writing from our first class, it might be this: to write is to love something enough that you want it to live on. That aim can sustain us through most all self-doubt.

Because few of us had yet selected our dissertation topic when we took this seminar, much less the setting in which we would conduct our dissertation research, Caroline ended our first class letting us know that one of the optional assignments that she'd introduce the following week would ask us to write about what brought us to doctoral work. "What do you want to commit your research to? What questions and settings and people are you drawn to that you want to know more about? What do you care most about?" She asked us to put forth our ideas now in class so that we might hear our own voices speak about our research passions. I don't remember what I said, but I know it *wasn't* that I wanted to study *writing*. And yet, here I am, your first narrator, your first guide on what I hope will be an exciting, occasionally trying, but ultimately rewarding read for you. This, the book of our class. Welcome.

QUESTIONS FOR FURTHER WRITERLY CONTEMPLATION

1. Consider a piece of writing that you love. What are the ways that the author has reached you personally? What parts feel like an intimate exchange?
2. What does it mean to be an expert? Who is an expert you respect and what is it about their work that encourages you to trust them?
3. Limerick (1993) urges us to avoid obscure prose. Is there a sentence from this chapter that gave you pause in that it felt obscure or inaccessible? If so, how might you clarify it for a reader?
4. Consider a piece of academic writing that has proved useful to you as a researcher. Are there sentence-level changes you might make to increase understanding for a future reader?
5. What is a story from your own research that you think is worth telling from your own experiences? How might this story benefit someone receiving it? How might it benefit you in offering it?

My Hopes for Class Two, by Caroline

During Class Two, I continued to point to what it means in method of inquiry and form to tell true stories about human beings who are not us, and to represent our understanding of those human beings in the contexts of their lives to an audience. I focused on several craft topics: bridging specifics to the larger universe of meaning, utilizing backstory/front story and wide angle/focused angle lenses in ways that bring stories to life. These craft topics bring out fundamental qualities of how narrative works. They point to the capacity of narrative to bring out connections between things. I assigned three readings to help us examine these craft topics: an essay by John Berger called "The Storyteller"; a *New Yorker* article by Katherine Boo (2001) called "After Welfare"; and my own essay, "Optilenz." I also introduced three optional writing assignments that I hoped everyone would work on in the coming week and perhaps read aloud during Class Three.

SUGGESTIONS FOR FURTHER READING

Agar, M. H. (1996). *The professional stranger: An informal introduction to ethnography* (2nd Revised ed.). Emerald Publishing.
Behar, R. (2014). *The vulnerable observer*. Amsterdam University Press.
Maanen, V. J. (2011). *Tales of the field: On writing ethnography* (2nd ed.). University of Chicago Press.

REFERENCES

Elledge, S. (1985). *E. B. White: A biography*. W. W. Norton.
Limerick, P. (1993, October). Dancing with professors: The trouble with academic prose (Book review). *New York Times*, 22–24.
Tuchman, B. (1981). *Practicing history: Selected*. Alfred A. Knopf.

CHAPTER 2

Before, Between, and Beyond
Communicating Meaning

Garo Saraydarian (followed by drafts of paper by Garo)

I have to admit that even as a doctoral student, the first thing I still check when I read a course syllabus is the assignments. My mind rapidly notes the total number, due dates, page length, and specific requirements in an attempt to assure myself that, yes, I can do this. And so, when Caroline formally introduced "informal, optional" assignments during our second class session, my classmate Allison and I turned to each other and silently mouthed the syllables "op-tion-al?" Was this "optional" in the sense that being asked to come in to work on a Saturday is optional? This first writing assignment (on the list were three possibilities; see Figure 2.1) *was* optional. But it *was* also assigned. And so, aiming to cover all my bases, I immediately decided that I was going to respond to all three prompts. I was glad I did.

Despite my initial apprehension, these introductory writing exercises initiated a journey in which I experienced myself as a subject. I gained awareness of the challenges of discovering and communicating the stories that live in my own memories, as well as in my research endeavors. As such, I was expected to be self-reflective, which is the basis for any growth, my own self becoming what Caroline called the "instrument for understanding." Writing about my life-world put me in touch with the place from which I view the world, an awareness important to all researchers. I was thus obliged to think through issues of ethical research, representation, and narrative structures *as a writer*. I was compelled to find the story, the stranger within me, and tell about him. I learned to dwell within the Other by learning how to dwell within myself. I think it is safe to say that the majority of PhD students in any discipline, even in the broad field of education, are not often, if ever, asked to develop a sense for writing. We are trained in citation practices, methodologies, and data collection. We are asked to look at our qualitative research data to see if they correspond or correlate to some wider theoretical construct. But how we then write the story of our findings—and *every* discipline has its stories—is not usually considered as important. Yet beyond correct style and grammar or simply aesthetic niceties, the craft of

Figure 2.1. Optional Assignment Prompts

1. What do you really care about in terms of the research you want to do that brought you into the program?
2. Write about yourself as a child telling stories: For instance, how were stories told in your family? Were stories expected to be the pure truth? Were you expected to have your facts completely right at all times? Were stories "supposed" to be happy? Were you encouraged to tell your stories?
3. Were we encouraged to speak? If so, under what circumstances and about what? Were fantasy and imagination accepted or did family discussions stick to the facts?

good writing has a large role in determining what our research *is*—it, in effect, creates the meanings a reader receives. How we *tell* our research, I've come to understand, is as important as how we *conduct* our research, and if we want our research to be meaningful, we must care about communicating that meaning to the reader.

The optionality of our first assignment gave us the space and safety to explore this new task without the pressure of meeting grading expectations or external rubrics of how we *should* write. I would imagine that gaining this insight into the inner life of students can help the instructor assess where we are as writers and, by revealing what our individual projects as writers are, better inform instructors in how to effectively help us convey our intentions.

I am dwelling on this particular assignment because it gave us several critical capacities. First, by discovering ourselves as *storytellers*, we became better acquainted with our own style and tendencies (both successful and unsuccessful) when writing, a process that would become important when we revised our own work. We also gained a sensitivity to the stories that dwell in our early experiences. There can be multiple stories for the same situation, and so we learned to choose which ones would better express what we were trying to represent. By working through our own attempts at narrative, we found ourselves in a better place to evaluate the attempts of others. Only by knowing our own stories can we develop a feel for whether the narratives we read "ring true"; attempting to write these stories down ourselves, we more readily ascertain how well other stories have been told.

Second, by writing about our own lives, we felt what it was like to have intimate parts of ourselves put on the page. We realized that effectively sharing our stories required opening ourselves out to the world. Writing about ourselves, we felt the vulnerability that comes with describing personal experiences, which hopefully creates empathy with the vulnerability of those with whom we engage in our research settings. Getting to know that which we research, what Caroline called "falling in love with our subjects," is very much a getting to know in the biblical sense, "a coition, so to speak, of our body with things" (Merleau-Ponty, 1978, p. 320). Such knowledge is ontological rather than epistemological—"to know" in the sense of *being* in another's flesh as opposed to knowing-that or knowing-how. There is no divide between body and reason in this most fundamental version of knowing. Listening for the narrative in research means seeing our participants not just as representations of facts, theories, or abstractions, but as the beloved. Toward a beloved, we do not just remember that they are so many feet tall and have such-and-such color hair; we notice the small details, the lilt of their gait, the flecks of gold and green in their eyes. And indeed coital knowledge presupposes an ethic of caring in narrative writing—for if one is to know another in this way, then one must approach another's stories and circumstances—and one's own attempt to represent them—with the same respect as any other intimate relationship.

Third, our optional assignments presented us with technical puzzles (see Figure 2.2), making us that much more receptive to some of the solutions this course would suggest. Instead of having us look at an abstract list of what a good writer does, we *wrote first* and discovered those conundrums ourselves.

By struggling to "give meaning to experience," as John Berger (2001), one of the authors assigned for this class, put it, we encountered the challenges of narrative writing through active engagement and reflection (p. 366). Then, when we read good writing and engaged in revision of our own writing (with input from classmates and Caroline), we were better able to recognize and incorporate specific craft techniques that strengthened our narratives. Indeed, if we had initially been assigned to tell someone else's

---

Figure 2.2. Narrative Puzzles

---

1. How do we convey the richness and complexity of a scene without engaging in reductive statements?

    Details! Through looking at the larger universe of meaning by way of <u>small</u> details, or "talismanic moments."

2. How do we contextualize our experience to wider issues, theories, and affairs?

    By using a wide angle and focused angle lens.

    By balancing explicit analysis with the implicit analysis provided by <u>small</u> details.

3. How do we make sure the reader understands the location of the event in our subjects' larger lives and present the webs of meanings that make these lives important to the reader?

    By skillfully weaving just the right touch of backstory to our front story.

---

story (which is what most of us will ultimately do when we engage in dissertation research), we would have been so preoccupied with data collection and coding that the skills of representing and *telling* would not have been brought sufficiently to our attention.

SO, JUST WHAT ARE WE REPRESENTING?

Seeing our research through the craft of narrative writing does presuppose a certain idea of the world outside of us. It assumes that our environment is a bountiful reality, and confirms a reality that can "testify to the always slightly surprising range of the possible" (Berger, 2001, p. 367). And yet, because of this complexity, taking any perspective results in the paradox that no matter how tight the weave, reality always flutters out of whatever conceptual net we attempt to catch it in. Such a world cannot easily be captured by propositional or discursive writing—it cannot be fully captured by narrative writing either. But what narrative writing *does* recognize is the incompleteness of this framing of reality, reflecting an attitude that writer and literary critic W. G. Sebald characterized as "willing to place great acts of attention on all things with the chance hope that revelation will occur" (Sebald, 2001, p. 85).

And so, we engage in writing that observes rather than instructs, that slows the reader down, that shows the reader the scene and allows them to feel and think about its impact instead of being told how to feel, how to think about the data. In answer to the question, "What kind of insight does narrative give into the nature of real events?," it can offer a truth that, Caroline (Heller, personal communication, 2019) explained, "is achieved not with an answer but with depth of inquiry." Rather than writing *about* a situation, we bring the reader *the situation itself*, leaving it to the reader to respond and to form an opinion. Indeed, by relying solely on propositional language, we make an editorial reduction—*this*, not *that* is the larger idea. By contrast, narrative writing is predicated on the idea that we represent reality largely by *showing, not telling*. You cannot understand a narrative by skipping to the "conclusions" section. Good narratives convey the "is-ness" of our research rather than the "ought-ness" of it so that our understandings are left open, our interpretations continue.

APPROACHING REALITY THROUGH CRAFT

Before turning to the three specific craft techniques addressed in our second class, it is important to point out that this course was not based upon an antagonistic relationship between quantitative, positivistic knowledge and qualitative, narrative knowledge. As Caroline stated at the beginning of our second class:

> In most research courses, we make our criticisms based on methodological standards, and we must never leave those behind. But here, we want to critique based on craft standards, which more imperceptibly (to most) permeate the making of almost all the representations of society. We want to learn to read as writers, not only as researchers—and I would add, as readers also. (Heller, personal communication, 2019)

For instance, upon reading "After Welfare," the assigned Katherine Boo (2001) article on the effects of Clinton-era welfare reform, it was clear that Boo's narrative was preceded by her own data-analysis and exhaustive research into policy papers, legal codes, local history, and statistics. Boo provided the "before" and the "beyond" that made the particulars she included in her article optimally meaningful.

As we discovered, the themes of any research story come from such data collection (see Figure 2.3). What narrative writing does, in balance with a rigorous research method, is add a realism that inoculates the data from the danger of being coerced into theoretical certainty. Acknowledging our imperfect understanding leaves our research open to further questions and meanings (Berger, 2001).

By writing, we attempt to represent an absence—a vision, a smell, a taste, a touch—through telling. But any telling, as Berger (2001) wrote, breaks the continuity of an "indivisible and continuous" (p. 366) life into a separate moment, abstracted by printed letters on the page. The goal, then, is to bridge this distance that writing creates, constructing, as Caroline (Heller, personal communication, 2019) explained, "the connection of the little moment of data available to the eye to a larger idea it connects to that is not necessarily available to the eye." Through narrative craft, storytellers join and glue events fragmented by the research process. We string experiences onto a thematic thread and regrow the connective tissue to the world

---

Figure 2.3. Questions to Ask Our Data

1. What does the reader need to know to find empathy in the situation?
2. What are the themes in my data? How can I take them from beginning to end?
3. Where are the small moments? Describe the gestures of a moment and hint at the intentions behind them.
4. What are the connections coming out of the data?
5. What is the little? What is the big?
6. What is the situation here?
7. What is the story?

beyond and before the situational frame. To accomplish this, narrative writers practice a "way of seeing that holds together seemingly random or disparate events" (Berger, 2001, p. 366). If creating connections defines a story, if we are involved in stringing together beads of experience, then the quality of our glue, the suppleness of our string, is important. Turning to this narrative glue, we come upon the use of three, often intertwined, narrative craft components on which our second class focused:

1. Wide angle and focused angle lens
2. Implicit and explicit analysis
3. Backstory and front story

Again, Caroline's choice of Boo's (2001) article for our second class served as an exemplary model of the effective use of these craft techniques in narrative writing. Boo adjusts the lens between a larger discussion of welfare-reform and its impact on single parent households within the specific world of Elizabeth Jones and her three children, Dernard, Drenika, and Wayne. Operating under the belief, as Boo wrote, that "the closer you get to families like Elizabeth's, the more clearly you see the flaws in the infrastructure that serves the children of the post-welfare world" (p. 94), her technique provides a complex, intimate portrait (focused angle) that opens the door to a broader picture (wide angle) of questionable public policy. In our research we all have grappled or will grapple with these often unanswerable questions—social justice, best practices, educational equity—but they become more compelling to the reader when we present them through the lens of specific situations, specific human beings.

Boo's piece also utilizes the small detail to reveal the wider universe of meaning. This narrative technique has two components: the small detailed kernel and the bridge to the larger meaning. Caroline advised that the particular must be "little, little, little." These details can be a gesture, an object, even a quote, but once discovered, details must be polished and honed. Am I using too many adjectives? Is my detail small enough? Am I explaining the detail instead of showing it? Is the detail redundant? Only then will the narrative magic of the apparently trivial moment that illuminates something larger take place. In addition, we have to care about that bridge to the larger ideas that these kernels express and be able to answer why these particular kernels are important in telling a larger story. For example, when Dernard's football team, the Bison, is invited to Disney World as part of the national youth football championships, in a short paragraph Boo (2001) opens up a world of contrasts between suburban affluence and the inner-city "Shrimp Boat" neighborhood of Washington, DC, where Dernard's family lives.

> Andre [the Bison's coach] reined in the Bison early for a good night's sleep before the game. As Dernard walked out of the theme park, his face tightened and he

grabbed my hand. A small red pool was spreading across the sidewalk. Melted Popsicle, I offered. He crouched, dipped a finger, resumed breathing. (p. 106)

Notice the three details: small, red, pool. Boo (*con permiso*) could have written: "A fallen, dirty Popsicle that oozed, like blood, into a pool of sticky, sugary liquid was spreading its tendrils across the sidewalk." Or, more significantly, Boo could not have noticed the moment at all, deciding to focus on writing a larger, analytical section that explained how differences in neighborhood crime levels affect the mental and emotional health of children. Instead we have three words, two adjectives, and a noun. We are punched in the gut with the immediacy of what Dernard is feeling. The implicit analysis—here, amidst affluence, a red pool truly is a melted Popsicle, not human blood—is balanced by the explicit analysis that Boo weaves throughout her essay of the poverty and unsafe conditions of growing up in the "Shrimp Boat."

Caroline's own autobiographical story, "Optilenz," (Heller, 2002) modeled for the class the use of front story/backstory in narrative writing. For "Optilenz," Caroline provided us with a graph (see Figure 2.4) that sketched out her own use of front story, backstory, slightly backstory, and further backstory to provide the reader with the significance of her father's introduction to the Optilenz machine, a mechanical reading aid for those with failing eyesight. Backstory/front story helps set for the reader the lifeworld of her father. Here the "present becomes interesting because of the past, the past interesting because of the present" (Heller, personal communication, 2019). In contrast to the more simultaneous pairing of wide-angle

Figure 2.4. "Optilenz" Plot Graph for Front Story/Backstory

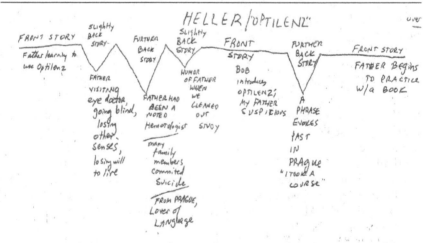

Source: Handout from January 30, 2019.

and focused angle, by offering backstory the writer provides a longer, chronological picture, a "before," from far in the past to the preceding day, hour, or minute, to contextualize the present situation, the front story, being described. Through becoming acquainted with Caroline's father's experiences when visiting the office of his ophthalmologist (slightly backstory), his surviving a death march between Auschwitz and Buchenwald in 1945 (further backstory), and his childhood and student years in Prague (way backstory), we see the relevance and meaning of Caroline's present experience (front story) of her father's struggle with a machine designed to help him read. An aging parent's grumpiness about failing eye sight, pre-WWII central Europe, the Holocaust, and Milan Kundera, the author whose book the Optilenz machine will allow Caroline's father to read, have nothing in common at first glance. But when woven together, as Caroline does in "Optilenz," they present a poignant study of universal themes of aging, lost worlds, the horrors of war, parent–child relations, and even a love affair with literature.

REVISING AND REFLECTING

It was also during our second class that we received our first Revision Worksheet (see Appendix A). These suggestions were to be used *along* with our writing, not as a checklist for afterwards. As with other elements of writing well, revising is located within the narrative quest of making meaning, not to check grammatical rules and formatting. Grammar is essential, but elements such as grammar are seen here as important *insofar as they add to this meaning*.

In revising, we are working on strengthening those bridges between the particular and the wider universe of meaning through writing, reworking, revising, and redrafting. We burnish that bridge, whittle that kernel of ordinary experience, and care about it until little by little, we find a way to express its larger significance. We begin to notice the gaps in our narrative that might need more backstory to better illuminate and invite the reader to care more deeply about the front story. We cut or lengthen sentences, deleting unnecessary adjectives, inserting an active verb to bring a more vivid picture of the "aboutness" of what we are aiming to convey. Being my own good editor requires asking: Do I tend to get to the point too quickly or too slowly? Do I tend to belabor the obvious? Do I rely too much on adverbs and adjectives? Do I sound too authoritative? Do I not sound authoritative enough? Our reading from Berger (2001) for this second class summed up the process of revision beautifully:

> And so the act of approaching a given moment of experience involves both scrutiny (closeness) and the capacity to connect (distance). The movement of writing

resembles that of a shuttlecock: repeatedly it approaches and withdraws, closes in and takes its distance. Unlike a shuttlecock, however, it is not fixed to a static frame. As the movement of writing repeats itself, its nearness to, its intimacy with the experience increases. Finally, if one is fortunate, meaning is the fruit of this intimacy. (p. 366)

Revising also amplifies our awareness of our strengths and tendencies as storytellers, which, as we discovered, are often influenced by how we were listened to as children, what our family and friends valued in our early storytelling. Were we encouraged to speak? If so, under what circumstances and about what? Were fantasy and imagination accepted or did family discussions stick to the facts? Circling back to the optional assignments, the third prompt (see Figure 2.1) invited us to explore this in terms of our own family stories. What follows is the final draft of my response to this prompt: "Write about yourself as a child telling stories." At first I drew a blank because, as you will see, I do not remember being a child who told stories, nor really having any stories told to me. Great, I thought, my first attempt at writing a narrative, and I can't come up with anything at all! I typed a first draft, really a kind of "brainstorming with myself" paragraph, where I tried to remember family stories.

> Stories—only metastory regarding how good a storyteller my great-grandfather was. Cigarette, pauses. Other stories were always mysterious, hidden. Perhaps it would have helped to tell the stories because there were some good ones: my grandfather's escape from death, my mom and dad's courage in getting married, my dad filing his mom's divorce from his dad, my grandfather as a priest, my other grandfather as a jeweler. All silenced, or told that I was too young (I'm in my 40s!) or not ready.

It was only a couple of days after this second class, as I was flying to California to attend my grandmother's funeral, that I realized that my first line, this lack of storytelling, *was* the story. The circumstances of being on a plane compelled me to jot down most of my ideas, even complete paragraphs, on beverage napkins—which, unlike other assignments for class, I had not yet learned to save. However, I do have a next-to-last draft that is a good example of my conscious revising using the craft techniques we were learning. I decided that the story of my great-grandfather telling stories would not make sense unless I included the front story of my aversion to telling stories to my own two children. Thus, I attempted to place this one memory in a larger context of meaning involving my own difficulties with storytelling (front story), the mystery surrounding stories while growing up (backstory), and the events the older generations of my family experienced (way backstory). Below is the complete final draft. It is followed by a comparative analysis of my revisions, in which I comment on my attempt to use the craft techniques discussed in this chapter—wide/focused angle, implicit/explicit analysis, backstory/front story—in order to make this narrative, hopefully, more present and meaningful to the reader.

Drafts of Writing

Finishing the Story

One of the difficult parts of being a parent is when my two children beg me to join them in their imaginative play. The moment they ask, my throat swells as if poured full of dry, dusty sand. Doing a puzzle together? Great. Coloring? No problem. Going for a walk in the woods to look for mushrooms? You bet. Building a new Lego set? Umm, yeaah! But when I'm expected to make a story with these same Lego figures, or when that walk in the woods morphs into an ongoing plot to continue the further adventures of Good-Bad Guy (my daughter's imaginary friend) I panic. I have nothing to offer.

I prefer history to *historia*, Thucydides to Herodotus. My children seem to have adapted by resorting to historical scenarios when Daddy is asked to play. I can rattle off useless, if (to me) interesting, facts, such as which president died a month into office from pneumonia he contracted during his inaugural speech (William Henry Harrison), or how to tell the difference between a Visigoth and an Ostrogoth (there isn't any). But threading these facts into an engaging story, juicy and dripping with flavor, is beyond me. Only the cracked pit is there. And so, when asked to write about storytelling in my childhood, that dry, dusty sand turns into a veritable Sahara. I wheeze and scratch out words in painful desperation. Every generation blames their parents for their own neuroses—God knows what my own children will write about me when they get older. Yet, for now, this is my turn in the intergenerational accusatory-finger game: and so, I begin with my father.

The only story, more like a metastory, that I can actually remember being continually told was how my dad loved listening to my great-grandfather, Garabed, during the evenings back in Jordan, his place of birth. Evidently, Garabed loved to have his grandchildren seated around him while he told stories of Armenian heroes like *Sassountsi Tavit* or the *djinn* that haunted the ruined Crusader castles outside Jarash. However, just when he got to a climactic point, he would pause and casually roll a cigarette of Turkish tobacco, slowly inhaling and enjoying every delicious moment as his grandkids moaned for him to continue. It was only after the cigarette became a fading stub in his fingers that he would put it out in the soft, cool desert sand, take a deep breath, and mischievously ask, "Now where was I?" before completing the story to the joy of his young audience.

My father and grandmother certainly had their tales as well. Yet, they could never seem to get past that cigarette. Stories were set up, the pieces put into place, and then the climax would dissolve with a shrug of shoulders or a dismissive wave of hand. "What would you know?" those gestures said to me, you're an American. One recurring story was how, rather, *that* my great-grandfather escaped from an Ottoman prison during World War I. But beyond that simple declarative statement lay silence. In response to the inevitable, yes, but *how* did he escape, what *happened,* my grandmother would always say, "It was a miracle, but you are not ready to hear it yet." This, when I was 42. She died the day after this past Christmas and so Garabed's miraculous escape remains a mystery along with the wise men and the incarnation. My father is even more oblique. When I was a child, he had an odd habit of walking around the neighborhood after dinner with a jasmine flower lodged in his nose. Depending on our ages, my sister and I used to giggle, tease, or completely avoid him when this occurred. Yet, when pressed for an explanation, he would only mention that his grandmother, my *ne-ne*, did the same thing. Later I discovered that *ne-ne's* name was Jamila, Jasmine, and that the lingering sweetness of jasmine petals reminded her of the gardens and orchards of her childhood home in Cilicia before she had to flee the Ottoman deportations.

And perhaps that explains my panic when asked to tell a story. The prologues are easy. You frame the facts and the scene, the background of what is to come. It is the climax, the emotional purchase and its denouement, that I never heard, never experienced as a child. Perhaps my father and my grandmother found it too painful to engage with such memories as they tried to survive in the United States. Later, I found out that my grandmother hadn't wanted to emigrate. Maybe, deep down, she felt that if the stories were never completed, they would not be lost in time. That somehow, avoiding ending her stories kept the door open to return to where those stories first took place.

Last year, for the first time, I took my 6-year-old daughter and 10-year-old son to my childhood home: California. Jasmine was in full bloom, a scent of childhood sorely missed since moving to New England, and I felt compelled to take a blossom and set it gently into my left nostril. My kids giggled and rolled their eyes at how silly their Dad was, but when they asked me why I did what I did, I told them. This time, I finished the story.

Revisions

Line 1: I originally had *"The most difficult part of being a parent,"* but changed to *"One of the difficult parts of being a parent"* upon Caroline's suggestion that calling my difficulty with engaging in imaginative play the *most* difficult thing seemed to ignore other, more difficult sides of parenting.

Line 2: I originally had *"[hot], dry sand"* but changed to *"[dry], dusty sand."* I thought "dusty" better conveyed the choking feeling I was trying to describe as well as the sense of confusion and even panic.

Line 8: I decided to have two ancient Greek historians, Herodotus (known for the fanciful tales in his histories) and Thucydides (known for his more "scientific" approach to history), stand in as more vivid explanations of my preference for fact over fiction.

Line 10: Added "to me" after "interesting" for specificity and clarity.

Lines 11–12: Originally had "*or why the unicorn on the crest of the British coat-of-arms on the Old State House in Boston wears chains (a defeated Scotland).*" I decided to use the Visigoth–Ostrogoth fact instead because it was less wordy and also a better fit as an arcane "useless" fact. Technically there is a difference, but it is based on the fact that part of the same Germanic tribe decided to head West while the other decided to head East.

Lines 12–13: Originally I had written just "*But [turning] these facts into an engaging story is beyond me.*" My final draft expanded this sentence into "*But [threading] these facts into an engaging story, [juicy and dripping with flavor] is beyond me. [Only the cracked pit is there.]*" I used "threading these facts" instead of "turning these facts" as a more accurate expression for what we do with narrative data. And I contrasted stories that are "juicy and dripping with flavor" with a "cracked pit" to convey my own feelings of inadequacy towards telling a good story.

Line 15: Added "*I wheeze and scratch out words in painful desperation*" to connect with the prevailing metaphor of the desert.

Line 20: Changed "*my Dad loved [sitting] in front of my great-grandfather*" to "*my Dad loved [listening] to my great-grandfather*" as being more to the point and not repeating the description in line 21 of grandchildren sitting around him.

Lines 22–23: I originally had "*told stories of Armenian heroes like [David of Sassoun, battles in Syria during World War I, and the hauntings of] ruined Crusader castles outside Jarash*" but decided to revise to "*told stories of Armenian heroes like [Sassountsi Tavit or the djinn that haunted the ruined] Crusader castles outside Jarash.*" Replacing "David of Sassoun" with "Sassountsi Tavit" and adding "djinn" provided focused details that revealed a wider cultural meaning of being Armenian and from the Middle East. The rhythm of the clauses also sounded more pleasant.

Line 24: Felt that "tobacco" needed the adjective "Turkish" to again polish that detailed kernel.

Line 25: Replaced "*[begged] for him to continue*" with "*[moaned] for him to continue.*" I felt like "moaned" was less of a cliché as well as providing a specific aural description that subtly connected to the hauntings of the Crusader castles.

Line 26: "*put it out in the [soft, cool desert] sand.*" Originally I did not have the adjectives. I added them to provide contrast to the dry, dusty sand that *I* felt when telling stories.

Line 30: As you will see, throughout the story I use the cigarette image as a "talismanic" detail that connects to the wider theme of telling stories as well as tying the whole narrative together. This technique will be labeled and discussed later in this book as the *objective correlative*. I also changed *"Stories [would be] set up"* to *"Stories [were] set up."* By getting rid of the passive voice the sentence becomes more vivid and present to the reader.

Lines 30–31: I replaced *"[would be] dissolved"* with *"[would] dissolve"* to, again, get rid of the passive voice.

Line 33: Originally the phrase was *"escaped from an Ottoman prison."* I added *"escaped from an Ottoman prison [during World War I]"* to add a specific detail. Later, this will become important as a hint of why my great-grandfather was in prison.

Line 37: I added the adjective "miraculous" to *"[miraculous] escape"* in order to strengthen the connection of Garabed's escape with my grandmother passing away the day after Christmas.

Line 39: I added the small detail of the jasmine flower to connect to the wider theme of family storytelling, or the mysterious lack thereof. At the end of the narrative, the jasmine flower will be a detail that connects my front story (telling stories to my children) to the backstory of my father telling, or rather not telling, stories to my sister and me.

Line 44: I used the phrase "Ottoman deportations" to hint at the context of rather than preach loudly about the Armenian genocide of 1915–1917, which is why my great-grandfather was in prison and how my family eventually ended up in Jordan.

Lines 45–52: This passage is where I engage in some explicit analysis.

Line 46: I replaced *"[set] the facts"* to *"[frame] the facts"* as a better verb to explain what storytellers do.

Lines 51–52: I changed *"[for returning] to where those stories took place"* to *"[return] to where those stories [first] took place"* as being a more direct and vivid sentence.

Lines 55–56: I added the detail of "left" nostril instead of just "nostril" to help bring the reader there at that moment. I figured that the reader would simply scan through a description of someone just putting a flower in their nostril but would be shaken out of automaticity by an unexpected, specific detail, such as which nostril it was.

Line 57: This was the key sentence for me that tied the whole narrative, the front and backstory, all the little kernels of meaning, together. I had originally written *"This time [I made sure] I finished the story"* but felt that I was being too insistent, trying too hard to make sure the reader got the connection. The sentence needed to be more subtle to work. So I took out the excess words and ended up with *"This time I finished the story."*

QUESTIONS FOR FURTHER WRITERLY CONTEMPLATION

Using our class's assigned readings (or other narratives that you enjoy), consider the following:

1. Locate other examples of the use of small details to "illuminate a wider universe of meaning."
2. How are the details described? What larger meanings do you understand from these details?
3. Highlight sections or create a graph representing the weaving of front story to backstory, wide-angle to focused-angle, and/or implicit to explicit analysis.
4. What are the metaphors that are used? Do they "ring true" to you?
5. How are verbs used? Are they specific and "strong?"
6. Read a passage out loud. Do the sentence lengths contribute to the meaning and effect of the narrative? Do they create a pleasing rhythm to your ear?
7. Are there places where the author is shouting what they want you to feel?
8. Does the narrative give you a clear sense of its meaning? Would you be able to state in a sentence what the meaning of the narrative is?

My Hopes for Class Three, by Caroline

During this third class meeting, we continued our focus on craft issues introduced in previous class: bridging specifics to the larger universe of meaning, wide angle/focused angle, and backstory/front story. But for this third class, utilizing Annie Dillard's essay "To Fashion a Text," along with a short fun piece by Katherine Boo called "Difficult Journalism That's Slap-Up Fun," we discussed how to tame the chaos of data collection and analysis, a necessary step toward laying the groundwork for composing narratives true to one's data. I invited volunteers to read their optional writing assignments out loud, hoping to forge a listening culture among ourselves, alongside our evolving reading and writing culture.

SUGGESTIONS FOR FURTHER READING

Abram, D. (1996). *The spell of the sensuous.* Vintage.
Clandinin, J., & Connelly, F. M. (2000). *Narrative inquiry: Experience and story in qualitative research.* Jossey-Bass.
Drucker, J. (2011). Humanities approaches to graphical display. *Digital Humanities Quarterly, 5*(1), 1–20.

Eisner, E. W. (1994). *Cognition and curriculum reconsidered* (2nd ed.). Teachers College Press.

Fisher, W. R. (1984). Narration as a human communication paradigm: The case of public moral argument. *Communication Monographs, 51*, 1–22.

Furman, C. (2019). Responding to the writer in student writing: Engaging in the descriptive review of written work. *Schools: Studies in Education, 16*(2), 1–21.

Harman, G. (2016). *Immaterialism: Objects and social theory*. Polity.

Harman, G. (2018). *Object-oriented ontology: A new theory of everything*. Pelican.

Havelock, E. A. (1963). *Preface to Plato*. Belknap Press.

Jankelevitch, V. (2003). *Music and the ineffable* (C. Abbate, Trans.). Princeton University Press. (Original work published 1961)

Lather, P. (1991). *Getting smart: Feminist research and pedagogy with/in the postmodern*. Routledge.

Merleau-Ponty, M. (1973). *Consciousness and the acquisition of language* (H. J. Silverman, Trans.). Northwestern University Press.

Ong, W. J. (1982). *Orality and literacy: The technologizing of the word*. Methuen.

Perkinson, H. J. (1993). *Teachers without goals. Students without purposes*. McGraw-Hill.

Polanyi, M. (1969). *Knowing and being*. University of Chicago Press.

Polanyi, M. (2009). *The tacit dimension*. University of Chicago Press. (Original work published 1966)

Putnam, H. (1988). *Representation and reality*. MIT Press.

Robson, C. (2012). *Writing for change: Research as public pedagogy and arts-based activism*. Peter Lang.

White, H. (1980). The value of narrativity in the representation of reality. *Critical Inquiry, 7*(1), 5–27.

Worth, S. E. (2008). Storytelling and narrative knowledge: An explanation of the epistemic benefits of well-told stories. *The Journal of Aesthetic Education, 42*(3), 42–56.

REFERENCES

Berger, J. (2001). The storyteller. In G. Dyer (Ed.), *Selected essays* (pp. 365–369). Random House.

Boo, K. (2001, April 9). After welfare. *The New Yorker*, 93–107.

Gessen, M. (2015, October 19). "The Memory Keeper," *New Yorker Magazine*.

Heller, C. (2002). Optilenz. *The American Scholar, 71*(2), 53–58.

Merleau-Ponty, M. (1978). *Phenomenology of perception* (C. Smith, Trans.). Routledge & Kegan Paul. (Original work published 1945)

Silverblatt, M. "A Poem of an Invisible Subject," in L. S. Schwartz (Ed.). (2007). *The Emergence of memory*. Seven Stories Press.

CHAPTER 3

Finding the Story in the Data

Denise Mytko (followed by drafts of papers by Denise and Thelma Goldberg)

I entered Class Three armed with two weeks of detailed class notes. I felt that I now understood concepts such as backstory, front story, wide lens and narrow lens, but had difficulty applying them to my own work. Having worked in technical fields and management for years, I'd trained my brain to skip across information like stones across a river, gathering observations to learn from, assess, and take action on as quickly as possible. I viewed my mind as a practical problem-solving machine. That started to change after our Week Two reading of *Optilenz* (Heller, 2002) about Caroline's father relearning to read. With this story and the diagram highlighted in the previous chapter, narrative craft features like front story and backstory transformed from vague terms into living concepts. *Optilenz*, the closeness Caroline felt to this story, as well as her capacity to explain these narrative elements, shined a new light on the power of narrative writing.

I had spent the prior week drafting our optional assignment, trying to write about my personal history of storytelling. However, I remembered my childhood only in little fragments. I felt that my memories were not complete enough to choose this prompt. Instead, I chose the other optional writing prompt: "What do you want to research and why?" After all, I had been talking about *this* topic most of my adult life, and as a doctoral student, I thought about it every day. I continued to consider my incomplete set of childhood memories. What if a researcher had studied my family when I was a child? Could that person's work have filled the gaps in my memory by asking me the right interview questions? Would I agree with a version of my life written by someone else? As PhD students, we either have already or soon will interview, observe, analyze, interpret, and write about others as part of our research. *How can we tell their stories when the data of a life is limitless?* Welcome to Class Three.

Week three of this course introduces:

1. What data to leave in and what to leave out (taming the chaos of our data).
2. What data details are helpful to a reader and what details are not helpful.

3. How data details shape a reader's images of the people we write about.

One of the pivotal points of a researcher's work is when they move from the information-gathering (data collection) processes to writing. In "Difficult Journalism That's Slap-Up Fun," Katherine Boo (2007) likens this transition to riding a bus. As a rider, she is *not* in control. It is her responsibility to open herself up to the processes of observing, of looking out the windows, and taking in that life as well as the life of the ride itself. She is openly gathering the information around her. We saw her do just that in the previous week's Boo reading discussed in Chapter 2. She closely observed her surroundings without influencing the direction of travel. In her essay, Boo explained that when observing as a journalist (and the same is true for us as qualitative researchers), she needs to lose control in a similar way in order to collect meaningful data. Ideally, she gathers data without influencing, and thus, in some sense, altering, her environment of study. To Boo, this means going where her participants are. Once having gathered data, she then must "change gears," so to speak, and take control as the driver of the story. Driving a story—as the writer—requires her to "exert maniacal control over those facts" (p. 6). She now "controls" the narrative, but always guided by what Caroline described as "keeping our oath to the data" (Heller, 2019). Boo analyzes. She interprets. She writes. Her challenge (and ours) is to create narratives that are true to the data collected.

TAMING THE CHAOS

We may choose to pursue methods of qualitative study that will include interviews alongside participant observation. During these observations and activities as researchers, we will take notes, create audio and/or visual records, and review primary documents and artifacts. At this stage, we are riding the bus. We don't know what information will be thematically important, nor which small details we hear and/or observe will illuminate those themes. So our work is led by access and openness to our surroundings and subjects. We record observation as completely as we can. At the end of this intense process, though, as we eagerly revisit our carefully constructed data record, what might we discover? It is *chaos*! We have likely ended up with binders of notes, hours of transcribed interviews, video and audio files, as well as countless folders with names like "Observation Day 1" and "Focus Groups 3–5." What to do?

The collected data is a complete record of situations that a researcher has observed, heard, touched, smelled, experienced within the context(s) of the research they have undertaken. Taming chaos is a process of finding themes/emblematic moments/stories from this body of data. In other

Finding the Story in the Data

words, in research language, *taming* is akin to coding, analyzing, interpreting. Like a sculptor, we remove what material is not applicable to our guiding questions and keep what is. Guided by our topic of study, by the questions that guide our research (with willingness to change those questions, for we *have* gone where the bus has taken us!), we begin to carefully examine and code our raw data. This process will slowly reveal important themes that will become the foundation of the story our research uncovers, and that we will one day soon aim to share with readers of our work. During the process of taming our chaos, complexities and contradictions in our data will no doubt arise. It is our role to consider these complexities, allowing room to explore and observe our themes as they overlap and influence one another. In Chapter 8 of this book, my classmate Thelma Goldberg dives into her approach for addressing complex and contradicting themes. As we comb through the data more and more, true to our oath, we may have to alter our originally proposed themes to align with those we have further uncovered. Not only does this practice strengthen our research moving forward, it controls the chaos! Themes are built from the ground of these connected data points. When our observations clearly illustrate a research theme, a bridge to a main idea begins to be created. As noted in Chapter 2, Boo (2001) makes these kinds of connections in her research study that became her *New Yorker* article, "After Welfare." In field observations, she recorded a child's reaction to the sight of a melting red Popsicle. Deep within the original chaos of collected data, the scene may not have seemed significant. However, the "small red pool" of melted Popsicle directly connected to the larger themes her research revealed—of a child's experience living in pervasive violence. Highlighting connections such as these strengthens a reader's understanding of the larger significance of her research. Boo noticed and cared about the melting Popsicle, as Garo Saraydarian noted in Chapter 2, because she cared deeply about Dernard's reaction to it and what it brought forth to her own growing consciousness about the pervasive effects living amidst violence have on a child's psyche.

The moments we narrate serve the larger ideas our data has led us to. Collected data that does not advance a reader's understanding of the research themes that have emerged through our careful analysis should be left (difficult as it may be to do so) on the *cutting room floor*. Figure 3.1 represents how Caroline chose to illustrate this concept on our classroom white board. The curving lines represent the themes Boo's research may have revealed, while the open circles on those lines represent key points where themes in the data intersect with small narrative moments, such as the moment Dernard noticed the melting red Popsicle. Underneath are the moments that landed on the cutting room floor—collected data points that do not advance readers' understandings of the themes of Boo's research—that do not advance the larger story her research evokes.

Figure 3.1. Visual representation of taming the chaos

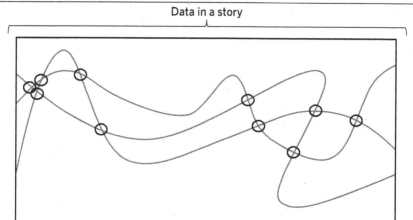

Source: Digital recreation of Professor Caroline Heller's white-board lecture content presented February 6, 2019 (See also, Appendix B)

A RESPONSIBILITY TO REPORTING

Shaping the chaos of a full data collection comes with great responsibility. As researchers and reporters of our studies, representing our participants honestly and well remains a priority of our work. We bear witness to people and landscapes, recording what we learn through scrupulous field notes. Emerging themes help us refine our "report" to include multiple aspects of an environment. We report what we discover to be the heart of the situation at hand. There is inherent audacity to sharing the story of another human being, and new researchers like me (and maybe you) likely feel the rawness of that audacity even more than seasoned researchers. In the readings for this third class, Annie Dillard (1987), as well as Boo (2007), introduced us to ways of managing this sometimes overwhelming feeling of audacity. As researchers, we are accountable to interpret our collected data with maximum credibility. This data holds the themes upon which we draw conclusions. As reporters, we are accountable to our research participants as well as to our readers. We do not place judgement on those we observe. For example, we may report on an individual who might be viewed unfavorably by readers. As a driver of that person's story, we decide what our words will be. They must paint an accurate nonjudgmental picture so that readers are free to form their own judgment. Detailing our observations of participants, as opposed to assigning value to their actions, is one narrative craft feature we use to accomplish this. In "To Fashion a Text," Dillard (1987) demonstrated this practice in the following description of her mother.

> My mother was both a thinker and what one might call a card. If she lay on the beach with friends and found the conversation dull, she would give a little push with her heel and roll away. People were stunned. She rolled deadpan and apparently effortlessly, her arms and legs extended tidily, down the beach to the distant water's edge where she lay at ease just as she had been, but half in the surf, and well out of earshot. (p. 63)

These lines convey Dillard's recollection and observation: just the facts, ma'am, without judgement. She has chosen to share interesting and unique information about her mother that renders her mother neither heroic nor villainous. She invites readers to form their own judgements by offering this memorable moment of her mother's rather unique form of mischief.

Including participants in the research process when appropriate can be important in achieving the goal of accurate, nonjudgmental portrayals. At a conference on narrative that Caroline encouraged us to attend, I learned that the participants in Boo's research, for instance, often reviewed her written observations in advance of publication (2019). And when writing about her family, Dillard (1987) promised them that she would "take out anything that anyone objects to—anything at all" (p. 6). It is up to us to decide how much editorial influence to share with our participants, while remaining true to our data. Participant collaboration can strengthen our work by encouraging talk across observer/participant boundaries. A researcher of literacy, Anne Haas Dyson (1995), whose work we would read for our fourth class session, which my classmate Rebecca Redlon describes in Chapter 4, explains the benefits of this approach:

"Stories," Dyson writes, "including those we tell about other people, are also

> about ourselves, written from our particular vantage points. In interaction, each speaker or writer infuses given words like *literacy* and *development* with new accents, new dimensions, because each is positioned differently in the social and ideological ground. Crossing conceptual boundaries is thus linked with crossing human ones: when we, with our diverse experiences and our common concerns, converse, we push each other out of bounds, we help each other attend to the world a bit differently. (p. 30)

Our published research captures snapshots in time. Despite our best efforts and hopes, we cannot fully predict future interpretations of our conclusions. Inviting our participant(s) into the research process can help guide our ability to understand and be understood.

A COMMUNITY OF WRITERS

The last 45 minutes of Class Three were devoted to an in-class read-aloud. Caroline invited us to read our optional papers, which she'd introduced to us the previous week, allowing time for group feedback after each volunteer read. I had never done anything like this before. I felt my heartbeat quicken *on behalf* of my peers—I wasn't even planning to read anything, but it was as though I entered my classmates' bodies. Having written drafts for two of the three prompts, I was still deciding if the meaning of "optional" meant that I could get out of doing this scary thing. The read-alouds began. The first volunteer began reading with shaking hands. The next volunteer opened her narration with an announcement of her nervousness. The third, with a background in theater, read her work like a seasoned pro. I was taken into each of their stories. My classmate Thelma wrote about her interest in researching tap dance education. As she read about why her research into this topic was important to her, I heard the taps from Thelma's 5-year-old feet, which she highlighted in her reading. My classmate Allison read her story *about* family stories, and it was as though I were sitting in the plastic chair where Allison sat during her hard conversation with her parents in Florida. My classmates Rebecca and Kat also read about memories of their families telling stories. Through Kat's reading, I sat around the dinner table with Kat's family of wordsmiths. Through Rebecca's I saw rivers in a brand new way. With each I saw again the vulnerable beauty of narrative writing. My peers received positive and careful feedback.

My own fast-beating heart persuaded me to wait to read my own optional writings out loud. Though this chapter was meant to cover the third week of our class, I want to mention that I *did* read my optional assignment the following week. In that paper, I shared the roots of my academic ambition. I recalled the day that I graduated from community college as a first-generation, nontraditional college student. I had never expected to earn an advanced degree. Once I had, I never imagined pursuing a PhD. I read my story of *why* I'd entered doctoral work, and recounted a few catalyzing experiences that remained and still remain personal and raw. I started to read in a nervous, tinny tone. I became more confident as I continued, and I heard my voice inflect in ways I hadn't heard it do since my read-aloud days teaching kindergarten. The text ran out. I looked up. My body braced. There was no need for worry. My new community of writers had connected with the sentiment of my work. I was going to be ok. I *was* OK.

Finding the Story in the Data

Drafts of Writing

Optional Seminar Assignment: What do you really care about in terms of the research you want to do that brought you into the doctoral program? Original rough draft written February 13, 2019 by Denise Mytko.

I'm one of thousands in a Texas conference hall. I move through the room with the currents of bodies for a while, eventually sitting on the floor with my back to a room divider. *This room gets bigger?* Chatter around me is indistinguishable. As the room quiets and the keynote speaker begins, I feel my heart start to beat faster. Pressure builds behind my eyes. "I'm now on my fourth or fifth study on food and housing insecurity in higher education . . . something I'd never thought I'd be an expert in," the speaker says. "The most under-resourced students attend the most under-resourced schools." She tells the story of her student who worked all night to pay tuition and attend her community college class. "Have you ever tried to go to college when you haven't slept and you haven't eaten?" she asks. The attendees around me clap softly. *I want her to stop.* Her examples of student hardship become more specific. *What is this? This talk is supposed to be about how college is expensive, but some of her examples are feeling a bit too personal.*

I don't hear the next section about ways financially independent community college students can struggle. I am fully engulfed in my own memories. I am looking into the trunk of my tan 1987 Honda Accord at five purple plastic buckets of clothes. One for my assistant Kindergarten teacher life, one for my Chili's life, one for my fitness center life, one for my museum manager/Park District life, and one for my student life, just in case I have the extra changing time on school nights. One bucket for each job. They're plastic, so the smell of working at Chili's doesn't spread more than it has to. I carry a backpack with a phone, a Nokia phone/pager, a regular pager, some books, and room for a bucket-worth of clothes that I will change in and out of a few times a day. Like my trunk, I keep my life roles in separate buckets. People rarely come over to my apartment. I make my friends at work. I would do anything for them, but they know little about me. I leave for the day at 3:30 a.m. or 7 a.m., and return at 10 p.m. or 2:30 a.m. every day. Because of this, that apartment is mostly remembered in the dark.

A round of applause brings me back to the speaker, who is transitioning to the topic of college financing faced by 87% of the undergraduate students attending nonresidential schools, how Pell grants designed to cover the cost of public college for under-resourced students no longer do so, and how many who take out loans often keep the loans without earning a degree. I flash forward to a short-term job that I was heavily recruited to. The company hired employees who had graduated from "Top 50" colleges only. I stand at my standing desk, feet from a kitchen that has three coffee makers, only one of which I can figure out how to get coffee out of. I look at my new boss as she warmly makes a judgmental comment about people who shop at Goodwill, which is where all of the clothes I am wearing happened to be from that day. She tells me that community college students hoping to transfer to a "Top 15 school" have a less than a 3% chance of doing so. I am to dissuade our well-resourced clients from considering community college. The most under-resourced students attend the most under-resourced schools indeed. At least I am a 3 percenter.

Back at the conference, the speaker asks why as a society, we can recognize how remarkable it is for a child to overcome significant challenges navigating their way to college, and not support that child through college. I pop a sweet raspberry into my mouth. I had brought them with me that morning. I had bought them from Whole Foods for $4.75 the night before. I remember feeling hot and smiling uncomfortably when the cashier rang them up. But hey, I could buy really expensive food at a conference, I've earned it . . . right?

As the speaker went on about how people paid for school, I remember how after transferring, I paid for Northwestern University as a commuter, in full, a few classes at a time using hand-written Tweety Bird checks. I thought of my friends, who sold their eggs when tips were low and how strep throat cost $139 to fix without health insurance. Most of all, I remembered how lucky I was to even *be* at that conference. Five dollars *was* too much for raspberries.

I have always known that parts of my story were common, because most of those closest to me lived a version of it. I know now that my story is common, because I study people far from me that have lived different versions of it. What I didn't know then, was that this common story isn't recognized as worthy in some places. Namely in competitive professional spaces. As a hiring manager, I have often heard "We have to pay her more because she went to Harvard" and "But those years (of community college or work) are just not relevant." That doesn't work for me. I am only one of countless people independent at or before the age of 18 in America, or in any other circumstance where one develops professional and academic skills in a way that is as unique as their own story. If I had held my jobs consecutively—*and I'm tremendously lucky to have had the work available to me*—I would have well passed 60 years of employment by the age of 40. That counts, and I'm far from alone.

The term "nontraditional student," in my opinion, is ridiculous. I feel so fortunate for this chance to research the challenges and benefits of working and learning. I hope to learn more about barriers to and in the workplace for nontraditional students. I hope that my research can influence policy to remove those barriers, making it a little easier for people to make more flexible and personal life choices.

Finding the Story in the Data

Drafts of Writing

Optional Seminar Assignment: What do you really care about in terms of the research you want to do that brought you into the doctoral program? By Thelma Goldberg

> *Listen to the rhythm*
> *Hear the gentle beat*
> *of a story*
> *Being told with dancing feet*

The anthropologist Behar (1996) describes memory as being at the heart of reflexivity, awakening emotions that remind us of stories that form our past and present. An experience from 60 years ago continues to fuel my love and inspire my interest in tap dance education today.

My memory of my first tap shoes is embedded in my mind, like the screws that affix my taps to my shoes. It was a Saturday in September. I was 6 years old and my father had dropped me off at the Bates School of Dance, three flights above the Hong Kong restaurant on Massachusetts Avenue in Central Square, Cambridge. A long hallway ran along the outside of a large studio on the left and two smaller ones on the right. Music filled the air. Muted laughter and an adult voice (the teacher? I wondered) shouting "and a 5 6 7 8" drew me to the low bench lining the hall where, through the glass windows of the studios, I watched children dressed in black leotards chassé across the floor. They looked about my age; will I be able to dance with them, I wondered? With my patent leather tap shoes carefully packed in a pink box-like container with ballerinas gracing the front, and my pink ballet shoes tucked in a special compartment with a snap closure, I patiently waited my turn to dance, happy to be in this magical place that (I had little idea that morning) was about to become my second home.

I remember the warmth of Grace's hand as she guided me into one of the small studios across from the reception desk. Hours watching Shirley Temple and Bill "Bojangles" Robinson dance across the black and white television screen in my living room had convinced me that I *must* learn to dance like them! "Shuf-fle," said Grace, as I lightly brushed the wooden floor with the front of my foot in response to her demonstration and direction to "stroke the floor, like painting." Today I use that same analogy, calling for my students to brush vibrantly colored shoes stripes onto my own wood floors. With Grace's gentle encouragement, I proudly shuffled, marched, dug, tipped, and stamped my feet. Grace taught me new words and showed me how to make amazing new sounds with my tap shoes. My heart was leaping and I felt like the "Star of the Day" on Community Auditions, the weekly talent show that aired on Saturday nights before Lawrence Welk. Even now I can hear the host, Gene Burns singing "Star of the day, who will it be?" Maybe me!, I thought on that memorable Saturday when I wore tap shoes for the first time.

Revisions

Line 9: I had originally used the phrase *"speaks of memory as the heart of reflexivity"* and based on suggestions changed that to *"describes memory as being at the heart . . ."* Ruth Behar did not speak but she very clearly described memory.

Line 10: I had written *"form our past and ~~inform our~~ present."* I didn't need to use inform. Stories form our past and present.

Line 11: I had written *"an experience that happened 60 years ago,"* but deleted *"that happened"* and substituted *from*, which is more concise.

Line 13: I had written *"My first memory of wearing tap shoes is deeply embedded."* I changed that to *"my memory of my first tap shoes is embedded in my mind."* Moving the word "first" shifted the narrative to my shoes, which is what the story is about.

Lines 16–19: I had started with *"there were three classrooms . . ."* but changed it to start with *"A long hallway . . ."* By starting with the hallway I'm inviting readers to walk into the studios with me.

Line 18 and Line 24: I inserted two parenthetical phrases *"(the teacher, I wondered?)"* and *"(I had little idea that morning)"* rather than separating them by a comma, which I had originally done.

Lines 21 and 22: I wanted to add color and texture to my descriptions of my shoes, so I added *"patent-leather"* tap shoes and *"pink"* ballet shoes.

Line 26: I deleted *"How excited I was to start tap dancing."* This was a perfect example of my tendency to write with sentimentality. I don't need to tell the reader how I was feeling—they can interpret that feeling from the descriptive details.

Line 28: By italicizing "I *must* learn to dance like them!", I replace the aforementioned sentimentality with a definitive statement that describes my determination.

Line 30: I clarified the subject to be *"my students."* I had originally written *"calling for vibrant red or mellow yellow to be brushed onto my own wood floors."* I'm calling on *"my students to brush . . ."*

Line 31: I originally wrote *". . . I remember feeling special and proud"* and changed that to *"With Grace's gentle encouragement, I proudly shuffled, marched, dug, tipped, and stamped my feet."*

Line 36: I originally wrote "Maybe it will be someday, *I remember thinking . . .*" I don't need the word *"remember."* The final sentence becomes stronger by being clear: *"Maybe me!, I thought on that memorable Saturday when I wore tap shoes for the first time."*

Finding the Story in the Data

QUESTIONS FOR FURTHER WRITERLY CONTEMPLATION

1. Observe a public space for a half hour. Write down 15 individual behaviors that you observe during that time. Reflect on the information you have captured using the following questions:
    a. Why did you choose to document these details? Do you see any commonalities in your observations?
    b. Do any of these small observations help you draw conclusions about the situation, or about the person you observed? How might the context of your life influence the conclusions that you draw or the judgements that you make?
    c. What is your participant role in this exercise, or how might this time of observation have unfolded differently if you had not been there?
2. Revisit Class Three's course reading, "To Fashion a Text." Select one page of this work, analyzing it using the following questions:
    a. What observational data or themes can you find in this selection?
    b. Why is the information in your selection important to the larger piece of writing?
    c. Put yourself in Dillard's shoes. If you were a researcher observing the material presented on this page, what other details might you have seen or recorded? What details do you suspect were "left out" of this selection?

My Hopes for Class Four, by Caroline

During this fourth class meeting, I opened with the topic I borrowed from Annie Dillard from last week's reading: "what to leave in and what to leave out." This idea is related to "taming the chaos of our data" also from last week. I leaned on my own beloved dissertation advisor, Anne Haas Dyson. In her (1995) *Children Out of Bounds: The Power of Case Studies in Expanding Visions of Literacy Development,* Dyson uses a case study to talk about issues Dillard talks about in regard to writing about her childhood. I introduced Dyson's introduction of terms, "bounded system," "unit of analysis," and "interpretive methodology," to link decisions nonfiction writers and journalists make with decisions qualitative researchers must also make when they write narratives based on their data. I love Dyson's notion of what is "in bounds" and what is "out of bounds" as one constructs cases and also as one constructs a narrative. Tonight, again, I hoped to save plenty of time for volunteers to read their optional writing assignments out loud.

SUGGESTIONS FOR FURTHER READING

Lopate, P. (2013). *To show and to tell: The craft of literary nonfiction*. Free Press.
Murray, D. (1995). *The craft of revision*. Harcourt Brace College Publishers.

REFERENCES

Behar, R. (1996). *The vulnerable observer: Anthropology that breaks your heart.* Beacon Press.
Boo, K. (2001, April 9). After welfare. *The New Yorker*, 93–107.
Boo, K. (2007). Difficult journalism that's slap-up fun. In M. Kramer & W. Call (Eds.), *Telling true stories* (pp. 14–19). NY: A Plume Book, Penguin.
Boo, K. (2019, March 23). *Katherine Boo and Matthew Desmond in conversation, The power of narrative.* Talk presented at 2019 Power of Narrative Conference, Boston University, Boston, MA.
Dillard, A. (1987). To fashion a text. In W. Zinsser (Ed.), *Inventing the truth* (pp. 55–76). Random House.
Dyson, A. H. (1995). *Children out of bounds: The power of case studies in expanding visions of literacy development.* National Center for the Study of Writing and Literacy.
Heller, C. (2002g). Optilenz. *The American Scholar*, 71(2), 53–58.

CHAPTER 4

The River Is Wide

Rebecca Redlon (followed by drafts of paper by Rebecca)

Reviewing the writing I did in Caroline's class, I see that the Saco River, which runs from the White Mountains in New Hampshire to the shores of Saco, Maine, plays at least a cameo role in each piece. It warrants a mention in the optional assignment Denise referred to in the previous chapter, and it makes a brief appearance in my family scene paper, which follows this chapter. In yet another assignment, I tackle my relationship with this river more directly, drawing an analogy between it and my earliest writing attempts. I described how I learned to swim in the Saco, how I at first "dabbled in the shallows, my small child's soul delighted and shocked by the water's cold and invigorating wetness, and then later I made daring leaps into it from a great height." In retrospect, I see that my history with that river accurately describes my experience with the class, and so I find myself turning toward the Saco yet again to provide a metaphor to convey the meaning I took from our fourth class session.

The Saco River, though untamed in many spots, is not a "wild" river; it is not known for tricky currents or frothy rapids. In fact, there are sections of the river that families rely upon for safe summer fun for children of all ages, offering miles and miles of clear shallow water with generous sandbars for picnicking. Even its deepest and fastest spots are easily navigable by canoe, with convenient portages around the occasional human-made dam.

In many ways, the flow of narrative writing *reminds* me of the Saco. The first few classes, where we delved into our own stories and began to think of ourselves—and trust ourselves—as writers, were like experiencing the shallows of this river as a child: a safe place in which I explored and paddled as I observed and drank in the details that surrounded me. The choices we were making about details to include in our "stories," focusing in and widening out, were the best kind of "play," where, like splashing in the shallows of the Saco, serious growth was/is fostered through creativity in the bounds of a safe environment.

The readings for Class Four presented a shift, as though we rounded a bend in the river to discover the safe shallows replaced with wider and deeper water—not menacing in any way—just more conducive to deeper study, to headier contemplation. A pause along this stretch of the river, perhaps in an inviting cove, allows us the chance to get wet beyond ankles and knees. We may not be able to see the river's bottom, but we trust it is fathomable.

During the last class, we looked at Annie Dillard's (1987) "To Fashion a Text" and considered the process by which she selected details to include in—and perhaps more importantly to omit from—her memoir *An American Childhood*. She wrote that the memoir is about "a child's vigor and originality, and eagerness, and master, and joy. It's about waking up" (p. 1). And so, the memoir is about *that* part of her life and the aspects of geography and family and class that informed her lived/remembered version of "waking up." Reading this piece invited us to view our own writing through a similar lens. In my narrative about childhood stories, this puzzle of what to leave in and what to leave out was the most plaguing; my family, being stereotypically Yankee, were reticent about feelings and emotions—they expressed themselves through stories, and so I had a great many to choose from. Even once I had narrowed my scope to one particular family storyteller, the number of examples from which I could select was dizzying. I spent most of my writing and revising time trying out and then trashing many of them before I settled on those that felt most fully emblematic of my memories of childhood.

THE RIVER IS DEEP, BOUNDLESS

The major reading for this week, Anne Haas Dyson's (1995) *Children Out of Bounds: The Power of Case Studies in Expanding Visions of Literacy Development*, plunged us into the deeper water of an actual *case* of qualitative research, the very subject we had been drifting toward all along. At the beginning of class, Caroline wrote several terms on the board that I copied into my notebook: Bounded System—the particular human experience being studied within limits defined by the researcher; Unit of Analysis—one's specific focus of interest; Case Study—every case is a case of *something*; Hermeneutic Axis—methodology of interpretation; Referential Totality—everything one winds up looking at and bringing into the research, from theories one has read that may relate to one's data, to the data itself. A quick glance around the room at the thoughtful and serious faces confirmed my suspicion that we were now dabbling in deeper waters, adding layers of complexity to our understandings of narrative writing for qualitative researchers.

Caroline further substantiated my hunch by proceeding to read aloud—something she rarely does—from Dyson's report, which to me indicated the importance of Dyson's work and the narrative instruction embedded in it. It was during this reading that the connection between the Dillard piece and Dyson's piece became clear to me, and I recognized the meaning of Caroline's choice in having us read them back to back. All of a sudden, the terms on the board became animated for me—they were no longer items I needed to define because I *knew* them already.

Dyson's piece tackles some weighty concepts, but the juxtaposition to Dillard's piece helps illustrate them in a concrete way. Dillard defines the boundaries of her memoir as a child's "waking up," and she refocuses those boundaries as she makes choices about what to leave in and what to leave out. Similarly, Dyson is "constantly making decisions about what is, or is not, within the constructed bounds, what is, or is not, relevant to such a case" (Heller, reading Dyson, 2019). The major difference, of course, is that as poet/memoirist/essayist Dillard has the advantage of artistic license and can manipulate her own story to suit her boundaries. As a researcher whose job it is to be concerned with the problems that arise when dealing with meaningful human actions and their products, Dyson does not have the luxury of making her subjects "fit" artificial boundaries a nonresearcher might be tempted to impose on a "case." As she noted, "I had begun by observing one child's writing but, soon, was enmeshed in a complex social drama featuring many children and the wider classroom and societal contexts in which their acts, and their writing, gained meaning" (p. 1). Basically, her case went out of bounds, thus forcing *her* to go out of bounds as well and to acknowledge the dynamic essence of qualitative case study as a method. Dyson commented that "Constructing or writing a case is a dialogic process, one that involves defining and redefining one's understandings" (p. 2). In working with complex human beings in a living research situation, we need to cultivate a spirit of elasticity to accommodate the shifting boundaries of our research territory.

And here the circle loops back on itself, and we are again reminded of Dillard (1987) who, though she has the advantage of intimate knowledge, is still in some senses observing herself and her memories in an attempt to understand what Dyson calls "some phenomenon" (1995, p. 3)—not *her* life, per se, but the inner life of children—and to render it in all its complexity. For Dyson (1995), the *something* "to be conceived and reconceived" (p. 3) is learning to write. In writing this paragraph, I am struck anew by the interplay of Dyson's and Dillard's pieces and how each writer used writing and observation (observation and writing!) to illuminate "some phenomenon." Each writer underscored the necessity of, as Caroline says, "thinking small as well as big" and "being present on every scale" (Heller, class notes, 2019). As Garo and Denise noted in Chapters 3 and 4 (respectively), the small things help make connections—they "keep it real" for the reader; the big things (e.g., theoretical and sociocultural issues) give us an opportunity to reflect and contextualize the smaller things in a "big picture." Each is necessary to capture the complexity of the phenomenon.

The pitfalls associated with case study analysis and writing are many, and both Dyson and Dillard commented on them. Case studies and memoirs are peopled with *people*—*real* people, whose lives are "other" to us and cannot be completely known, whose secrets and inner selves are sacrosanct. The lives of these people continue beyond and outside the page, and that fact should give the writer pause. What are the possible implications of what I am about to write? In what ways might my interpretation—biased as it must be—impact the situation, the person I am writing about? These are just a few of the questions a qualitative researcher must address in order to acknowledge the nuances involved in writing about human beings. As Dillard (1987) noted, "Things were simpler when I wrote about muskrats" (p. 6). Dyson (1995) cautioned against the treatment of the individual as part of a "collective word that distances and dismisses" (p. 5), one that tends to sanitize, dehumanize, or homogenize. She also cautioned against speaking *for*, reminding us that a researcher's own history and experiences can impede understanding, just as they might allow it. She went on to note that researchers "*as writers* [my emphasis] can work to make another's life more perceptible, more accessible, by respecting the details of that world, the recurring themes and rhythms of the other's life scenes" (p. 4). This quote alone provides ample justification for a course like this one to be available to qualitative researchers.

THE RIVER IS NOT SENTIMENTAL

In the end, both Dillard and Dyson want to reach an audience: Dillard because she thinks there is something interesting, something worth considering, about a child's inner life, and Dyson because she wants to add knowledge and understanding to educational theories and practice. Dillard's audience is not just women of a certain age, ethnicity, and socioeconomic class who grew up in Pittsburgh, and Dyson's audience is not just academics. Each knows that to reach the scale of audience she wishes to attend to her work, she must use the writing to appeal to those whose lives do not necessarily intersect with hers. How each portrays the people at the center of her work is part of that appeal. Handouts from Caroline on characterization (see Appendix C) and sentiment (see Appendix D) versus sentimentality directly address the problem of portraying complex human beings.

According to Caroline, part of the answer to the puzzle of rendering complex lives on paper is a matter of sympathy, of feeling the gamut of human emotions one's participant is apt to have. "This is an essence of characterization," Caroline wrote, "and this is an essence of qualitative research: thoughtful, deeply humane research that endeavors to affect the reader and the world" (Heller, class handout, 2019). Easy to say, not so easy to do. What about when the researcher's ethos is fundamentally opposed to that of her subject? What strength of will or character does it take to sympathize with racist behavior, for example? Or how does a narrative writer expose the foibles of a person they love? These are scenarios that one must expect to arise and that must become part of the "dialogic process" Dyson described.

In addition to the difficulty of rendering people with sympathy, writers/researchers should also be chary of using sentimentality rather than sentiment in characterizing both people and events. Sentimentality, Caroline cautions, invites readers to "surrender the intellectual, the mindful, aspect of their make-up (Heller, personal communication, 2019) and to hand themselves over to greeting-card emotion. The sentimental writer relies on heavy-handed use of modifiers and hackneyed expressions, making feeling for the sake of feeling the main point of writing. In the end, this communicates nothing. Sentiment, on the other hand, is "evoked by restraint, by relying on brute detail" (Heller, 2019) to convey meaning. T. S. Eliot (1920) suggested that the only way to express emotion in art is by finding an "objective correlative," something Caroline shared in another handout during our fourth class (see Appendix E). Eliot used this fancy term to denote "a set of objects, a situation, a chain of events which shall be the formula of that *particular* emotion" (p. 92) the writer hopes to evoke. While Eliot no doubt used the word "formula" with a touch of irony, surely effective use of objective correlative defies any formula, just as Boo's deft reference to the melting Popsicle that frightened young Dernard defied formula, but evoked for the reader a world of emotion.

Combined with the connection between Dillard and Dyson, the discussions around these concrete tools for becoming a more effective writer of narrative had my head reeling by the end of Class Four. I had already been thinking about what scene I wanted to write about for our first "real" (as opposed to optional) assignment, and I could already see where the issues around characterization and sentiment would be paramount. Without Class Four, the issues could easily present a problem; after Class Four, I viewed them as an opportunity. The "something" I wanted to explore was my family's dedication (unspoken, of course!) to dying at home, and my plan was to try to draw a connection between the recent death of my mother and my first experience of a family member dying at home. Between the complexity of the people and the necessarily charged emotions involved, I knew I had my work cut out for me. Looking back on it now, I realize that the only reason I was able to write about the two experiences at all was because I now had the tools to render the scenes in a way that would be true to the people and events. I leaned into the concept of the objective correlative to render my family's grief with as much clarity and with as little sentimentality as possible. I *could* use word to create world.

THE RIVER IS A COMMUNITY

Class Four concluded with more of my classmates reading their optional assignments. This had already become one of my favorite elements of the course—I reveled in hearing my classmates read their work, and I was inevitably blown away by an insight, a turn of phrase, or an image that brought my imagination to its knees. Writing is such a personal endeavor; there is always the risk of our self-destructive comparisons or odious jealousy getting in the way of genuine appreciation of each other's work. By the time of this fourth class, however, the class had already fostered such a sense of fellowship that there was no room for such petty, albeit very human, feelings to spring forth. Instead, we saw in each other's work new possibilities for our own, and we saw our own work through someone else's eyes—a gift indeed.

Like the river, the nature of qualitative inquiry is not linear; it does not progress in a straight or straightforward line. Sometimes it meanders across familiar landscapes, sometimes it seems to loop back on itself, and at other times it rushes along silently, if swiftly. The nature of writing is the same, and has the same power to help the researcher/writer discover truths and new understandings. At times, we take to the river solo, cruising along at our own pace and taking in the sights. At other times, we seek companions and feel lucky when we find them. We enrich one another's experiences with a variety of perspectives, we remind one another of the richness and complexity of human nature, and we learn from one another along the way.

Each week we drifted off to our separate lives after our class, it was easy to imagine each of us wrapped up in our own thinking about what that class means to our work. But once again, Caroline brought us together in our separateness by asking each of us to consider how our new insights would bear on next week's assignment, which was to read anthropologist Michael Jackson's (1995) *At Home in the World* and compose questions for him in anticipation of his visit. You'll be part of that visit in the next chapter.

Drafts of Writing

The Threshold (final draft)

1. My parents' room is a tidy square with bright white walls and yellow-painted woodwork. The hardwood floor gleams, and the straightforward lines of the furniture assert function over form. The king-sized bed dominates the room as it has always done, but the inert form of my mother lying in it no longer commands as she always did. I have just administered pain medication, the routine of which has replaced traditional concepts of time; the earth no longer moves around the sun, dictating the shift from one day to the next. Our days have come to a halt in this land that Time denounced—or did this land of Dying denounce Time? Either way, it has ceased to be. Days now exist in three-hour increments and revolve around my mother. This, at least, has not changed, for she was always at the center. We set alarms, but we don't really need them, our hearts and minds

tethered as they are to this new instinct: to keep pain an arm's length from my mother while she decides when to leave us forever.

2. I squeeze some lotion into my palm and reach for her hand, the small bones rolling through my fingers like pick-up-sticks. The room is still, though noises from the rest of the house reach us from time to time. I can hear my father running water in the kitchen sink and my brother speaking quietly on the phone. His voice grows occasionally louder; he must be pacing back and forth in the dining room.

3. Just a few days ago, my father called to say that he got a wheelchair. My mother had fallen twice, and he was eager for the wheelchair's arrival. "I'll be able to wheel her out to the porch," he told me on the phone. "Maybe even take her for a walk down the lane."

4. Later that day I stopped by, and sure enough, there on the porch sat the wheelchair, my mother propped up in it, an unlit cigarette in one hand and a vacant look on her face. My father met me at the door with a wide smile and something like hope in his eye. Mom did not acknowledge my presence at all, and when I bent down close to say hello, it took a few moments for her gaze to settle on me. She smiled and waved the cigarette in my direction. While my father talked about the wonders of the wheelchair, I kept my eyes on Mom. Two days before when I visited, she swore at me and told me she didn't want any company. THAT was my mother. Where did THAT mother go? THIS mother waved the cigarette around the vicinity of her mouth, as though her lips were a moving target. In spite of the July heat and the perspiring glass of water beside me, goosebumps rose on my arms. Changeling, I thought.

5. Just outside the bedroom door, my brother's voice rises in a tight arc; he is, I can tell, speaking with his wife, but my imagination stalls before it can conjure a conversational context—my emotions are single-track, devoted to one enterprise only. I pick up my mother's other hand and smooth the skin moving loosely across the bones.

6. The day the wheelchair arrived, I asked my father if he wanted me to stay the night. With his head cocked to one side, he said, "No, of course not. Why would I want you to do that?"

7. I was still watching Mom, who had finally gotten the cigarette in her mouth and was now fumbling with the lighter, her eyes pegged on a distant point, one disconnected from anything going on here. I wondered what Dad saw when he looked at her.

8. "Well," I said, "things don't look so good today."

9. He insisted: they-were-fine, the-wheelchair-was-great, don't-worry. But at nine o'clock that night he called, and I drove the fifteen miles at 90 mph. When I arrived, Mom was in bed, unresponsive, her legs jerking around, her arms chopping at the air. While dad called hospice, I climbed into bed with my mother and tried to soothe her, holding her arms down so she wouldn't smack herself or me in the face. After some time, she stopped

flailing, but she moaned and moaned, an animal sound that sliced the air. My father paced the room and chanted her name "Janie-Janie-Janie" until the nurse arrived with drugs to take, at least, my mother's pain away.

10. I place my mother's hand on the quilt and pick up a hairbrush, running the soft bristles over her hair, and time folds itself away leaving me lodged in a snapshot memory of her, pregnant with my brother, sitting in an armchair with her feet up and me, aged four, brushing her hair over and over until she falls asleep.

11. The memory is disrupted by the thunk of a car door in the driveway, and I wonder who it is. Moments later, there are voices in the kitchen—men's and one woman's. My father is talking to my Uncle Jim (my mother's brother) and Aunt Lynn. Uncle Jim comes every morning and stays for hours. He seems to have lost time, too, and is easy to have around because he requires no company. He sits on the porch reading the paper until the day gets too hot, then drifts inside to work on the jigsaw puzzle somebody set up on the dining room table. Sometimes he drives off and comes back with sandwiches or doughnuts; taciturn by nature, his gifts give voice to the helplessness I sense lurking just beneath his skin, so pointed I don't dare touch him. I have seen him hovering outside the bedroom door, but I have yet to see him enter.

12. I hear my aunt laugh and imagine that she is sitting at the kitchen island, her hair perfectly coiffed, her nails perfectly polished, outfit strictly coordinated—she is a stalwart presence—and I think of her thumbing through the basket of photos I set there to give visitors something to look at, something to do with their hands. I have learned that grieving people need tactile occupations: a puzzle, spoons to stir their coffee, pictures to pick up and share, hand to hand, with others. The photos—a surprising number of them, given how much my mother hated the camera—are easy to look at: in them she is always Janie. Even frozen in time, you think she is about to laugh, offer you a glass of wine, invite you to eat one of her capacious meals, tell you a wildly embellished story, ask you to jitterbug with her. It is hard to reconcile Janie of the photographs with the shadow lying in the next room.

13. In these last few days, my father and brother and I have become Master Consolers. People come, take one look at us, and fall apart; their faces collapse, and we embrace, pat, shush. "She loves you very much," we say. "You are so important to her." And we mean it—it is true. We are grateful for their grief; it saves us from being swallowed by our own. At the end of each day, I no longer smell like myself, having absorbed the colognes and perfumes of our visitors; I climb into the shower not to refresh myself but to relocate my own scent.

14. Someone has started another pot of coffee—I can smell it—and a second woman's voice has joined the small chorus. My mother is snoring, a light whistle, and I tip my head to better hear the new voice. It is my father's sister, my Aunt Dixie. She and my mother were once close, plotting

get-rich-quick schemes when they were young. My father always shook his head when they tore off in a car—he knew they would return with something to make his life more difficult: a heavy piece of furniture ("It's an antique!") needing repairs; a box full of piglets, not-quite-weaned; once, a cross-eyed sheep; another time, fifty baby roosters. Dixie's voice, firm and light, reminds me of another time, another bed.

15. I was living in Seattle when my father called to tell me I needed to come home if I wanted to see my grandfather before he died. The train dragged against its tracks and slipped infinitesimally east, each mountain, each plain, each train-track city neighborhood marking my journey into the past. At home, I drove fast on icy country roads once so familiar now grown strange after months on the opposite side of the country where everything was green all the time. The whiteness of the landscape—ice, snow, birches hip-deep in their cold banks reaching bone-like arms to the sky—scorched my eyes in spite of the clouds. Driving against the current of the river on my left made it feel like I wasn't moving at all and—just for a second—I closed my eyes to make it all go away.

16. And then I was there, moving through the dim barn, grasping the smooth porcelain kitchen doorknob, pushing my way into the warmth of the house. The washing machine was running, a testament to the ordinary while my grandfather lay in a rented hospital bed in the living room, dying—extraordinary. And yet also ordinary. I thought he was asleep and lightly touched his wrist, the knobby bone there evidence of cancer's thrall. My grandfather was not a bony man and yet here was a bed full of bones and loose flesh. Then one eye flicked open and he saw me. "I didn't think I could wait," he whispered, "but I did." He smiled the trickster grin—the grin of someone who glued a dime to the floor every April first—and for a moment we were in the backyard on a summer day, lighting a firecracker under the lawn chair where my unsuspecting grandmother sat.

17. One afternoon I sat alone with Gramps. I was tired from strain and sleeplessness, propped up by the armchair in which I was slouched, a half-attended book in my lap. With the exception of a low-watt bedside lamp, the room was dim, sharpening my other senses. Gramps's breathing was slow but unlabored, an intermittent sigh. The sound of voices and the smell of coffee wafted in on occasional high and low notes. "The adults" (though I was in my twenties, I could never think of myself as anything but a child in that house) were talking to the minister. The deeper voices of the men translated as an indistinguishable rumble punctuated at times by a discernible word spoken by the higher voices of my mother or my Aunt Dixie. Behind their voices hummed the engine-workings of the house, the machines that carry on, oblivious to pain and sorrow. In that moment I gave thanks to Furnace, Dishwasher, and Clothes Dryer whose background refrain signified the persistence of order, of life.

18. In spite of the contrasts, I feel the same peace in this house now surrounded by all that is ordinary—ordinary people, ordinary routines—all while keeping company with a family member waiting at this unknowable threshold. To keep vigil in this timeless country is a gift, and I mean to be awake to every moment, present for every touch, every breath. Back then, when my grandfather was dying, my mother told me she didn't want to be such a burden to her children at the end, that we should put her in a nursing home. Noticing the slender crease in the quilt where my father occasionally lies down to rest, I can't imagine those words of hers remain true. My hope is that she knows her husband lies beside her, that she can hear us when we speak to her, that she smells the coffee and the freshly cut flowers I place by her bed every day. I hope that she knows the house—her house—is full of friends and family every day and that we won't leave her alone until she leaves us.

WRITING PROCESS ANALYSIS OF THE THRESHOLD

Paragraphs 1 and 2: As is typical of my writing process, this opening paragraph did not spring to mind easily; in fact, my original draft began with several pages describing me picking flowers for the vase I mention just briefly in my final draft. Several paragraphs into that description, I knew I would wind up throwing it all away; I came close to giving up to start over, but I pressed on hoping something useful would come of it. When I finally found myself in my parents' bedroom, alone with my mother, I knew I was onto something. Still, I continued to write, spewing memories and remembrances in no particular order. Soon, the writing folded over me and held me in a cocoon of recalling and recounting. To me, this is the best kind of writing. In academia, we use writing primarily to show what we know—to prove that we have read and understood texts, to demonstrate that we have synthesized materials. Rarely are we asked to write in order to discover what we think. It is, in my opinion, a missed opportunity.

For this assignment, when I finally wrote my way into my parents' bedroom, I knew something I didn't know before: my family was organized in a series of concentric circles. The outermost ring contained extended family and friends; the next contained my immediate family, including my brother and his children; the penultimate circle consisted of my parents and their marriage; finally, within that sacrosanct circle, my mother existed as the central being in my father's life. This realization was not something I would have come to just sitting around and thinking—I found it through writing—and it provided me with the frame through which I wanted to view my family scene.

I had three goals for the introductory paragraph: first, to establish my mother as the atomic center of the family scene; second, to capture that sense of timelessness engendered by witnessing the slow passing of a loved one; and, finally, to establish a tone of quiet observation that would carry throughout the piece. Opening with my mother in her marital bed was a conscious choice that I hoped would underscore her location at the center; I also hoped it would provide a central focus for the writing, a "homebase" I could return to over and over without becoming repetitious. To bring time into focus and to convey the immediacy of the experience, I decided to narrate this part of the scene in the present tense. After Class Four, I knew my success with this piece would hinge on my ability to render this scene without sentimentality. I had written the initial flower-picking pages before our class, and when I returned to them, I could see sentimentality oozing from nearly every line—partly because I was at the center of those pages. For example, in the very first paragraph, I wrote, "I need to get out of the house for a few minutes, and I can't bear to sit on the porch with yet another cup of coffee." I thought I might be able to achieve some of this by making use of a quiet and observational tone. This choice turned out to be crucial; it helped situate me at the periphery, where I could more easily observe (in this case, my memories) and share the sentiment of the experience.

Of course, picking those flowers was an experience I had, as was the conversation I had with my Uncle Jim later that day, and which I recounted in my first draft. These details, while true and important to my experience, were not important to the meaning I wanted to convey with this piece of writing. In her essay "How I Wrote the Moth Essay—and Why," Dillard (1985) likens writing about personal experience to creating a mosaic: just because you have a lap full of tiles does not mean your mosaic will be better if you use them all. I like this simile; it is an apt comparison for writing personal narratives and for writing one's research. Dillard goes on to say that all a writer needs to cull unneeded details and experiences from their writing is "nerves of steel and lots of coffee" (p. 11). I would add to that an unswerving and unsentimental view of one's writing. There is no room for preciousness in the revising process.

Paragraphs 3 and 4: I switched to the past tense to help cue my readers to the fact that I was providing some near backstory to help them understand how we came to be in this present. I gave some context for my mother's decline and, hopefully, showed how devoted my father was to my mother.

Paragraph 5: I returned to the present, indicated by a return to the present tense. I wanted the readers to feel as though they were in my parents' room with me, as this vigil required being in the present, even as memories and thoughts interceded from time to time. This paragraph also provided a model for the remaining structure of the piece. The things that happened outside this room were noticed, but they remained peripheral to my mother's experience, one that I was observing, one that was mysterious and unknowable.

Paragraphs 6–9: I returned to the near backstory I started earlier, providing the readers with even more details to help them see my mother's rapid decline, something I sensed was happening but that my father couldn't/wouldn't.

Paragraphs 10–13: I made the decision to continue the familiar pattern of me describing what was happening in the present while reaching into the past for memories that flesh out the present. Because the Janie readers meet is inert in the present, I wanted to give them some indication of who she once was and what she meant to people. For this reason, I offered details about people coming into the house to visit and their relationship with my mother. I also wanted the reader to see the irony (without being ironic!) in our roles as consolers.

Paragraph 14: I introduced my father's sister in paragraph 14. She was an important bridge to one of the messages I wanted to convey with this piece: that dying at home is a sacred part of our family culture. In my first draft, I included a long conversation Dixie and I had at the time. In revising, I realized that the conversation felt like a huge interruption—that it intruded on the flow between memory and present, that it was *too loud*. I decided I could convey the same message through the established structure, and so I used hearing Dixie's voice to launch a memory of another bedside vigil, that of my grandfather.

Paragraphs 15–18: The memory of my grandfather's last days (far backstory) occupy the final paragraphs. In them, I hoped to reflect the similarities between the two experiences (my grandfather's death and my mother's death) through a focus on time, the comforts of home, and the dying person being at the center even while everyday life carries on at the edges.

My goals for the final paragraph were to be explicit about the connections between the two vigils and about why they were personally important to me. I also wanted to echo motifs I established in the introduction, which I did by alluding to my parents' marital bed with the detail about the crease in the quilt where my father slept. In my original draft, that detail was much earlier in the narrative, but when I got to the end, I felt it would have a greater impact in the conclusion. I also wanted to return to my mother as the central and deciding figure she was in her living life, and so the final words "we won't leave her until she leaves us" mirror the last words of the introduction, "while she decides when to leave us forever."

At one point in the semester, Caroline alluded to a passage from Vaclav Havel's *To the Castle and Back* (2008) in which he writes that language "can never completely capture something as connected as reality, experience, or our souls" (p. 347). Writing my family scene made me experience the abiding truth of these words. At certain points in the writing and rewriting, I felt I was approaching the "truth" of the scene; more often than not, I felt bound by the constraints of my tools. In the end, through a studied and careful application of craft in conjunction with collaborating with my peers, I am satisfied that I landed on at least an approximation of the experience I described for my readers. If nothing else, it has brought me closer to *a* truth, if not *the* truth.

QUESTIONS FOR FURTHER WRITERLY CONTEMPLATION

1. To practice developing sentiment rather than sentimentality in your writing, try one or more of the following writing prompts:
   - Write a brief imaginative scene in which you describe a building (barn, apartment complex, seaside cottage, etc.) from the point of view of a person whose child has died—without ever mentioning the fact of the death.
   - Write a dialogue—real or imagined—for two people in which the conversational topic is superficial, hiding a more serious subtext; for example: a couple on the brink of a break-up deciding what movie to see.
   - Select a piece of personal writing you have done and isolate all the "I" statements (I + verb OR I + verb + a few other important words). Do the "I" statements tell a story of their own? Are the "I" statements self-focused or focused outward ("I felt so sad for her" vs. "I laid my hand on her arm")? Are there changes you can make to your "I" statements that would change the way your reader receives emotion?
2. Choose a favorite narrative—or select a reading from this book—and read it closely for evidence of what T. S. Eliot calls the "objective correlative," details or sets of details that convey the emotion of a single scene or that point toward an overarching feeling. (See "Thoughts on SENTIMENT vs. SENTIMENTALITY" handout in appendix.)

My Hopes for Class Five, by Caroline

That my students got to meet the soul and the work of anthropologist Michael Jackson. I became interested in Jackson's work after browsing through his books at the Harvard Coop one rainy evening. I opened *At Home in The World* almost by chance and felt that I was in the presence of an anthropologist whose work invited me to both think and feel deeply. Reading this book allowed me to ponder the question: what are the ingredients of an author's prose that let the reader feel that the author is fully inhabiting his research, not just reporting it? Once I was lucky enough to get to know Michael Jackson, I realized that the dynamic intensity in any story can only come from what the author has *felt*, not just thought about.

SUGGESTIONS FOR FURTHER READING

Bruner, J. (2004). Life as narrative. *Social Research*, 71(3), 691–710.

Elbow, P. (1998). *Writing with power: Techniques for mastering the writing process* (2nd ed.). Oxford University Press.

Josselson, R. (2004). The hermeneutics of faith and the hermeneutics of suspicion. *Narrative Inquiry*, 14(1), 1–28. https://doi.org/10.1075/ni.14.1.01.jos

Polkinghorne, D. E. (1988). *Narrative knowing and the human sciences*. State University of New York Press.

Richardson, L. (2000). Writing: A method of inquiry. In N. K. Denzin & Y. S. Lincoln (Eds.), *The SAGE handbook of qualitative research* (2nd ed., pp. 923–948). SAGE.

Richardson, L. (2001). Getting personal: Writing-stories. *International Journal of Qualitative Studies in Education*, 14(1), 33–38. https://doi.org/10.1080/09518390010007647

Schaafsma, D., & Vinz, R. (2011). *Narrative inquiry: Approaches to language and literacy research*. Teachers College Press.

REFERENCES

Dillard, A. (1985). How I wrote the moth essay—and why. In T. Cooley (Ed.), *The Norton sampler* (pp. 8–15). Norton.

Dillard, A. (1987). To fashion a text. In W. Zinsser (Ed.), *Inventing the truth* (pp. 55–76). Random House.

Dyson, A. H. (1995). *Children out of bounds: The power of case studies in expanding visions of literacy development*. National Center for the Study of Writing and Literacy.

Eliot, T. S. (1920). *The sacred wood: Essays on poetry and criticism*. Alfred A. Knopf.

Havel, V. (2008). *To the castle and back*. Random House.

Heller, C. (2019). Thoughts on sentiment vs. sentimentality (Class handout). Lesley University.

Jackson, M. (1995). *At home in the world*. Duke University Press.

CHAPTER 5

Meaning Through Journeying
Krysta Betit (followed by art work and drafts of chapter by Krysta)

Figure 5.1. Class Notes 1

Source: Student Krysta Betit's in-class notes created February 20, 2019

Our fifth meeting as a class was different from previous classes in that we tackled our first book-length text and, rather than turn to Caroline for guidance and craft suggestions, we were given two new guides—the poet, philosopher, and anthropologist Michael Jackson and his intimate study of the Warlpiri people of Central Australia, *At Home in the World* (1995). Though the text and the author are deeply intertwined in a generative sense, in the context of our work as researchers the delivery of information from each is markedly different and offers new ways to consider how research is done, how people are represented, and how the means by which we communicate both our own positions and those of our participants figure into the larger schemas of representation and authority. The author himself served as a model of behavior and style, while the text served as a research exemplar and an instruction manual for narrative writers. Dr. Jackson's visit with us also served as inspiration for my own pages of sketches alongside my notes, excerpts of which I've included.

When doing research with human beings, the voice of authority is (traditionally) given to the researchers themselves and the task of representation is often in the hands of an individual who is privileged by some form of dominance in the broader cultural hierarchy of our world relative to the individual or individuals being studied. To represent another person with integrity is an act of authority because a researcher's writing becomes the means through which research participants' voices are represented and heard. Researchers are not writing about themselves for the purpose of publication, and while research interlocutors may be invited to have input into a text, it is ultimately the researcher who shapes the final text that others will read. The voice through which this authority is communicated is at the heart of why hearing from Michael Jackson in person, after hearing the *voice* of Michael Jackson *through his written text* offer us two routes through which to consider the ever-shifting and sometimes competing roles of researcher as listener, recorder, curator, and finally *teller* of others' stories.

To prepare for our meeting with Jackson, Caroline asked us to create a list of questions and asked a member of the class to serve as discussion moderator. Our questions fell into distinct categories:

1. Questions Around Processes of Field Work
2. Jackson as Researcher/Interpreter/Analyzer
3. Jackson as Writer
4. Jackson's Inspirations/Reception
5. Challenges of Research
6. Advice to New Researchers

Though a few of our questions focused on Jackson's fieldwork and the relationships he built with his participants over time, more centered on the written voice through which he communicated. We were already developing a sense of responsibility as future "voices of authority."

In reading *At Home in the World* (1995), I was struck by the scope of Jackson's ambitious undertaking as well as the assured voice with which he communicated to his readers. Early in the text, he stated his desire to create something new: "I wanted to develop a style of writing which would be consonant with lived experience, in all its variety and ambiguity. Nowadays, one must have recourse to art and literature if one is to keep alive a sense of what hard science, with its passion for definitive concepts and systematic knowledge, often forgoes or forgets" (p. 4). His voice is clear; he intends to write something new about what it means for persons to exist where they are in the world, and to do so Jackson will turn to influences that don't always "live" within the social sciences realm. An example of this is when he described another researcher's thoughts on a signature aspect of Warlpiri life: "Fred Myer speaks of a distinction between the immediately visible world and the Dreaming—a noumenal dimension of Being out of which everything emerges, in which all life forms are steeped, but which people must be taught to see" (p. 26). Jackson goes on to describe an experience of camping in the outback with his wife—and he brings literary beauty to

Figure 5.2. Class Notes 2

Source: Student Krysta Betit's in-class notes created February 20, 2019

a moment of cooking and steeping tea: "That night we cooked a spinach risotto, and boiled a billy can of tea made from the wild lemongrass that scents the air at night at Ngarliyikirlangu" (p. 26). In this one sentence, he gives readers access to his own field experience as well as the atmosphere of the world of people he wants to understand (p. 26). His voice is deft, lyrical, and polished on the page.

In person, while he spoke deftly and lyrically, too, he also revealed a shy and vulnerable quality that gave us another window onto how a researcher may operate in the service of those they write about.

As she introduced Jackson to the class, Caroline said of *At Home in the World* that "everything spoke to [her] on a thinking level and a feeling level" (Heller, personal communication, 2019). This brought forth Jackson's opening remarks about his relationships with his research interlocutors and the fidelity he hoped for in his work, not just in his interpretations of interlocutors' lives and values but in fostering authentic relationships with them. Hearing Caroline's opening comment, I was brought back to an early moment in Jackson's book (1995) when he explained the scope of his project: "By going to Aboriginal Australia, I hoped to explore the ways in which people created and sustained a sense of belonging and autonomy when they did not build or dwell in houses, and *house* was not synonymous with *home*" (p. 4). I scribbled a comment into my notes as Jackson spoke: "home is something to do with feeling unconflicted in a place . . . feet planted firmly on the ground." Similar sentiments, but different ways of voicing bring us to a vision of this place as a place of simultaneous homeyness and borderlessness, which ignited both my intellectual and emotional response. In turn, it gave me two ways of seeing Jackson the author, a celebrated intellectual with command of the written word, as well as Jackson the generous visitor, a kind and sage speaker whose verbal musings on the world, though no less poignant, are steeped in the vulnerability and gentleness of a person for whom research is not a clinical academic exercise, but an ongoing sense of respectful, honorable immersion in and openness to what surrounds him, be it Warlpiri culture or a visit to our seminar.

Evoking much of what Rebecca's chapter just discussed about the value of sentiment over sentimentality, Jackson's work conveys the fullness, in all its complexity, of his own experience; "Her lachrymose tone irritated me" (p. 45), his straightforward words regarding a research interlocutor's pleas for a ride, are juxtaposed with the words of one who cares so deeply for the people he strives to represent that he begins one of the book's chapters simply with, "This is Ringer's story" (p. 74), followed by Ringer's words standing alone, sans the social science researcher's more typical interpretive overlay. This was also true of the reminiscences Jackson shared with us about his work. His ability to paint both his research interlocutors *and* himself using all shades and nuances of human motivation and experience is what helped me understand his immense talent and largesse as a researcher—we can close our eyes and see through to the heart of his messages about home, place, belonging, and the responsibilities of representing self and others.

I found the shyness and humility with which Jackson spoke to us in person startling and deeply moving, for he is considered an authority on a wide range of topics and on qualitative research itself. Looking at my classmates' (and my own) copies of his text, I observed hundreds of post-its, paper clips, and highlighter markings—but in coming together the following week to reflect on our meeting with him, I realized that few of us had written extensive notes about his presence with us, taken, as we were by Jackson's grace and forthcomingness, diminishing distance between sage researcher and graduate students.

For me, two moments particularly stood out from our meeting with Jackson. The first was when Caroline told the story of stumbling into the Harvard Coop during a rain storm and finding Jackson's work serendipitously; the second was when Jackson told a story of his first wife's death and of starting a new marriage years later while engaged in the research that led to *At Home in the World*. They stood out because the universe suddenly felt as random as it may truly be. It didn't seem right or fair that Jackson had suffered such an immense loss, but I also took in the idea that balances are always swaying, often bringing together objects and people that need to be brought together. It was after sharing the story of his second marriage that Jackson turned to our questions and began an answer that at once affirmed *and* brought into question the roles he assumed as a researcher. Of his own understandings as a White New Zealand-born man choosing to "study" native aboriginal peoples, he said, "I grew up aware that I was an heir to a great historical injustice." He did not seem conflicted about this, but instead sat with the paradox and pointed to it as easily as one points toward a destination down an unpaved road.

Regarding the potential harm of representing the lives of others, he responded to our worries, present and future: "We live in a world where we're told that we all belong in a category," he said. His response reminded me of a line in his text: "Definition is itself at the roots of racism: the way we reduce the world to a word, and gag the mouths of others with our labels" (p. 14). These two thoughts are conceptually similar but they were delivered in different manners—the voices here speak to different ways in which researchers may conceive of themselves. In the first, spoken moment, that we were privileged to witness in our seminar, the researcher is, along with all of humanity, a potential victim of labels; in the second, written moment, the researcher considers how he may victimize others. Each statement is given from a different perspective. The written voice of the researcher can feel far away, even lofty, while the oral voice of the author sitting across the table from me, felt as near as my classmates were near, as Caroline was near. And neither voice is less or more powerful than the other. At the heart of each is a desire to lean in toward emotional and intellectual honesty, truth, fairness.

In his book (1995), Jackson questioned the potential for a researcher's bias as a form of betrayal. He wrote about moving from fieldwork to the generative process of creating a text: "Sometimes one feels that this transmutation involves a kind of betrayal. The question arises time

Figure 5.3. Class Notes 3

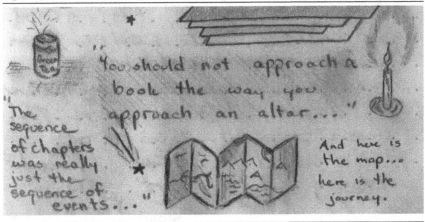

Source: Student Krysta Betit's in-class notes created February 20, 2019

and time again: how can one keep faith with the people who adopted one into their world and transformed one's understanding? How can one reconcile the different conceptions of knowledge that obtain in the field and academe?" (p. 156) Here I could see and feel his determination to do right by those he considered so closely, and among whom he was (soon, in the course of his fieldwork) considered an embraced member.

In looking through my notes about Jackson's visit to our class and my subsequent drafts of this chapter, I was struck by how difficult it was to write this chapter in a way that would be useful and instructive to those attempting to capture and convey the lived experiences of other human beings. So much can be gleaned from Jackson's book and our collective experience of meeting and speaking with him, and yet to distill the impacts feels monumental. I am brought back to Jackson's simple advice to each of us in our various stages of research and writing, his warning not to take ourselves and our research too seriously: "You should not approach a book the way you approach an altar," he said with a rather mischievous smile. Garo, in reviewing one of my earlier drafts of this chapter, told me that he remembered Jackson sharing with us that *At Home in the World* had been dismissed by certain scholars in the broader academic world for being "too narrative." Funny that this is precisely the reason Caroline brought Jackson into our lives—our class's stated permission/invitation to tell the stories of our research undertakings free of the jargon and pretense that is pervasive in social science scholarship. Perhaps this is why this chapter was difficult for me to write. I'm denied the possibility of hiding behind esoteric language. I must instead share the story of Jackson's visit as clearly and straightforwardly as Jackson offered us—in his book and in his presence—the story of the Warlpiri people he met and hoped to understand.

I spoke with my classmates right after Jackson's visit. "Why did he affect me so much when he came into the room?" Denise asked. "He was humble and shy, and yet he managed to add order to the randomness of life." In writing about the sometimes confusing expansiveness of the definition of home for the Warlpiri people, Jackson the author walks the reader through the meanings of home with ease and authority. Jackson the *embodied* author visiting our class took it one step further, distilling his work in this way: "Doing ethnography at this level is like being a guest in someone's home and yes they tell you to take anything out of the refrigerator, but of course you don't . . . ." This relatability, this humor, is a hallmark of Jackson's work. Even when writing about something as serious as working with one's fieldnotes, he wrote rather cheekily, "But fieldwork cannot be willed into happening. Inevitably, it proceeds by fits and starts. Anxieties and doubts beset you, no matter how good your language skills, how thorough your background reading, how extensive your ethnographic experience in other cultures" (p. 21).

At the end of our conversation with Jackson, Caroline asked if I would accompany him to the elevator and show him which bus to take on his route home, for he rejected our offers to drive him home, insisting that he loved to take the bus. I was nervous but excited to speak to him, and overcame my nervousness by telling him that I would be his "temporary Virgil." This announcement made him laugh, and we eased into a conversation about journeys, both academic and personal. As I think back on our conversation, alas, unable to remember it completely, I am struck by a final note from his book: "Meaning resides in the journeying, not the destination, and the authenticity of ethnographic knowledge depends on the ethnographer recounting in detail the events and encounters that are the grounds on which the very possibility of knowledge rests" (p. 163).

Drafts of Writing

Supplement to Chapter 5—Revising My Initial Paragraphs

This entire chapter is a wild palimpsest—the story of how I wrote the story of another person who was visiting our class to tell the story about how he wrote a story about and on behalf of people whose stories were drastically different from his own. In Figures 5.4–5.8, you will find my notes and revisions on three different drafts of this chapter as it came together—I hope they offer useful reflections about revision as both an act of contraction and an act of expansion.

Figure 5.4. Betit Writing Drafts 1

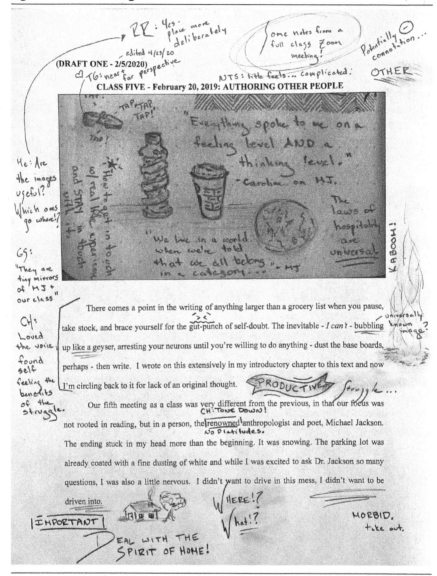

Source: Student Krysta Betit's writing draft, 2019

Figure 5.5. Betit Writing Drafts 2

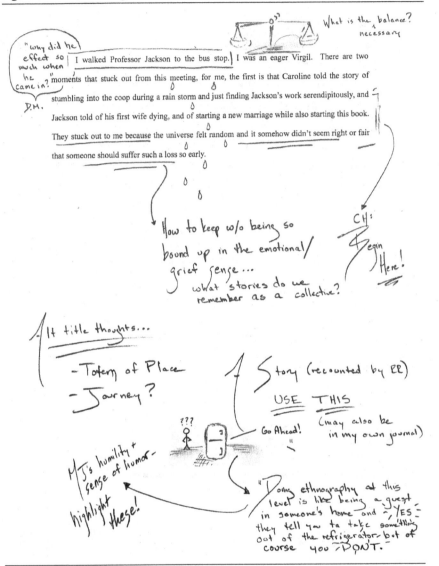

Source: Student Krysta Betit's writing draft, 2019

Figure 5.6. Betit Writing Drafts 3

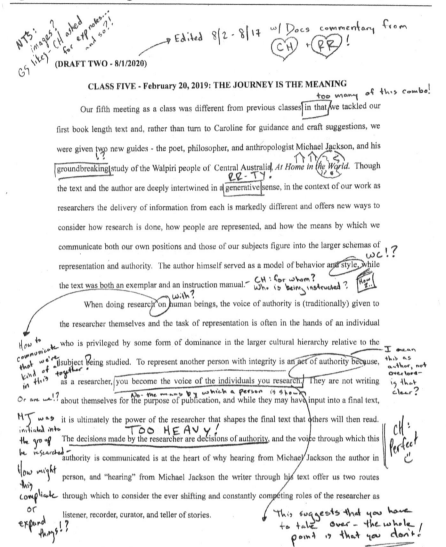

Source: Student Krysta Betit's writing draft, 2019

Meaning Through Journeying

Figure 5.7. Betit Writing Drafts 4

[handwritten: was said in class...]
[handwritten: I chose this image b/c it was one of the 1st things CH said in class]

(DRAFT THREE - 3/7/2022)

[handwritten: ✓ NOTES 6/ 3/4-3/7 - after review of journals, previous drafts, and various scraps of paper/correspondence.]

CLASS FIVE - February 20, 2019: MEANING THROUGH JOURNEYING

[handwritten annotations on image: ...or the artist of another person's chewed up pear... / That's the scary part: becoming the author of another person's story...]

Our fifth meeting as a class was different from previous classes in that we tackled our first book-length text and, rather than turn to Caroline for guidance and craft suggestions, we were given two new guides - the poet, philosopher, and anthropologist Michael Jackson and his intimate study of the Walpiri people of Central Australia, *At Home in the World*. Though the text *[handwritten: changed from "groundbreaking" by review committee.]* and the author are deeply intertwined in a generative sense, in the context of our work as researchers the delivery of information from each is markedly different and offers new ways to consider how research is done, how people are represented, and how the means by which we communicate both our own positions and those of our participants figure into the larger schemas of representation and authority. The author himself served as a model of behavior and style, while the text served as a research exemplar and an instruction manual for narrative writers. He *[handwritten: Added for clarity.]* also served as inspiration for many pages of sketch notes, excerpts of which are included.

[handwritten: Kept from previous draft.]
[handwritten: Added for Clarity]

When doing research with human beings, the voice of authority is (traditionally) given to *[handwritten: team effort]* the researchers themselves and the task of representation is often in the hands of an individual who is privileged by some form of dominance in the larger cultural hierarchy relative to the individual or individuals being studied. To represent another person with integrity is an act of authority because, as a researcher, one's writing becomes the means through which other voices

[handwritten: changed from subject - Even as we write away from systems of dominance - language + habit struggle to keep up!]

Source: Student Krysta Betit's writing draft, 2019

Figure 5.8. Betit Writing Drafts 5

are represented and heard. Researchers are not writing about themselves for the purpose of publication, and while they may have input into a final text, it is ultimately the researcher who shapes the final text that others will read. The voice through which this authority is communicated is at the heart of why hearing from Michael Jackson *the anthropologist and author* in person, after hearing the voice of Michael Jackson *through his written text* offer us two routes through which to consider the ever-shifting and sometimes competing roles of researcher as listener, recorder, curator, and researcher as teller of others' stories.

[Handwritten annotations: "removed 'power'"; "Expand to clarify!"]

Source: Student Krysta Betit's writing draft, 2019

QUESTIONS FOR FURTHER WRITERLY CONTEMPLATION

1. In what ways might we, as researchers, position ourselves to remain in conversation with our subjects? How can we maintain professional relationships and boundaries while also becoming reporters on the lives and experiences of other people?
2. What does authenticity mean to you as a researcher? How might your answer be similar to that of your participants or, as Jackson refers to his participants, interlocutors? How might it be different? How can these similarities and differences prove fruitful or generative?
3. In envisioning fieldwork, what stumbling blocks are most likely to prevent you from doing your best work on behalf of your participants? What are some steps you can take before fieldwork begins?
4. What biases or preconceived notions about your participants are you aware of yourself holding? How might you best acknowledge these while also working through them?

My Hopes for Class Six, by Caroline

Some years ago my undergraduate anthropology professor, Dr. Milton Singer, recommended Carla Cappetti's (1993) book, *Writing Chicago: Modernism,*

Ethnography, and the Novel. I loved this book, particularly the opening chapter, "Between Literature and Science: Chicago Sociology and the Urban Literary Tradition," which seemed to me a perfect endorsement for our class! Cappetti sees qualitative research studies connecting deeply with the work of novelists, for both aim to lead readers to the stuff of real life. She illuminated the origins of the Chicago School of Sociology, and the degree to which novels about Chicago were used to teach young sociologists not only how to do sociology, but how to write. With Cappetti's insights, alongside those of Laurel Richardson, who heralds writing's deep importance to the process of qualitative inquiry, which I also assigned for class six, we reexplored craft topics, with a special focus on bringing a scene to life. I hoped that we have plenty of time toward the end of our 2 ½ hours together for students to read their scene papers aloud.

SUGGESTIONS FOR FURTHER READING

Jackson, M. (2012). *Lifeworlds: Essays in existential anthropology*. University of Chicago Press.
Jackson, M. (2013). *The accidental anthropologist*. Random House New Zealand.
Jackson, M. (2014). *The politics of storytelling: Variations on a theme by Hannah Arendt* (Critical anthropology, 2nd ed.). Museum Tusculanum Press.

REFERENCE

Jackson, M. (1995). *At home in the world*. Duke University Press.

CHAPTER 6

Representational Adequacy
Bringing My Scene to Life

Jeanne Lima

Our first nonoptional writing assignment for Narrative Writing for Qualitative Researchers asked us to write a scene; our scene papers were due at the end of our sixth class. Caroline had provided us with two alternatives for scene consideration: (a) for those of us who were already working within a research setting, we could *"bring to life a scene from that setting or a slice of its 'life' that captures the excitement of what you are studying"* OR (b) we could write *"a sketch of our family—a slice of life that would portray the culture of our family that somehow evoked a larger truth about them."* Caroline appended the assignment with a reminder to think deeply about elements of narrative that we already discussed: backstory, front story, wide lens, focused lens, characterization, and sentiment versus sentimentality, and to apply these craft elements to our scenes.

Because I had just spent my holiday break horseback riding at the Flying E Ranch in Wickenburg, Arizona, I decided to write a scene from that trip. I felt that my experiences contained the color and sensations not just of a good scene, but a *great* one: wranglers dressed in dusty leather chaps shouting directions amidst galloping horses kicking up dirt between the paddocks and the barn; the Sonoran Desert, which yielded plants bearing names like Soap Tree Yucca; the insistent calls of the vermillion flycatcher birds echoing between the craggy slopes of the Vulture Mountains, their voices piercing the silence of the desert; the ranch's rustic dining room with its table constructed of heavy oak planks, inviting guests and wranglers who'd worked up appetites riding on the warm desert trails.

Caroline also reminded us that *the scene should have meaning—it should serve a larger purpose evoking the themes of one's research or the life of one's family.* Mine, I felt, did, but its meaning was not one that I was accustomed to sharing. It certainly involved family, but usually I kept the story of my family tucked away in the caverns of my mind—caverns that, even when alone, I hesitated to enter. Nevertheless, I realized that this story should imply important meanings behind "the scene," just as a researcher chooses scenes from her field observations that speak to the larger themes of the research, as Denise Mytko discussed in Chapter 3. Furthermore, I started to feel that if I were to represent the lived meanings of my future research participants, I needed to understand the vulnerability that such unearthing entailed. Without evoking the *meaning* of my holiday vacation, vis-a-vis avoiding the pain of being with my family over the holidays, my scene would be shallow, meaningless. The chapter from Cappetti (1993) also reminded us that scenes are important in narrative writing because life *happens* in scenes.

Still, I wrestled with myself about whether I would write about my Christmas trip and certainly whether I would read it aloud.

My passion for writing—no, rather, my *yearning* to write something notable, something true about the human condition—*my* human condition, as well as the human conditions of my future research participants—triumphed over my fears. I would write the scene of my week at the ranch, even though in doing so I would likely have to depict events in my life that led me to that week. The narrative meaning, as we were coming to understand, would require this. My comfort lay in drawing upon those events in the skillful writing manner that Caroline had been describing all semester, utilizing only those details essential to create the threads of narrative logic that would lay the foundation for my scene. I would carefully weave together the narrative elements that would facilitate an authentic representation of the scene—no histrionics, no melodrama, no sentimentality. In order to achieve this, I relied on the technique that we'd discussed in previous classes, and which Rebecca Redlon discussed in Chapter 4: T. S. Eliot's (1920) concept of the objective correlative, which, as Eliot described, constitutes "a set of objects, a situation, a chain of events" (p. 92) through which the writer evokes the emotional richness inherent in these details rather than directly stating the emotion itself. The scene I would describe would indeed carry within it the emotion of my trip, but I would never directly state that emotion. Perhaps, too, that would enable me to venture into those precarious mental abysses. I would write a scene that flowed naturally from the characters and events that precipitated it, pleasing T. S. Eliot, along with Caroline.

The reading assignments for this week were the chapter from Cappetti (1993), which Caroline indicated could on its own lay the foundation for a course like Narrative Writing for Qualitative Researchers. We also read Laurel Richardson's (2000) *Writing: A Method of Inquiry*, which highlighted narrative writing goals and exercises, but stopped short of actual instruction in narrative writing. The previous week, to prepare for our discussion of Cappetti and Richardson, Caroline offered guiding questions for us to ponder. A question related to the Richardson article piqued my interest: *Richardson (2000) talks about micro-process writing-stories (p. 932). What does Richardson mean by her term and how have you experienced the impact of micro-process writing in this seminar and in other areas of your writing lives?* Caroline had expressed some disappointment that Richardson did not actually focus on *craft* in her article, but I viewed the microprocess of writing-stories as a means of clarifying my writing and honing my skills as I developed my text. Richardson asked, "Who has not looked at the computer screen, read a paragraph he or she has written, and then chosen to alter it? Who has not had their subsequent writing affected by what they have already written? How does the process of writing passages and reading them back to yourself open new questions and issues that feedback and emanate from the earlier passages?" (p. 932). She went on to allude to the influence of computers on our writing processes. I related to that. Years ago, before personal computers became commonplace, I wrote my papers in longhand. I was constantly crossing out and using caret marks to insert new words, sentences, paragraphs. I performed all my revisions pencil on paper so that I could then transfer them, using my Olympia manual typewriter—a clumsy machine, now obsolete. This process forced me to retype an entire page or even the entire paper if I decided to alter a word or portion of the text midtyping. That challenge has been alleviated by computers, of course, allowing us to revise *while* typing and thus obtain instant feedback about whether we have preserved textual cohesion. We can immediately determine the effectiveness of an alteration—whether we have properly secured the links that unite sentences or paragraphs, and/or enhanced the clarity of the text through our revisions. Thus, "story-micro-processes," as Richardson described them, enable us to view more immediately where our texts are going and how we can clarify the details that can best get them there.

In thinking about this guiding question for our read of Richardson's article, I shared with the class how my scene assignment, "Christmas on the Trail," underwent several digital revisions—12, to be exact, as evidenced by the document name for the final version I would submit for Class Six (and, if courage prevailed, even read aloud)—"Scene Assignment Draft XXXXXXXXXXXX.docx," each X standing for a version. While writing, if I didn't have access to a computer I immediately copied any notes on the story into a new version when I reached home. In that manner, I could see immediately how my hastily chronicled thoughts fit into the printed text and whether they added value and meaning to the scene. I also made extensive use of the online thesaurus to replace words with more specific choices. I could examine the value of my substitutions online and click the little undo symbol if I didn't like them. This immediate feedback enabled me to clarify—not only to the reader, but to myself—what I had seen in the desert and how I felt on the back of a horse. Micro-process-stories also enabled me to realize the value of applying narrative craft to research because the ease of revision allowed me to position/reposition the details of my scene in such a manner that they served the larger meaning. Moreover, while I relied on the immediacy of feedback on the computer when I composed previous academic papers, I now adjusted my techniques on the scene writing assignment to achieve what I hoped was an evocative narrative voice that would draw readers into the world I was creating.

I also thought a great deal about another guiding question for the week. That question too, helped me write my scene, if more indirectly: *Based on reading Cappetti (1993) and Richardson (2000) and anything else we've thus far turned to in our seminar,* Caroline asked us to consider, *do you see value in the literary traditions of Chicago Sociologists returning to a prominent place in the social sciences? If so, what is that value?* I again looked for parallels between the elements of narrative that I was thinking about for my scene paper and those that Cappetti described in the first chapter of her book. She noted that the Chicago sociologists relied on personal life records, journalism, and literature to evoke the experiences of (in the case of their own literary focus) urban life. Likewise, William Isaac Thomas (1931), a founder of Chicago sociology, whom Cappetti references (p. 21), recommended gathering letters, diaries, and autobiographies—published or unpublished—and in the author's native language. Robert Parks, another early Chicago School sociologist, endorsed the literary works of Goethe, Tennyson, Whitman, Tolstoy, Dickens, Twain, and many others, as resources to address the social issues of industrialization and urbanization. Parks was more interested in gathering details through keen sensory observation than in forming generalizations—a practice which, upon transferring to writing, enables sociologists to *notice* small moments (see Chapters 2 and 3) and include them as observed reality. Finally, Robert Redfield, Park's sociology student, contributed to the second generation of Chicago School sociologists by employing literatures of immigration, the family, and the city, represented by authors such as Upton Sinclair, Edith Wharton, James T. Farrell, and H. L. Mencken. I noted authors from my own reading who brought forth human action and behavior through the characters in their stories. For instance, Twain's (1884) masterful use of dialogue between Huck and Jim in *Huckleberry Finn* engages the reader in Huck's conflict over whether to surrender Jim to authorities as a runaway slave: "That's just the way: a person does a low-down thing, and then he don't want to take no consequences of it. Thinks as long as he can hide it, it ain't no disgrace. That was my fix exactly" (Chapter XXXI.). Similarly, Wharton's (1911) characterizations of Ethan and his wife, Zeena, in *Ethan Frome* yield an insight into a poor farmer's dissatisfaction, propelling the narrative toward an ending that is wholly unexpected, but at the same time entirely plausible.

The Chicago School sociologists suggested many narrative elements that would help me compose my scene paper. In lieu of the native language that Thomas recommended, I would incorporate the cowboy jargon of the wranglers. Instead of industrialization and urbanization, I would describe the Sonoran Desert setting in contrast to the suburban setting in which I grew up. Finally, I would rely on Edith Wharton's sharp characterizations of Ethan Frome and his wife to inspire my sketches of my own family members.

I had readied the first draft of my scene paper for submission and christened it with the title "Christmas on the Trail." During our five previous classes, Caroline had offered writing advice that my fellow students have already shared in previous chapters. As I thought about reading my scene aloud, I performed a mental checklist: *Did I bring my scene to life? Did I evoke this particular time and this particular place and these particular people?* Well, I *had* diligently described the dirt paddock from which I had mounted my horse and even incorporated the wrangler's dialogue, "Git on up, Jeanne." (Later, as we commented on each other's papers through Google Docs, Caroline and several of my classmates suggested that I start with the wrangler's dialogue to draw the reader in right away. It was good advice.) I asked myself, *did I evoke the purpose of the scene? Life happens in scenes,* Cappetti had said and Caroline had reminded us when she introduced this writing assignment. *Life is built in scenes.* Okay, but the unsettling part was that it was *my* life that was built into my scene. My job as a writer was to relate what happened and let the reader judge, so I wrote: "I was on my own journey: an escape from the family Christmas in Massachusetts." In class we'd talked a great deal about how important it was to provide context—backstory to give meaning to front story; wide angle to give meaning to focused angle. Well, my front story depicted how I sat perched on Ponder, the bay quarter horse I was assigned, ready to ride into the Sonoran Desert. I had also added a brief flashback to more fully explain my front story: "For two days since I had arrived at the ranch, I had been on horseback, traveling the trails through the mountains and flatlands of the Sonoran Desert—four hours all-told, two in the morning and two in the afternoon." However, I felt my scene still needed more context to evoke the larger meanings: the backstory, the story behind the story. I'd started to hint at this purpose in the second paragraph: "Even though the staff had prepared all kinds of Yuletide festivities that day—singing, tree decorating, Christmas cookies—that was not what I cared about. As a matter of fact, I could have done very well without them." Then, transitioning into the third paragraph, I expanded my backstory, providing context for it that included details that would explain the logic behind my vacationing at Circle E Ranch on Christmas Day: "A little history about my aversion to family Christmas would do here." I tried to provide just enough detail to let the readers experience the events of that backstory and judge everything, including my own character, for themselves.

Caroline had given us a handout entitled, "Everything You Wanted to Know About Writing, but Were Afraid to Ask." In it she recommended *Concision, crisp verbs rather than -ing construction. E. B. White at Work: The Creation of a "Paragraph." Active voice. Rhythm. Letting objects and actions speak for themselves as long as possible. Strong verbs, long/short sentences. Just before the period is what we remember! Scenes that hold meaning.* I wrote the following line: "She was sitting on the side of my parents' bed, which she had commandeered for her visit." I realize now that "propped" would have been a better verb to use than "sitting."

What else had I jotted down in my notes during class? What could help me write this story? I eyed my scrawled notes that included reminders/writing tips—*milk narrative tension; keep things moving; have eye on something bigger; utilize both wide-angle and focused angle lens*—and the following lines resulted: ". . . three silhouettes on horseback atop the mountain" and then "I peered to the side of Ponder's hooves at a plant comprised of clusters of thick barreled stems . . . no more than 8 inches high."

I thought of our discussions about using sentiment rather than sentimentality: *When lots of drama, tension there, back off or you have melodrama. Sentimentality. Back off.* "We already knew that our mother was sick and not in the way that most people were sick. There was no crying, no 'I want Mommy' hysterics."

. . . look at the particulars of situations in their own universe of meaning. Which includes the effect of the macro on the micro, the wide angle on the focused angle. Thus, lots of context features needed!!! "Walking on, leisurely and rambling, horses and riders scaled the crescent-shaped sides of the Vulture Mountain Range. Ponder likes to do what I can only call a cross between a jump and a little gallop when he climbs the ledges."

Caroline had also given us a handout about using dialogue in our scenes. *Dialogue*, I pondered: *Keeps narrative moving—advances it. But we shouldn't give the reader meaningless exchanges. We should only use dialogue when a person is saying something that no amount of trying will allow us to say it as well, and/or when those words are endemic to the emotional tone and really bring out who the speaking person is.* I recalled the text that my sister, listed as "wireless caller" in my cell phone, had sent me the previous Christmas: "Jeanne, you did exactly what I said you would do. You put the responsibility on me and made this all about you." It was one of many texts that prompted my escape from the family Christmas fest, and its sting would become a major catalyst to my story: the reason for my exodus to the Flying E Ranch in Arizona.

Early in the semester we'd discussed the differences between *implicit and explicit analysis* when presenting the story of one's data—that is, figuring out when we needed to be explicit about what something means and when, such as our iconic melting Popsicle example, it would be more powerful to let an incident speak for itself. *Implicit versus explicit analysis*: "The fuzzy like quality and the translucent spines of this cactus make it beautiful to behold, but that beauty is deceiving. The slightest contact with a jumping cholla will cause its spines to detach themselves from the branch and thrust themselves like needles into your skin or clothing. And yes, it hurts, and they are hard to pull out." I wasn't altogether sure if this passage counted as implicit or explicit (I think likely explicit! What do you think?). But I knew that the written sentences felt meaningful and satisfying to me, bringing readers into the desert scene, but with a bit of instruction/warning about what to watch out for while there.

My reverie concerning my hope that I had adhered to the writing craft tips we'd discussed and read about also involved different ways of approaching revision. Tonight, Caroline reminded us that *most every piece of writing has life and promise. But the real potential is in one's willingness and ability to strengthen the whole; to live up to its promise. And this is difficult.* She advised us to ask ourselves, *with the skills I have now, can I make it better?* And she went on to discuss two categories of revision: structural and fine tuning. The latter, she said, is often more palatable, more inviting because structural revision implies changes in organization that can feel daunting, but that are important—questions such as: *Should I present this material chronologically? By scenes? By connected stories? By highlighting and organizing around characters? By organizing around the data themes?* Caroline suggested that all of these are strong organizational options, but added that one element of narrative is not optional. Like in a good piece of music, *the beginning and end should reflect each other, the end in some sense being a recapitulation/an echo of the beginning.* Oh, please God, I thought, don't let me have to perform any major changes in structure!

The time arrived for me to share my paper. Yes, I raised my hand to read aloud. I don't remember much about reading my scene paper to my classmates, which is not unusual for me. I tend not to remember the details of scary events. However, I do recall a couple of occurrences as I read aloud. At home I had perused my paper repeatedly, but I had done so silently. Reading it silently, I felt that my scene flowed. However, reading aloud before others, my voice faltered a couple of times. It was as if the flow of my story suddenly hit a dam—perhaps a word that didn't quite fit or a thought that didn't quite link to what went before. At these moments, the flow of thought seemed to roll backward or disperse, and I paused each time, *hearing* the dams of impeded meaning or logic and knowing that more revisions might be needed. My hesitation may also have ensued from relating events of my life which for years I had tucked into the depths. I had to redirect the river of my thoughts quickly—many pairs of eyes and ears were waiting. I did so by pushing my story over each dam and wading through. Yes, it was intimidating, but my classmates and Caroline offered my Arizona scene a warm reception. I was grateful for our class agreement when offering comments on our writing: *Always start with positive feedback.* The warmth that emanated from those listening to me made me realize that with their help, I could eventually refine my story and transform it into the living thing I wanted it to be. Perhaps I could even reconcile myself to the idea of incorporating myself into the story to give it larger purpose—to faithfully render the human condition, including my own.

QUESTIONS FOR FURTHER WRITERLY CONTEMPLATION

1. Daniel Taylor (2016) discusses how sentimentality, as opposed to sentiment, abuses emotion: "Sentiment is a synonym for emotion, and in storytelling, as in life, it is a positive and inescapable force. Sentimentality, on the other hand, is the abuse of sentiment for manipulative purposes. It is, in brief, the manipulation of emotion to elicit responses not supported by the circumstances" (p. 38). He further argued that it is the "specificity of revelatory details of description" that renders the story "emotionally engaging" (p. 31). These details may occur in any element of the story, including setting. One such notable setting in classic literature occurs in Willa Cather's novel, *Death Comes for the Archbishop* (1927), which tells the story of a Catholic bishop who struggles to institute a diocese in New Mexico territory. The final lines of the novel read as follows:
   > When the Cathedral bell tolled just after dark, the Mexican population of Santa Fé fell upon their knees, and all American Catholics as well. Many others who did not kneel prayed in their hearts. Eusabio and the Tesuque boys went quietly away to tell their people; and the next morning the old Archbishop lay before the high altar in the church he had built.

   How does the setting of this final scene elicit emotion in the reader without relying on sentimentality?

2. Taylor (2016) also notes the following: "Irony—perhaps the most intellectual of literary devices—exploits the gap between appearance and reality, and in this case releases a thunderclap of emotion. And it does so without the need for any direct statement or elaboration regarding emotion or significance" (p. 28). Do you think that the final scene in *Death Comes for the Archbishop* makes use of the literary device of irony to convey emotion?

3. The following appeared in the *American Scholar* on October 28, 2014:
   > Ernest Hemingway—perhaps at Harry's Bar, perhaps at Luchow's—once bet a bunch of fellows he could make them cry with a short story six words long. If he won the bet, each guy would have to fork over 10 bucks. Hemingway's six-word story was, "For Sale: Baby shoes, never worn." He won the bet (Lehman).

   Hemingway was known for employing a simple writing style in which prose was direct and unembellished. He is also famous for utilizing very specific details that convey emotion. How does the legendary short story, "For Sale: Baby shoes, never worn," evoke emotion? Could you rewrite this story in a manner that might be overly sentimental? Would your rewrite have the same effect?

4. The following quote is extracted from *Ethan Frome* (1911) by Edith Wharton:
   > The other woman was much smaller and slighter. She sat huddled in an arm-chair near the stove, and when I came in she turned her head quickly toward me, without the least corresponding movement of her body. Her hair was as grey as her companion's, her face as bloodless and shriveled, but amber-tinted, with swarthy shadows sharpening the nose and hollowing the temples. Under her shapeless dress her body kept its limp immobility, and her dark eyes had the bright witch-like stare that disease of the spine sometimes gives.

   How does the characterization of the "other woman" convey emotion in this story? What details contribute to eliciting this emotion?

5. The philosophy of "Show, don't tell" in writing cautions the writer to employ sensory details to convey emotion rather than simply telling or stating it. This philosophy is reminiscent of Hemingway's employing specific tangible details to express emotion—a technique that saves his novels from becoming overly sentimental. With this in mind, note Huck's inner dialogue in the following extract from *The Adventures of Huckleberry Finn* (1884) by Mark Twain: "I was mighty down-hearted; so I made up my mind I wouldn't ever go anear that house again, because I reckoned I was to blame, somehow." Clearly, Huck is telling rather than showing his emotions in this dialogue, but does the use of the dialogue itself in the story prevent the character from becoming overly sentimental? Why or why not?

6. Death is often used in a narrative to evoke emotion. The following passage comes from *The Return of the Native* by Thomas Hardy:
   > They stood silently looking upon Eustacia, who, as she lay there still in death, eclipsed all her living phases. Pallor did not include all the quality of her complexion, which seemed more than whiteness; it was almost light. The expression of her finely carved mouth was pleasant, as if a sense of dignity had just compelled her to leave off speaking. Eternal rigidity had seized upon it in a momentary transition between fervor and resignation. Her black hair was looser now than either of them had ever seen it before, and surrounded her brow like a forest. The stateliness of look which had been almost too marked for a dweller in a country domicile had at last found an artistically happy background.

   What details in this passage elicit emotion in the reader? What if you wrote a version of this passage that simply stated the emotions that the onlookers felt in gazing at the corpse of Eustacia? Try it and see if it has the same effect.

7. In his essay, "Hamlet and His Problems" (1920, 2015), T. S. Eliot described the "objective correlative" as follows:
   > The only way of expressing emotion in the form of art is by finding an "objective correlative"; in other words, a set of objects, a situation, a chain of events which shall be the formula of that particular emotion; such that when the external facts, which must terminate in sensory experience, are given, the emotion is immediately evoked (Eliot, "Hamlet and His Problems" from *The Sacred Wood*, 19191920, 2015).

   Choose one or two of the passages cited in questions 1–4 and see if you can describe the "objective correlative."

My Hopes for Class Seven, by Caroline

How can we resist a movie break? Everyone had been working so hard to understand the craft of narrative. Documentary films are enhanced by strong narrative every bit as much as written qualitative research is. I loved this collage-like film that, in my first viewing, seemed to bring forth many of our craft topics. Backstory/front story and wide angle/focused angle can perhaps be seen even more clearly in film than in written text. And then there's the narrative instruction that comes through our ears—*listening* to film, as well as watching it. What can our ears tell us about narrative that our eyes alone cannot?

SUGGESTIONS FOR FURTHER READING

Gingerich, J. (2012, October 24). *Understanding the objective correlative*. LitReactor. https://litreactor.com/columns/understanding-the-objective-correlative

Taylor, D. (2016). "Didn't our hearts burn within us?" The use and abuse of emotion in storytelling. *Christian Scholar's Review*, 46(1), 27.

REFERENCES

Cappetti, C. (1993). *Writing Chicago: Modernism, ethnography, and the novel*. Columbia University Press.

Cather, W. (1927) *Death comes for the archbishop*. Alfred A. Knopf.

Eliot, T. S. (1920, 2015). *The sacred wood: Essays on poetry and criticism*. Alfred A. Knopf.

Elledge, S. (1986). E.B. White at work: The creation of a "paragraph." In *E.B. White: A biography*. W. W. Norton & Company.

Hardy, T. (1999). *The return of the native*. Penguin Classics. (Original work published 1878)

Richardson, L. (2000). Writing: A method of inquiry. In N. K. Denzin & Y. S. Lincoln (Eds.), *Handbook of qualitative research*. SAGE Publications.

Twain, M. (1865). *Adventures of Huckleberry Finn* (eBook edition, Project Gutenberg). Charles L. Webster and Company. https://www.gutenberg.org/files/76/76-h/76-h.htm

Wharton, E. (1911). *Ethan Frome* (eBook edition, project gutenberg). Scribner's. https://www.gutenberg.org/files/4517/4517-h/4517-h.htm

CHAPTER 7

Finding Narrative Gifts in Film

Allison Horváth-Tucker

Because I work in the theatre, I have found my way into scholarship by telling myself that I am a researcher/storyteller. Indeed, the role of theatre is to tell other people's stories. As actors we stand on the stage, visible mouthpieces of stories that extend far beyond our individual experiences. And if we are to be successful on stage, we must do our homework, so to speak, to tell an accurate story and do justice to the characters we try to embody. The magic of theatre is its urgency and sense of direct and immediate presence. Directors bring their own concept of the story to the script and actors working on the production bring layers of their own backgrounds and perceptions to the characters they portray. Perhaps most important, audience members interpret the performance in their own nuanced ways. Nothing is straight-forward or objective about theatrical storytelling.

Even before we watched *I Am Not Your Negro,* a documentary film by Raoul Peck (2016), that builds from the writings and oratory of James Baldwin, I began to recognize that theatre artists and documentary filmmakers are qualitative researchers in their own right, engaging in inquiry about particular people in particular context, whose words, history, and behaviors (data, yes) tell a story. I'd never felt that connection more than I felt it tonight as we packed ourselves into the tiny conference room across the hall from our usual classroom, where, unlike in our own classroom, the sound and video equipment actually worked.

We sat shoulder to shoulder as Peck embarked on the journey of a researcher–storyteller in his own unique way, aiming to bring James Baldwin's unfinished manuscript *Remember This House,* to life alongside curated imagery, songs, quotes, and videos showing the America of today juxtaposed with Baldwin's America of decades before. We ate popcorn. I was in my element.

The subject of the film is also Baldwin's elegiac memories of his friends, Martin Luther King Jr., Malcolm X, and Medgar Evers, all assassinated. Baldwin does not hold back in his writing and neither does Peck in his curation of Baldwin's words. The film's first scene until its last utilized powerful juxtaposition—for instance, text scrolling across the screen with titles such as "Heroes," "Witness," "Purity," and "Selling the Negro," set against footage of an interview from 1968 in which Baldwin pushes back on the White interviewer who tries to convince viewers how good life is for Black people in America. This interview and others Peck includes, as well as videos of Baldwin speaking extemporaneously, are captured in quotes in the accompanying book (Peck, 2017). Unlike the book, though, the film gives us access to Baldwin's exquisitely poised demeanor, the anger we see in the twitches at the edges of his mouth, his gaze, the look in his eyes as he speaks about Martin, Malcolm, and Medgar, and others he lost to the cause of Civil Rights, the exhaustion that can be seen in the way he holds his cigarette. This energy cannot easily be conveyed in text. Caroline tried not to interrupt the film more than a few times, but at opportune moments she paused it to ask us to consider how we might achieve similarly evocative power through text alone, a question that, even without her asking, guided our viewing. This was one important reason for narrative writers to watch film, listen to film—to discover which craft elements we can call upon at any given moment that could help us find written substitutes for the evocative qualities of film. After all, many films come directly from already published novels and stories, less often the other way around. Perhaps documentary films could emerge in similar ways from our written qualitative studies about education. A powerful thought.

Many of the film's moments captured me. For instance, just when I found myself fully drawn into Baldwin's speeches, Peck cuts away from the grainy 1960s footage to offer graphic images of more recent police brutality. We hear Baldwin's words, but they now underscore images of the world as it is in the 1990s, 2010, 2015, *and*, I thought as I watched, today. One of the most arresting moments came as I watched and listened to Baldwin speak about the murders of Black children in the 1950s, while the names and pictures of victims of modern-day police brutality appear on the screen.

> *I know how you watch as you grow older, and it is not a figure of speech, the corpses of your brothers and your sisters pile up around you. And not for anything they have done. They were too young to have done anything.*
> *Tamir Rice. Darius Simmons. Trayvon Martin. Aiyana Stanley-Jones. Christopher McCray. Cameron Tillman. Amir Brooks*

It wasn't only the recent video clips that held my attention. The incorporation of videos from the 1950s and 1960s were equally effective in telling Baldwin's story. In the film and the book, a White "Woman in the South" is quoted saying, "God forgives murder and he forgives adultery. But he is very angry, and he actually curses all who do integrate." Peck places her quoted words above a photograph of three young White men holding hand-made signs: "We won't go to school with Negroes." "We the pupils of Clinton Hi don't want Negroes in our school." What an experience it was both to "hear and watch" the woman speak her words while also seeing the conviction in her eyes that God supports her views. The narrative impact of that visual was a profound moment, and again, I wondered how the narrative craft elements we were learning might offer similar effect.

Maybe this last paragraph succeeded in doing a bit of that. I hope so.

Countless moments in the film strengthened and elevated the narrative and the period music—Ray Charles performing the longing, hurting words of "What'd I Say" juxtaposed with Doris Day lightly singing "Should I Surrender" from the 1961 film, *Lover Come Back*. Words, images, and music flavored the decades for those of us who did not live through them.

The film captures energy and movement as we watch high school student Dorothy Counts, who is Black, walk resolutely toward her destination while surrounded by a White mob. We are not asked to imagine. We see. How might our written texts accomplish such "seeing?" Minutes later, we did not have to rely solely on Baldwin's description of actor Clinton Rosemond's performance of a Black janitor wrongly accused of raping a White girl. We watch the terror in his eyes, the gloss of sweat covering his face, the refracted glint from the fancy spectacles worn by the White male interrogators, each of whom towers over him. In this way, imagery communicates tangibly and vividly, differently than if it were received from text alone. I realized that just to think about the camera coming close to Rosemond's face helped me register the meaning of focused angle writing more fully. As I think about representing my future research participants, I well may always ask myself, "What would the camera see?" Again and again such images helped us to recognize how much we needed to understand about writing craft in order to do justice to moments in our research settings that we want our readers to see and to "get." Here was an image of the small detail (a White man's fancy spectacles) dramatizing something monstrously larger—power, hate, racism. This is what I wanted my own writing to be able to accomplish.

By the time—our seventh class together—that we watched this film, we'd spent six weeks discussing craft: bridging little moments to big meanings; engaging in implicit or explicit analysis; presenting people in complex ways rather than as heroes or villains; offering backstory and front story; offering wide angle and focused angle; using dialogue effectively; evoking themes without shouting them; writing with sentiment, not sentimentality. Here in this film, I realized, were all of these elements. A strength of the film is its ability to take large topics and connect them to small moments. Symbolism is clear in Baldwin's writing, but becomes even more apparent when paired with the visuals offered in Peck's documentary. When Baldwin writes about the 1950s and 1960s characterizations of Black men as simpletons or fools, Peck pairs that with tangible examples of American advertisements depicting exaggerations of Black men, women, and children. When Baldwin writes about the loss of Black children, Peck widens the lens to reflect on contemporary examples, ongoing losses.

It would have been easy for Baldwin to romanticize the memory of Martin Luther King Jr., Malcolm X, and Medgar Evers and turn them into face-value heroes. However, Baldwin and Peck worked to show the impact of these men, while also revealing their frailties, their humanness. Dialogue was preserved in Baldwin's writing and then brought to life in Peck's film. The backstories of all three men were brought to life through images, videos, and direct quotes.

Although Baldwin no doubt didn't intend to teach doctoral students how to become better narrative writers, inhaling his precise, beautiful use of language inspired my desire to represent my thinking, my seeing, and that of my future research participants, in well-chosen words. And surely, even if I had closed my eyes, just listening to his words in the film I would know more about writing. I would register when my attention waned (which, in this film, it never did), a sign that revision may be needed, for, as we had discussed already in our seminar, we *hear* when prose is boring or when it hits a wrong note much more readily than when we read prose silently. Similarly, Raoul Peck, in paying homage to Baldwin's words, made creative decisions about how to bring forth Baldwin's thinking and *being* as fully as possible, as well as how to hold our attention as fully as possible, how to keep us alert and engaged. His task involved research and editing and ended as a documentary work that married Baldwin's source material with the research material that Peck brought in. This is a similar process to how we will approach writing our dissertations and that all qualitative researchers take conveying the story that their data reveals.

When approaching a story that is not one's own, whether as an academic researcher/writer, theater artist, or filmmaker, one must acknowledge and understand one's own biases. To have bias, educational researcher Lee Shulman (1988), wrote, "is not a flaw of research; indeed, it is an essential feature of all scholarship that the research practitioner should learn to recognize and acknowledge if he or she is not to develop an unearned air of objective omnipotence or blind faith in putatively dispassionate inquiry" (p. 4). The visual nature of the film helped address intrinsic bias. When possible, Peck had us hear directly from Baldwin, either through direct quotes or through videos of him speaking. Peck's choice to position Baldwin's words with other images, songs, and videos of the Civil Rights movement helped to contextualize Baldwin's work. This was enhanced by the parallels Peck emphasized by including modern-day images. For me, *I Am Not Your Negro* served as an example of narration brought *to life*. Visual arts such as film or theatre lend themselves to telling stories in visually stimulating ways, but I was starting to understand that strong narrative writing can bring us close to life as well. Text can be rich with imagery, while imagery and performance can be rich with text. To do justice to a story that belongs to a person or people (particularly when one's

Finding Narrative Gifts in Film

life is quite different from theirs), it is vital to support one's interpretation with a wealth of context, research, and deep analysis of one's own biases. If visual narrative is to become a viable method of communication or an ethical presentation of research and stories, it must be backed by a series of tools and processes that hold it accountable for the integrity of the subject at hand. In a best-case scenario, researchers and artists alike do the most justice to the stories they wish to tell by turning their microphone of privilege to the voices of those who have lived the stories. However, when that is not a possibility, the task falls to the responsible researchers/storytellers to acknowledge their biases, investigate fully the world and context of the subject of the story, and then present it as completely and evocatively as they are able.

My strength has never been writing. However, as I said, I'm a theatre artist. Among my classmates watching this film with me tonight, our shoulders touching, are dancers, visual artists, musicians, and orators. As we sit, I wonder how this film works for them, how it intersects with their own art-forms. And I wonder how it would work for you. How might you, your students, or your classmates be drawn into the experience of James Baldwin through the combined power of the visual, the auditory, the textual? And how might we widen our understanding of what forms our research narratives will take when we consider the power of film? In Chapter 8, Thelma Goldberg will add to this conversation, and in Chapter 9, Avigail Shimshoni will add her own insights to these questions.

QUESTIONS FOR FURTHER WRITERLY CONTEMPLATION

1. Baldwin's goal, if he had had the time to write the book he planned, was to see Dr. Martin Luther King Jr.'s, Malcolm X's, and Medgar Evers's lives "bang up against one another to reveal the story of America." Do you think Raoul Peck, the filmmaker, succeeded in making that happen? How and how not?
2. What does film do that written text might not? What narrative craft topics thus far discussed might allow written text to come close to the power of film?
3. Baldwin narrated: "The line that separates witness from actor is a fine line indeed." As a researcher/writer, have you ever felt similarly? Explain?
4. "I am saying that a journey is called that because you cannot know what you will discover on the journey, what you will do with what you find, or what you find will do to you." How is this quote related to qualitative research and writing? How does it resonate with you in your own present or future work?

My Hopes for Class Eight, by Caroline

I had been a huge fan of the work of the late anthropologist Barbara Myerhoff since I saw the film *Number Our Days*, and then read the book, her more complete anthropological study by the same title. Watching and reading Myerhoff was a great way of pushing some of our narrative craft topics even further, as part of our three-week look at film narrative and its embedded "instruction" about research and writing. In both the film and the book, we saw lots of examples of objective correlative, complex characterization, and even a window on sentiment vs. sentimentality.

REFERENCES

Peck, R. (2016). *I am not your Negro (From texts by James Baldwin)* (film).
Peck, R. (2017). *I am not your Negro*. Vintage Books, Penguin Random House.

CHAPTER 8

Number Our Days
A Study of Community

Thelma Goldberg (followed by drafts of paper by Garo Saraydarian)

Like anthropologist Michael Jackson (Chapter 5) and Wendy Luttrell, the educational researcher you'll meet in Chapter 10, the late Barbara Myerhoff cared deeply about sound research method *and* sound representation through narrative writing. She sought to enter as fully as possible the experiences of others and allowed herself to be an intriguing and trustworthy character in the "story." Since the documentary film, *Number Our Days,* directed by Lynne Littman (1976), was followed by the complete book (1978) of the same title, I focus my chapter on examining and comparing these renderings. In both, we see Myerhoff striving to back her meaning-making by presenting clear data, in narrative form, to her viewers/readers. Somewhat like Allison Horváth-Tucker revealed in Chapter 8, watching the film, then reading the book, we get a taste of the complementary ways a study can be narrated and represented. In the film we get to *see* Myerhoff as an interviewer, which helped me prepare for and think about our seminar's soon-to-come "interview a stranger" assignment.

NUMBER OUR DAYS

The film *Number Our Days* opens with images of the Venice Beach boardwalk juxtaposed with the sounds of Hava Nagila, the joyous Hebrew song. The camera pans across the beach and parking lots and rests on the Israel Levin Senior Adult Center, where older adults, dressed in their finest hats and coats, accessorized with canes and umbrellas, wave to friends as they leave the concrete boardwalk to enter a room already filled with music and dancing. The scene of the Center contrasts sharply with the scene of the boardwalk, where we see a youthful bicyclist carrying a surfboard, people swimming and sunbathing, and palm trees swaying against the backdrop of the sea. At the Levin Senior Center, a singer welcomes everyone to take out their cameras for the Horah, and dancers—some of whom remain seated—hold hands, sing, and greet each other like old friends. As the camera captures the circular movement of the dance patterns, it speeds up and creates a dizzying effect—like a merry-go-round or spinning top—and I wonder if this image is a harbinger of chaos to come.

Number Our Days, the book, an ethnography of the community that forms at the Levin Center, was published in 1978, shortly after the film won the 1976 Oscar for Best Documentary Short Subject. An involved participant observer who bonded deeply with the Center participants and as an outsider—a qualitative researcher, decades younger than the Center participants—Myerhoff, though Jewish, never experienced the losses the elderly Jewish refugees had endured.

During our seminar we had already studied characterizations in the writings of Boo (2001), Dillard (1987), Dyson (1995), and others that offered meaning and examples of careful narrative representations of individuals' lived experiences. Here was a film, quite unlike *I Am Not Your Negro*, that aims to tell research participants' stories. As with narrative writing, documentary film aims to translate complex human experiences to an audience. In our seminar, we'd already discussed the researcher/writer "exercise in imagination" that Myerhoff described in her introduction to the film. In "The Historian as Artist," Barbara Tuchman (1981) identifies imagination as an essential quality, along with sympathy, that enables the historian "to *understand* the evidence" (p. 47). In "Optilenz," Caroline (Heller, 2002) characterized her father as crabby and difficult, yet she found a way to bring forth his wonderful attributes too, and we end up sympathizing with the frustration both she and her father experience as he struggles to read with the aid of a text projector. In another example of narrative representation/characterization that allows for the full range of human traits to come through, Annie Dillard (1987) identifies her mother as a "force for disorder," who "liked to step on the drawstring of a crawling baby's gown" (p. 4), yet the reader finds her mother endearing because in other narrative moments Dillard brings out the fullness of her humanity. Myerhoff offers similarly full characterizations of the Center participants without reverting to sentimentality. She doesn't say that the Center participants were sad or lonely, yet the sentiment she evokes in the opening scenes already revealed this. The rich details she offers lead the reader and viewer to sensory experiences, such as the whirling dervish of the opening film scene, and this brings us increased understanding of the lives of the Center participants and of the larger meanings: people in their 80s and 90s, some over 100, continuing a sense of culture and community that sustains them.

Number Our Days, both book and film, examines how culture can be represented and studied through words, but also through ceremonies and rituals. The Israel Levin Senior Adult Center was the setting where for several years Myerhoff, her film director Lynne Littman, and a camera crew, followed elderly Eastern Europeans as they participated in everyday activities, rituals, and ceremonies that maintained their connection to their roots in Eastern European Jewish culture, as well as to each other. We enter the Center's function room, participants' tiny apartments near the Center, and their lives, where Littman's camera (and Myerhoff's senses, and later, her pen) record not only the landscape filled with sounds and conversations, but also artwork, photos, and memorabilia, symbols of the residents' rich pasts.

How did the book and the documentary differ in helping viewers and readers understand the Center community and the lives therein? Myerhoff, interested in the many cultural meanings of aging, initially wanted to study an aging Chicano community, but was challenged by friends' and colleagues' suggestion that it may be time to "study her own." In making the choice to study aspects of her own culture and religion, she openly wondered if her motives are academic or personal. "An anthropologist," she said in the film's opening, "tries to feel the inside of a native's hand. That's the way you know the culture." She asked whether anyone can *truly* know others and expressed her excited readiness to study this population: "I will be a little old Jewish lady one day," she said (to the camera and then in her book text). She is eager to learn about that experience. To gain that knowledge required her to balance dual identities—qualitative researcher/anthropologist and "surrogate grandchild" (p. 36). Boo (2001), as well as other researcher/writers we read, also balanced the tension between her responsibility as researcher and her growing sense of friendship and connection with the people she set out to understand. Each had to navigate the tricky terrain of balancing what at times felt like dueling identities, and as a tap-dance teacher planning to write her dissertation about the lives of tap-dance teachers, I knew that one day I would have similar balance challenges.

Myerhoff chose to focus on a deep study of specific individuals rather than try to present a general commentary on aging. "My interpretation, therefore, must be read as pertaining to these particular people at a given period of time—how much they have in common with others must be determined by someone else" (p. 29). In her ethnographic study of a program for pregnant teens that Kat Marsh discusses in Chapter 10, Wendy Luttrell (2003) avoided generalizing the meanings her research participants presented by respecting and representing each girl individually and not claiming that they embodied a universal response to being a pregnant teen. Likewise, in the book and documentary, Myerhoff captures the individual expression of being a "little old Jewish lady" by making visible the choices and sacrifices that defined each Center participant's unique life. "I *see* old people in a new way, as part of me" (p. 19).

An early scene in the film introduces us to one of Myerhoff's first participant "teachers," Bertha, whose daily work is feeding pigeons. She walks two miles every day and seems to easily tell personal stories to Myerhoff and to the camera, including one where she encounters young men on the

Boardwalk who rather menacingly ask her if she believes in Jesus. We hear dignity and humor as she retells her story of standing up to them with confidence and courage. A new scene unfolds when Myerhoff joins Bertha and Bertha's friend, Mike, while they visit with each other on a bench, their morning ritual. Bertha talks about the death of her husband and her children, revealing both her vulnerability and her commitment to living independently now. "Men are helpless," she responds to Myerhoff's suggestion that she might marry again. In fact, Myerhoff reminds us in a voice-over that follows that scene, Bertha's friend Mike "*is* helpless to protect Bertha from her painful memories." In the film version, music enters the scene, and the camera zooms in on tears that Bertha quickly wipes away, while Mike touches her shoulder and urges her to stop thinking about the past. This technique of offering us a close-up, accompanied by a beautiful melody is employed throughout the documentary, and I couldn't help but wonder if the music made these moments veer toward sentimentality. Both writers and filmmakers face the challenge of letting readers respond to emotional content without being guided on *how* to respond by soaring music or similar cues that text might offer. Boo (2001) demonstrated this element of narrative writing in her story, evoked by Garo Saraydarian in Chapter 2, of a family living in a violent neighborhood of Washington, DC. In that narrative, we sympathize with older sister Drenika's need to care for her two brothers, not because Boo paints her as sad or overwhelmed, but because Boo provides rich details of the violence she saw and heard during a lunchtime visit to the family's apartment.

Myerhoff is as adept at infusing her narrative text with sentiment that resides in her characters, without benefit of background music and camera work to cue us emotionally. Early in the book we meet Shmuel, who is not in the film. During one interview, he recounts the terror he felt as a young child singing a hymn for the governor of his home city in Poland by standing and singing the same hymn in front of Myerhoff, "his tears and laughter," as she describes those moments, "spill(ing) out freely" (p. 56). Myerhoff brings us into his cramped apartment where Shmuel shares stories of his childhood and his love of Judaism and the Yiddish language. We can almost see Shmuel "nattily dressed except for the disorderly newspapers and magazines and scraps of notes poking out of his pockets" (p. 62). This use of objective correlatives, as described in earlier chapters, is an important element in a narrative writer's toolkit. As we enter Shmuel's small apartment, we see "rickety bookcases . . . a huge bare-breasted ceramic woman in yellow harem pants (holding) a tiny, fluted lampshade . . . and a brave little table bearing heaps of magazines and papers" (p. 44). Again, Myerhoff deftly avoids sentimentality by describing what she saw and heard rather than what she felt or signaling what the reader should feel.

One of my favorite scenes in the film is a visit to the small apartment of Paulina, one of the Center participants. We see a sewing machine prominently placed, and observe Myerhoff demonstrating the fine art of interviewing, and most important, listening. We get to *see* a sensitive interviewer/listener at work—a smile, a touch, a nod, a shared song and dance. Earlier in the semester, Michael Jackson (1995), in his study of the Warlpiri people, revealed to us similar capacities, understanding that his research participants, like Myerhoff's, were seeking witnesses and validation. Both consider the interviewees to be the necessary narrators of their own stories. Myerhoff accomplished her goals by asking broad questions that invite the interviewees to tell stories. We observe Myerhoff in action when she interviews Cosimo in his apartment. Her gentle but probing questions invite Cosimo to tell stories that end up amplifying the meanings of loneliness and old age introduced by Bertha and then Bertha and Mike in earlier scenes. We *see* Myerhoff as she actively listens, engaging her body, her eyes in the interview experience—inviting Cosimo in this way to recognize that she knows that his story has rich and important meaning. She establishes an environment of trust by directing all her focus to her participants. She didn't lower her head to write notes or move her eyes to a cup of tea.

For an assignment a few weeks after this class session where we studied and discussed Myerhoff's work, we were asked to interview a stranger. At that time, too, I was on the cusp of beginning my dissertation research, which would include interviewing. I took note of all that Myerhoff did, including her frequent examination of her actions, motives, and relationships with the individuals, as well as the issues they raised by their words and enacted in their lives. By reflecting on her role as researcher, while growing into the roles of friend and surrogate daughter, too, she revisited again and again her responsibility to represent the participants and the topic of aging with clarity, compassion, and honesty.

Jumping ahead to my own "narrative" as I write this chapter, I have *finished* my dissertation. Like Myerhoff, I had to balance a dual role during interviews for my research. The participants were colleague tap-dance teachers, and we shared some of the same experiences I was ostensibly studying *through their* teaching stories. I was vigilant in similar ways as Myerhoff that *their* stories come through in my narrative descriptions without my opinions influencing either their comments during the interviews or my narrative representations. I often thought of Myerhoff and her nods, smiles, eye contact, and I tried to practice her active listening and seemingly unbiased acceptance.

Both the film and book offer frequent glimpses into the tension between insider and outsider status that many researchers navigate. Several of our readings addressed this topic. Luttrell (2003), for instance, would refer to this tension as being "split at the root" (p. 171). To honestly represent another, she believes there is a need to be both analytically distant and emotionally present. To accomplish this, she constantly considered three dilemmas: (a) On what basis could she claim knowledge of another? (b) How would she maintain (through representation) the individual characteristics of her subjects? and (c) Who would benefit from her study?

Myerhoff engages in frequent self-reflection about her place in the growing story of the Center participants. In the film, she is physically present in many scenes, sometimes as an active participant and at other times sitting alone on a step, observing her participants from a distance. She alternates from holding the video camera to being the sole object of the camera's lens. In these latter moments, we see Myerhoff the researcher exercising her imagination and empathy as she shares her process of understanding the experiences of those she is trying to understand and represent. In the book, unless she is interviewing someone, she is an observer of her participants *and* of herself. Through narrative description, she makes her participants visible to the reader as they engage in activities and rituals that represent life in the Center. She also reflects on her own story and the significance to her present study of her relationship with her grandmother Sofie, "who taught me that everyone had some story . . . and stories . . . could transform the world" (p. 240). I suspect she had to "harden her heart" (p. 171), as she described her own emotional challenges in telling the story in her data, in this case, to write the story of the crisis between Center participants Sadie and Anna. The concept of hardening the heart is a technique the Center participants used to protect themselves from being hurt when tensions escalated, as often happened. They depended on one another, and their family-like interactions brought forth all the complex emotions of any family. Their ongoing emotional revelations inspired Myerhoff to write honestly about herself, while representing the individuals she studied as the imperfect, complex people they were.

Another example of Myerhoff's insider status occurred on Fridays at sundown when the community gathered for an important ritual. In the film we observe Bertha recite the prayers and light the candles that signify the beginning of Shabbat. This scene is described in much greater detail in the book, and I wondered how much Myerhoff's personal, as well as anthropological quest brought additional significance to this weekly practice of faith. "Basha chanted the traditional Hebrew prayer, encircling the flames three times with open hands, drawing their holiness to her face, covering her eyes with her hands, finishing with her own private prayer as tears spread through her fingers down her cheeks" (p. 255). Again, Myerhoff describes what she saw and heard, and we come to understand how this ritual validates their identities and keeps their memories alive.

I imagine Myerhoff and Littman ended up with hours and hours of videotape that they edited down to create the 29-minute film we see. As

Denise Mytko described in Chapter 3, in one of our early readings, "To Fashion a Text," Annie Dillard (1987) asked, "What to put in and what to leave out?" Myerhoff asked herself a similar question when, in the book, she wondered "how to cut up the pie of social reality" (p. 28). This phrase landed in my notes to become my own question as I faced my dissertation research. Littman and Myerhoff let us know that they intentionally left out some of the troubles and disagreements that Myerhoff then detailed in the more comprehensive book so that the film could serve as a thank you to the Center community. The participants became "visible" by the sensitive portrayal of them as survivors, which included explication of their individual strategies in response to age and adversity. The film succeeded in bringing increased funding and attention to the Center, assuring that it would remain a place to rejoice, to grieve, and to continue to build community that preserved their Jewish culture and the Yiddish language.

The book does what the film did not do by describing specific incidents and sociocultural dramas that threatened the order and balance of the community. Myerhoff crystalizes the paradoxes the Center people face to become more visible in and to their chosen world. One is their need to engage in meaningful, passionate experiences, which risks the loss of dignity and harmony. The story of Kominsky and the graduation ceremony he organized for his Yiddish history students is a good example of the tension that frequently presented itself during important gatherings. One of the attendees at the celebration gave an unplanned speech about the topic of Jewish persecution that raised harrowing memories and caused discomfort in the guests. As often happened, a joyful event could not occur without reference to a sad and painful past, and I began to understand why Myerhoff included an image of uncontrolled whirling in the film's opening scene.

The first time I watched the documentary, *Number Our Days*, I cried from beginning to the end. Although the film is a triumphant story of aging with dignity, it is also a tale of mourning and loss. I was grieving the recent death of my husband and the scenes of joyful dancing hit me like a tidal wave. During subsequent viewings to help me write this chapter, I was able to watch the documentary as a student of narrative writing. My personal experience with death brought a deeper appreciation for the techniques Myerhoff used to record the secrets of aging with dignity. Yes, the film did what the book could not do quite as fully—capturing the joy in people's eyes, the lightness in their bodies as they danced across the floor, the sounds and rhythms produced by the musicians, and the memorabilia present in their homes. Myerhoff selected images that provided a rich sensory experience not easily described through text. But I'm not a filmmaker and until I decide to become one, I can only try to come as close as I possibly can—with well-chosen words that will aim to tell the story of *my* data.

SUGGESTIONS FOR FURTHER READING AND VIEWING

Barbara Myerhoff completed another documentary, "In Her Own Time," which followed her research of the Fairfax neighborhood of Los Angeles, a population of ultraorthodox Hassidic Jews known as Chabad. During this time, she was diagnosed with cancer, and this documentary became her personal story of facing death. It is available on YouTube:

https://www.youtube.com/watch?v=RrUB58a3ZrI

Kaminsky, M., Weiss, M., & Metzger, D. (2010). *Stories as equipment for living: Last talks and tales of Barbara Myerhoff*. University of Michigan Press.

Garo Saraydarian's "Craft Paper" assignment that focuses on Myerhoff's dexterity with Sentiment vs Sentimentality

The "Graduation-Siyum" scene in Barabara Myerhoff's *Number Our Days* is a siren-song for sentimentality. A writer could easily drench the pages with emotions that force upon the reader a sad sight of abandonment and neglect of the elderly by their children. Superficially the scene dares the writer to indulge in the pathos of the elderly clinging to some sort of meaning in their lives. Dr. Myerhoff skillfully avoids this. By juxtaposing third-person narrative and analysis with the participants' own dialogue and text, Barbara Myerhoff is able to depict the Graduation-Siyum in a way that invites the reader to explore for themselves the nuances that are suggested.

I will specifically look at pages 83–112 in the chapter "We Do Not Wrap Herring in the Printed Page," excluding the introductory *bobbe-myseh* from Myerhoff's Living History class. Pages 83–112 consist of lengthy intellectual discussions and third-person narrative punctuated by short quotes, text, and dialogue from the participants. Structurally, these abstract sections slow the absorption rate of the descriptive scenes, thus modulating the emotional level. I have undertaken a count of line length (see below) that is coded according to six categories: third-person narrative/description, anthropological analysis, dialogue, quotes from speeches, text, and participant commentary. Out of 1,198 lines, 513 of these lines, or 43% of the passage, is theoretical analysis of the Graduation-Siyum. On a large structural level, then, the passage (pp. 83–112) has a high ratio of unemotional, distanced analysis that stabilizes a scene from becoming too maudlin. More importantly, these analytical sections are placed in key points in the scene, interrupting the narrative where an emotional section risks slipping into sentimentality. For instance, the two largest sections of analysis come after two intense scenes: 136 lines on pages 96–98 after Hannah's "embarrassing" speech regarding the Munich tragedy at the Olympic Games; the other, 150 lines on pages 106–110, appears amidst discussion by the elderly regarding emigrating to America, the ambiguity they felt towards the rupture with the past, and the challenges of finding meaning and identity in America.

Throughout the Graduation-Siyum passage we are constantly, but subtly, reminded of the age-world of the young contrasted with the age-world of the elderly through very specific and detailed descriptions. This contrast begins right at the setting of the scene beginning on page 83 where Myerhoff describes the "carnival flavor" of a sunny day at Venice beach after several days of rain. We have sound: steel bands, conga and bongo drums, bottles, garbage can lids, a piano, and a flute. We have motion: skateboards and roller skates, pogo-sticks, the flautist playing while pedaling his bike, the piano being pulled on a wheeled platform. We have characters: winos, musicians, kids, a squad car, and a clothed monkey. And finally, we have the pungent smell of weed.

Weaved within this young and busy scene are the elderly: a couple in an electronic golf cart, Sam in his motorized wheelchair, and Eddie (blind) and Harry (deaf) teaming up to cross the road. What we see, hear, smell is a dizzying whirl of youthful energy being navigated steadily but carefully by the elderly. This contrast between young and old is laid out without shouting: "The elderly have lost their vibrancy and the world ignores them!" In fact, the idea of carnival, of a celebration, is literally appropriated by Nathan who, in answer to Hannah's skepticism of the appropriateness of the ceremony, shares a memory of his amazement upon seeing a carnival as a young boy.

Ironically, Myerhoff's judicious use of quotes and dialogue acts as a counterweight, a more sober *midrash*, to the very sentimental speeches by Kominsky and Abe during the ceremony. Myerhoff is the objective referee toggling between speeches and, often critical, participant commentary. When Kominsky opens the ceremony on page 88, he speaks about the old people in terms of neglect: "Nobody gave them attention," "These are humble people, not much education," and "How they are forgotten is a disgrace." In response, Myerhoff uses the participants' own words to dilute Kominsky's sentimentality quoting Hannah as saying, "I, for one, would appreciate it if he wouldn't make us out to be quite so humble," and regarding the absence of so many of their children, "I told him that my daughters got more important things to do with their time than to come watch Mama make herself stupid" (pp. 88–89). Hannah often takes on the role of reality-checking whenever the rhetoric of the speakers soars towards generalizations and platitudes. In answer to the rabbi's paean to scholarship, Hannah asks, "What about the girls who were never taught Hebrew?" (p. 90). Even Abe's speech, lamenting the way the elderly are abandoned and taken for granted while praising them as role-models of learning elicits a "So because Abe makes an announcement and Kominsky makes a big party, suddenly we are sages" from Hannah (p. 94). Indeed, Hannah's take on the whole Graduation-Siyum is simply, "what is the fuss for?" (p. 100).

Myerhoff also uses other voices to ensure that the scene is not overly-romanticized. In response to Kominsky's exuberant exegesis of the children's lyrics to "Oyfn Pripetchol Brent a Fayerl," Nathan offers a different perspective of his early school experience in which corporal punishment by the *melamed* was routine. Even Sofie, who begins the Graduation-Siyum chiding *Hannahleh* for being so skeptical, ends by stating that instead of spending money for the ceremony it would have made more "sense to send the money to Israel and not make such a fuss over us" (p. 100). Sophie even feels "ashamed to be in here today" after hearing Hannah's speech and seeing the way the refreshments were devoured afterwards (p. 100).

Yet, Myerhoff does not allow the participants' skepticism to distract the reader from some very real and conflicted feelings on the part of the elderly graduates. Again, she accomplishes this through direct quotes, and even more effectively, through actions. Thus, Myerhoff reports that the graduates framed and hung their diplomas next to newspaper cuttings of the day's events; Moshe is described relating a story from Martin Buber that allowed the Graduation-Siyum to be seen as part of an evolving tradition of Jewish adaptation. Kominsky's passion is evoked by the image of his "abundant white curls . . . not kept in place by his red velvet, gold-trimmed skull-cap" (p. 88). Although, a constant skeptic of the proceedings thus far, Hannah's inner emotions are revealed through the objective correlative of the diploma that she held, "tightly with both hands" (p. 94). Josele Masada's emotions are also depicted through the objective correlative of the "large rip in his coat lapel" (p. 95). One can even notice a scent of hurt beneath Hannah's proud but dismissive words, "One daughter is a doctor, the other one a teacher. These are busy people. For this business here I should ask them to give up an afternoon?" (p. 89). Does she protest too much? In such a manner the depths of both Hannah and Josele's emotion are thus implicitly shown and heard, not stated. When emotions are stated explicitly they are in the participants' own words, as in Hannah's speech regarding the Munich tragedy (p. 94).

When Myerhoff does use third-person descriptions, they serve to either quickly move the narrative along—"Jacob Koved, as president emeritus, was called on next" (p. 91)—or, report factual details.

> Seated at a table at the front of the room behind bouquets of blue and white flowers sat the various dignitaries, Abe, and Kominsky. The graduates, 26 in all, were arranged in rows flanking the head table. They wore their finest clothing beneath blue and white satin ribbons that crossed the breast from shoulder to waist. Most were solemn and flushed with excitement. Young ushers with armbands bearing the Hebrew character for "order," shooed away the itinerant curious outsiders and the neighborhood winos who regularly patronized the Center bathroom. (p. 87)

This description sticks exclusively to the facts. The only adjectives used to express emotion are "solemn" and "flushed." Contrast this passage with (forgive me, Barbara) this poor attempt of mine.

> Seated at a table at the front of the room behind bouquets of blue and white flowers sat Abe and Kominsky and the various second-rate dignitaries Kominsky had shamelessly begged to show up for the Graduation-Siyum. The flowers seemed to be the only fresh life-form in the drab, gray, crumbling Center building where youth was perennially absent amongst the wilted petals of the aged and forlorn in a forgotten garden of dashed hopes and crushed dreams. There were only a paltry 26 graduates in all, arranged in funereal rows like abandoned, mossy headstones flanking the head table to make them look more substantial. They tried to wear the finest clothing that they could afford on their meager pensions, blue and white satin ribbons hiding a loose stitch or a torn seam, or a stain of ketchup that no one had bothered to help them wipe off even though they had cleaned their children's clothes for years. The only young people present were young ushers with bored countenances and armbands bearing the Hebrew character for "order," shooing away the itinerant curious outsiders and the neighborhood winos who regularly patronized the shabby Center bathroom that reeked of incontinence and helplessness. Rolling their eyes they wondered what commandment they had broken to put them in such a Geriatric *Gehenna*, a Sickly *Sheol*. Indeed, the noises of mirth and merriment outside on the boardwalk mocked the self-importance of the Graduation-Siyum. This was a futile and vain attempt to make meaning against the sounds of a virile, youthful world that didn't give a damn, that would never give a damn, that could care less of the sacrifices these people made year after year after year. It was reprehensible and sad and it made one worry about one's own aging. Will the child who now looks at you with loving eyes leave you to rot and be impatient for your death as you age? Will we eternally play the part of Kronos to precocious Zeus? Such ingratitude could only be found in America.

And so Myerhoff deftly dances around what has probably the greatest potential to be fodder for preachiness—the absence of family and children at the Graduation-Siyum. A count shows that the word "children" appears 20 times between pages 83–112, nine of those times, almost half, in the analytical sections on pages 92–93 and pages 106–107. Again, Myerhoff packs an emotionally laden word into more academic prose.

When the topic of children does appear in the narrative sections it is approached obliquely, with the elderly as a mirror reflecting contradictions and absence. Myerhoff matter-of-factly states that "Sonya's daughter, Rachel's granddaughter, and about a dozen representatives from Jacob Koved's family constituted the entire contingent of the graduates' kin" (p. 87). Kominsky and Abe's speeches highlight the gap between ideal and reality. Kominksy explains that the Graduation-Siyum is a chance for "you the children . . . to honor them [their parents]" to which Hannah replies "And tell me please where are all the children who are supposed to be here to see us?" (p. 88). Abe turns to the audience to address the children who "are here to show them [their elderly parents] you understand what they have done" (p. 94). A nice sentiment until you realize he is speaking to no one who fits that definition.

Myerhoff also uses the objective correlative to signify the children's absence. The diplomas are, "commercially printed forms intended for children's temple confirmations and graduations from Hebrew School" while each person's nickname and childhood name was used on the form, a name the elderly had not heard since "they had left *their* [italics mine] parents decades ago" (p. 90). The choice of the graduates standing instead of doing a procession was an idea Sofie borrowed from her grandson's graduation, a grandson who is not in attendance for *her* graduation ceremony. The one child that does speak, Dovid, is related to no one in the Center. The class song is a Yiddish children's song. In a way, this infantilization of the elderly serves to turn them into substitutes for their own children. In fact, it is only the sudden appearance of schnapps and cognac, as announced by Moshe, that brings some adult material into the celebration. Thus the theme of children is the nonpresence around which many of the ritualistic aspects of the ceremony circle.

And then there is Shmuel. Shmuel's role in *Number Our Days* is much larger than the Graduation-Siyum scene. For most of the Graduation-Siyum passage, Shmuel fills the role of a critical sounding board against Myerhoff's observations. However, in the last paragraphs of this chapter Myerhoff allows Shmuel to express some sadness, from which he shares his story of Rabbi Ben Levi sitting in his study praying, "Look at us now. We have forgotten the prayer. The fire is out. We can't find our way back to the place in the forest. We can only remember that there was a fire, a prayer, a place in the forest. So Lord, now that must be sufficient" (p. 112). Thus the richness of emotion that the Graduation-Siyum evokes is held carefully and lightly until the end by Myerhoff, allowing a chapter fraught with feelings to unfold its richness at its own pace, like the elderly, with dignity and poise. The sentiment is sufficient.

APPENDIX

37 lines (pp. 83–84): Third person description of Venice beach boardwalk—"All week it had been raining . . ."
46 lines (pp. 84–85): Third person description, background on Eli Kominsky—"Eli Kominsky had extensive connections . . ."
24 lines (p. 85): Dialogue between Hannah, Sofie, and Nathan regarding their impressions of Kominsky and his ideas—"This Kominsky has . . ."

49 lines (pp. 86–87): Analysis of Graduation-Siyum as ritual; two themes of being a Jew and learning—"It is not surprising . . ."
2 lines (p. 87)—Quote from Hannah commenting on the Graduation-Siyum—"We are all crazy . . ."
40 lines (pp. 87–88): Third person narrative/description of the people present and the decorations of the Center for the Graduation-Siyum—"Despite Hannah and Shmuel's doubts . . ."
18 lines (p. 88): Text of Kominsky's opening speech—"This is a mitzva . . ."
4 lines (p. 88): Third person description of Kominsky—"Kominsky's eyes blazed bright blue . . ."
14 lines (pp. 88–89): Commentary by Hannah on being labeled "humble" and on the absence of the graduate's children—"I, for one . . ."
11 lines (p. 89): Third person description of Sonya the valedictorian
1 line (p. 89): Quote from Sonya's speech—"the land of freedom . . ."
2 lines (p. 89): Third person transition to Jacob Koved—"Following her, Jacob . . ."
4 lines (p. 89): Quote from Jacob's poem about his mother—"a poor women . . ."
2 lines (p. 89): Third person transition to Kominsky again—"Kominksy then introduced . . ."
3 lines (p. 89): Quote from Kominsky introducing Dovid and theme of Jewish education—"This boy, Dovid . . ."
3 lines (p. 89): Third person narrative—"Dovid read a passage . . ."
6 lines (p. 89): Text from poem by Bialik that Dovid had translated "You are/Silent and humble . . ."
2 lines (p. 89): Dialogue by Hannah and Nathan regarding being called "humble" again—"Oy vay . . ."
10 lines (pp. 89–90): Third person narrative of other speeches by public officials and the rabbi—"At once, the chorus of hushing . . ."
8 lines (p. 90): Commentary by Hannah on women not being allowed to learn to read Hebrew—"That's right—the luckiest man . . ."
5 lines (p. 90): Third person background on Hannah's previous commentary
20 lines (p. 90): Third person narrative/description of handing out diplomas—"Kominsky began to pass out . . ."
5 lines (p. 90): Commentary by Sofie on no procession being her idea—"This part was my idea . . ."
24 lines (p. 91): Third person narrative of ceremony after the diplomas—"After the diplomas . . ."
7 lines (p. 91): Quote from Kominsky's "Charge to the Class"—"For Jews, study is . . ."
1 line (p. 91): Third person transition to Jacob Koved—"Jacob Koved . . ."
15 lines (pp. 91–92): Quote from Jacob Koved's speech regarding study being a religious act—"What Kominsky has told you . . ."

73 lines (pp. 91–92): Analysis of the Jewish pursuit of learning—"Learning, one of the major sacred symbols . . ."
1 line (p. 93): Third person transition to Abe's speech—"Kominsky called upon Abe next . . ."
6 lines (p. 93): Quote from Abe's speech—"You are our parents . . ."
1 line (p. 94): Third person transition to Abe concluding his speech—"He turned to the audience . . ."
18 lines (p. 94): Quote from Abe's concluding remarks—"How proud you must be of your parents . . ."
8 lines (p. 94): Dialogue between Sophie and Nathan and Hannah about Abe's comment about age and learning—"This is true . . ."
3 lines (p. 94): Third person transition to Hannah's speech—"Nevertheless, she held her diploma tightly . . ."
2 lines (p. 94): Quote from Hannah's introduction—"I couldn't go on in this way . . ."
3 lines (p. 94): Third person description of Hannah becoming emotional during her speech.
10 lines (pp. 94–95): Quote from Hannah's speech [Munich Olympic Games tragedy]—"Jews have always been scapegoats . . ."
17 lines (p. 95): Third person narrative/description of reaction of audience to Hannah's speech. Description of Josele "Masada" and rending his coat—"Hannah sat down to an embarrassed silence . . ."
1 line (p. 95): Quote from Kominsky to Josele—"We don't forget, Josele Masada . . ."
136 lines (pp. 95–98): Analysis of meaning of being Jewish: Great Tradition, Little Tradition (Yiddishkeit), and Eretz Yisroel. Ambiguities and conflicts between these three aspects. Jewish identity in America—"Hannah and Josele's unplanned, dramatic references . . ."
3 lines (p. 98): Third person tradition to Kominsky—"Following Hannah's and Josele's outbursts . . ."
1 line (p. 98): Quote from Kominsky introducing the class song—"Now we all sing."
3 lines (p. 99): Third person narrative of Kominsky leading the singing—"He led the class . . ."
12 lines (p. 99): Text from the song "Oyfn Pripetchol Brent a Fayerl"—"On the oven a little fire is burning . . ."
4 lines (p. 99): Quote from Kominksy explaining song—"In this song, we got everything . . ."
4 lines (p. 99): Commentary from Nathan with a different perspective on school—"What he could also say . . ."
7 lines (p. 99): Third person narrative of conclusion of ceremony
3 lines (p. 99): Quote from Sonya thanking Kominsky and showing donation of class to Israel—"We want to make this honor for our *chaver* . . ."

- 3 lines (p. 99): Third person narrative of reaction to Sonya's announcement—"There was a burst of applause . . ."
- 15 lines (pp. 99–100): Dialogue between Sofie, Hannah, and Moshe regarding the whole experience of the Graduation-Siyum—"This Kominsky has very strict ideas . . ."
- 5 lines (p. 100): Third person description of food, including schnapps—"On the table . . ."
- 5 lines (p. 100): Commentary by Sofie regarding people eating—"Look how they stuff themselves . . ."
- 7 lines (p. 100): Third person description of community response to the ceremony—"For days afterward . . ."
- 64 lines (pp. 100–102): Commentary by Shmuel about how the Graduation-Siyum was artificial and "made-up"—"Characteristically, Shmuel was quite outspoken . . ."
- 82 lines (pp. 102–103): Analysis of Shmuel's commentary discussing differences between an American graduation and a Jewish Siyum and the metaphor of combining them—"Shmuel's statement . . ."
- 4 lines (p. 104): Commentary from Sonya reflecting on the ceremony—"It was a miracle . . ."
- 5 lines (p. 104): Third person summary of graduates appreciating presence of young people—"Some felt the most important part . . ."
- 3 lines (p. 104): Commentary from Hannah criticizing presence of Rabbi's daughter—"What kind of rabbi was this . . ."
- 6 lines (p. 104): Third person description of graduate's response to ceremony and absence of their children—"No one talked openly . . ."
- 10 lines (p. 105): Commentary on ceremony by Moshe at Living History class—"This comes from Martin Buber . . ."
- 5 lines (p. 105): Text that Moshe referenced by Martin Buber—"If you put on Sabbath clothes . . ."
- 8 lines (p. 105): Commentary by Moshe on the referenced text about it being all right that the Graduation-Siyum was not traditional—"This I am liking very much . . ."
- 23 lines (pp. 105–106): Analysis of ritual in terms of emigration to America—"The ritual was . . ."
- 10 lines (p. 106): Quote from Sonya regarding experience of coming to America—"Life in America . . ."
- 150 lines (pp. 106–110): Analysis of ritual and establishing meaning and continuity in reference to emigrating—"Emigration brought some fulfillments to the elders . . ."
- 6 lines (p. 110): Third person description about final impression of Graduation-Siyum and a transition to Shmuel's critical view—"A few days after the Graduation-Siyum"

Figure 8.1. Peer Review Comments

Comments for Garo from Jeanne	Comments for Garo from Rebecca
Garo, nice work. You've skillfully incorporated dialogue and comment to depict how Myerhoff avoids creating sentimentality in her writing, despite the many situations that invite it. I particularly like how you depict Kominsky in comparison to Hannah at the Graduation-Siyum. It made me realize how overly sentimental Kominsky was in contrast to the elderly at the Center. His words are full of pity and anger: "Nobody gave them attention. These are humble people, not much education . . . How they are forgotten is a disgrace." The reader becomes embarrassed for Kominky's overly sentimental speech when Hannah retorts, "I, for one, would appreciate it if he wouldn't make us out to be quite so humble . . ." Garo you pointed this out right beautifully. It made me view Kominsky's character in a fresh way—in terms of sentimentality vs. sentiment. Really enjoyed your analysis.	Garo—I thoroughly enjoyed reading your interpretation of BM's portrayal of a sentimental occasion using sentiment rather than sentimentality. I remember being very uncomfortable reading this section—as you say, the graduates seemed infantilized by the ceremonial leaders, and that bothered me a lot. I appreciate the way you show how BM (and indeed, they themselves) saves them from such a fate. They emerge with their dignity intact thanks to their own poise and BM's treatment of the scene. Your explications are clear and often beautifully/empathetically phrased, indicating your own reverence for BM's writing and the participants themselves. Very nicely and neatly done!

Source: Student peer review exercise notes, created during the week of March 20, 2019

89 lines (pp. 110–112): Commentary by Shmuel criticizing the lack of a sense of reality and an exaggerated sense of importance by the elderly at the Center—"This just gives them more encouragement . . ."

19 lines (p. 112): Shmuel's story about losing knowledge—"When the great Hasid . . ."

My Hopes for Class Nine, by Caroline

I was lucky enough to see *Sweetgrass* when it premiered at the Kendall Theater in Cambridge, MA in 2009. Ilisa Barbash, curator of visual anthropology at Harvard's Peabody Museum of Archaeology and Ethnology, and Lucien Castaing-Taylor, director of the sensory ethnography lab at

Harvard, spoke at that event about their experience making the film and their hopes that they found a way to do right by the story that their data revealed. I knew then and there that if I was going to teach a class on narrative writing for qualitative researchers, I wanted my students to see *Sweetgrass* and, if possible, meet Ilisa and Lucien in a similar way to how I met them in 2009. After all, they worked just up the street from us. What a perfect way to end our three-week focus on narrative film. Lucien was away working on a new film, but Ilisa graciously accepted our invitation. I hoped and believed that we would not only be captivated by Ilisa's discussion of narrative, but also be drawn to the sustenance from the very idea of visual anthropology and sensory ethnography and what they can convey about narrative evocation of data. (Note: Little did I know then, that one member of our seminar, Avigail, would become so enamored of the film that she would invite Ilisa for tea months later, and then interview her classmates and me about our reactions to *Sweetgrass*.)

REFERENCES

Dillard, A. (1987). To fashion a text. In W. Zinsser (Ed.), *Inventing the truth* (pp. 55–76). Random House.

Heller, C. (2002, Spring). Optilenz. *The American Scholar, 71*(2), 53–58.

Jackson, M. (1995). *At home in the world.* Duke University Press.

Luttrell, W. (2003). *Pregnant bodies, fertile minds: Gender, race, and the schooling of pregnant teens.* Routledge.

Peck, R. (2016). *I am not your Negro (From texts by James Baldwin)* (film).

Peck, R. (2017). *I am not your Negro.* Vintage Books, Penguin Random House.

CHAPTER 9

Sweetgrass
A Chance to Feel

Avigail Shimshoni

The following chapter is based in part on my personal communications with Ilisa Barbash, Caroline, and my classmates 6 months after our seminar ended.

Narrative writing for qualitative research is like climbing a mountain. We go up the mountain. We come down the mountain. Sounds simple, but it isn't! We prepare and climb with purpose. But, along the way, we might find that the path we have planned leads us to a dead end, and we retrace our steps, or we might discover new paths to the top of the mountain. Back at base, we hope to convey in text what we found in fresh and intimate ways for our readers. But, which story and whose story among the many that might be embedded in our data should we tell? And how should we tell the story? Would Denise, my classmate who climbs the mountain with me, tell the same story from the same data? And once told, will our readers hear, see, and feel our stories the way we hoped they would?

As I became better equipped with the practices of narrative writing craft during our course, I found that when working as a visual artist, which is my fundamental training, I've faced similar challenges. I've applied paint on canvas to tell stories. But of course, as a writer, I only have text to work with, and as a doctoral student in education I need (and want!) to use that "medium" to paint images.

Telling a story through film, as we've studied for the last three class sessions, became my link between capitalizing on words and capitalizing on images. Film adds layers of complexity because embedded in it are moving sequences of images, activity in action, and sound (often including conversation, text or narration). I chose to write this chapter to expand upon the idea of storytelling in another medium and because I wanted to explore how a closer look at the film *Sweetgrass* (2009), to which I deeply related, could sharpen our understanding of the craft of narrative writing and the kind of choices we need to make to convey the purpose of our work. I also hoped that I might have a chance to meet with Ilisa Barbash, who works at another famous academic institution in Cambridge, just down the street from Lesley, one-to-one to talk more in depth about the film and the process as she experienced it. To my happiness, that hope came true.

THE STORY IS SIMPLE

> A river of sheep ... sheep move like water when in groups ... loud, aggressive sheep shaving ... stillness of cold ...
>
> —Denise Mytko, reflecting on *Sweetgrass* during my interview with her

The story of *Sweetgrass*, as summarized by one of its creators, Ilisa Barbash, is straightforward: the sheep go up the mountain for summer pasture and then they go down the mountain. We learn in the film that the journey of the last herders to lead sheep into Montana's Absaroka–Beartooth mountains for summer pasture began back at the ranch, where we witness the shearing of the sheep in the winter and lambing and docking of the lambs. The film continues with the herders leading about 3,000 sheep through town and up the mountain to graze, and then back down the mountain and back through the town at the end of summer. This reminds me, too, of Caroline's advice that the one quasi "rule" of strong narrative writing is that the ending of the "story" should in some way recapitulate the beginning, even if the nuances and meanings of the end differ from the beginning.

Threads of the herders' *backstories* are interwoven within this simple overarching framework. My classmate, Denise Mytko, highlighted this in one of her comments about *Sweetgrass*: "The ranchers were *so* practiced that their history doing that work was obvious." Another classmate, Rebecca Redlon, "made a quick note of all those sheep being run through town and how that was a community experience—a thread of tradition."

FINDING THE STORY ALONG THE WAY

> ... hearing about making the film was a whole story in itself, connected to, but also separate from, the content of the film.
>
> —Kat Marsh

Creating *Sweetgrass* took Barbash and her collaborator, Lucien Castaing-Taylor, 8 years from when they first started filming in Montana to bringing it to the public. From the beginning, they set out to create a "salvage documentary with a twist" (Barbash, personal communication, 2020). They would shoot a film within a genre that documents the last ritual performed in far lands, but theirs would be close to home in the rural western United States. They wanted to offer viewers the experience of the sheep drive up the mountain as they experienced and witnessed it while shooting the film. As in other projects Barbash has embarked upon, the "narrative was created along the way" (Barbash, personal communication, 2020). Barbash (the producer) and Castaing-Taylor (the film recorder and in qualitative research terms, the "participant observer") did not know what the narrative of *Sweetgrass* would be until they were well into the later process of editing the footage and sound recordings, a kind of "coding" of the "data."

Barbash (personal communication, 2019) spoke to this when she visited our seminar to show the film and then later explained this further when I interviewed her:

> I embark on a project, knowing the story I want to tell—and this often had to be articulated in grants. Then the footage gathering/shooting is a kind of research, some of which may support the story and some of which might contradict it or take new directions. Of course, I (the filmmaker) get to choose what to shoot and what not. Then in the editing room, I look through all the footage and see what I've got. Gaps in a story can be filled with title cards or narration or even shooting more footage. But I really have to go with what's there if it's to be a true documentary.

Barbash and Castaing-Taylor did not have a lot of time to *gather information* and do research in advance of filming. The opportunity to film the last sheep drive into the Montana mountains fell into their laps suddenly and quite by chance, exactly at the time in their professional lives when they wanted to create a documentary film about the American West. They first learned about this opportunity in February 2001, and by that summer they were in Montana filming. Their children traveled with them for, initially, they intended to immerse themselves in the experience of going up the mountain with the sheep and herders as a family. But as happens in many research projects, they quickly learned that logistics presented challenges. Going up all the way into the mountains would be too dangerous for their young children. Alongside the ranchers and herders' family members, friends, and neighbors, Barbash and her children got up at 4 in the morning to join the first part of the journey with the sheep's long trek. But then when Castaing-Taylor headed up the mountain with the sheep and herders, Barbash returned to town with their children, filming events around town such as the rodeos, the Sweetgrass county fair, the shooting contests, and the haying of the grass.

Over three summers, but mostly during the summer of 2001, they shot several hundred hours of footage and sound recordings. Then, through an editing process that lasted 8 years, they continued the extensive research to help them better understand sheep ranching and the social and biological history of this area of Montana.

Several themes emerged from this vast amount of data—and each theme, Barbash told me, could have warranted a film of its own. But the decision they made early on to focus on the sheep drive informed their first step of *taming the chaos* (the concept Denise Mytko discussed in Chapter 3; also see Appendix B) of the data. Focusing on the sheep drive meant cutting out the 40 hours of footage that Barbash shot while Castaing-Taylor went up the mountain with the herders and sheep and leaving behind the stories that could have emerged from the footage Barbash shot in and around town. Because they had culled the data from the sheep drive for the themes the data told, much of the data from town ended up on the cutting room floor.

Centering the story of *Sweetgrass* on the sheep drive also meant taking out anything that would distract viewers from the purpose and urgency of the journey: that the sheep, the herders, and their accompanying anthropologist Castaing-Taylor make it to the mountain basin in time for summer grazing. For example, scenes alluding to the controversies over the impact of sheep grazing on the natural habitat in these mountains and the strict regulations the herders needed to abide by were present throughout the film in *implicit* ways but were not explained. A bear that was a threat to the sheep and may well have killed several during one night is seen and spotted by the herders, but was not shot; wild goats are seen backing away as the sheep head up the mountain; and towards the end of the film, we can spot a sign on a tree indicating that they are leaving the Absaroka–Beartooth Mountains Wilderness as the sheep and the herders pass in front of the camera on their way off the mountain.

In some cases, focusing on this chosen purpose meant leaving out other stories that Barbash wished they could have included, such as the herders' Norwegian and Irish/British/Scottish heritages and their lively culture of storytelling. The filmmakers decided to include a scene of the herders joking around while docking the lambs right before the sheep are herded to the mountain, and the joke they included in the film is told well, but jokes that followed, reflecting one of the herder's Norwegian heritage, were eliminated in the editing process. Barbash felt that including another joke would slow down the pace of the scene too much. It was time to head up the mountain.

Finding the narrative was not only a matter of deciding *what to keep and what to leave out*, placement or *sequencing* shaped the narrative as well. *Sweetgrass* includes two text tiles; the first one, at the beginning of the film, only states the geographic location, Big Timber, Montana, USA. The second text tile appears at the end of the film and informs viewers that *In 2003, over three months and one hundred and fifty miles, the last sheep trailed through Montana's Absaroka-Beartooth Mountains*. The filmmakers deliberately chose not to inform the viewers at the beginning of the film that the sheep drive in 2003 was to be the last one. When they first experimented with switching the placement of these two text tiles, Barbash felt that they would be guiding the viewers on how to interpret the film, including looking for reasons in the film why the sheep drive would be the last. She and Castaing-Taylor did not want to give too much explicit interpretation, which is something we had discussed in our seminar regarding decisions about narrating our own research. It was exciting to hear now-familiar narrative craft topics discussed by these renowned ethnographic filmmakers.

When I met her for our interview, Barbash (2020) added:

> Entire scenes can be placed in different parts of the film editing, and this changes the pace of the film, and the way the narrative unfolds. For example, we'd thought about putting sheep shearing at the end of the film, but then it would have been two different endings—almost like two deaths. So, we put the shearing near the beginning.

TELLING THE STORY OF SWEETGRASS...

> We need to trust the viewers more. Let them look, feel, contemplate and interpret for themselves... without narration, interviews, text-tiles or sound effects.
>
> —Ilisa Barbash

To offer the viewers the opportunity to "look, feel, contemplate and interpret for themselves," as Barbash described during our interview (2020), she and Castaing-Taylor crafted *Sweetgrass* in the observational documentary style: scenes unfold as the filmmakers witnessed them while shooting and recording the film. Off- or on-camera narration, text tiles, soundtracks, interviews, or explicit directing are deliberately done away with. In their absence, the filmmakers rely on the editing process of the sounds and shots recorded on site. But like qualitative researchers and writers, Barbash and Castaing-Taylor do not pretend to be absent from the film's "text." For example, in a scene that takes place in the herders' tent up in the mountains, Lucien Castaing-Taylor's presence is made known when one of the herders says, "Lucien fell asleep." The filmmakers' expressive hand is in the choices they made filming and integrating camera work, visual images, and sound. Below, I illustrate a few examples of the *crafts* Barbash and Castaing-Taylor used (in collaboration with Ernst Karel on the sound editing and mixing) to create the sensory experience of *Sweetgrass*.

With Camera Work:—Shots—Zoom—Position—Movement

Length of the shots, range of zoom, positioning and movement of the camera, work together to create atmosphere and the sensory *feel* the viewer experiences watching and listening to *Sweetgrass*. According to Barbash (2019), they purposely included long takes to give viewers the opportunity to immerse themselves in what is going on and make sense of it for themselves. In the longest take of the film (about 5 minutes), positioned in one place, Castaing-Taylor slowly pans the camera to follow one of the owners of the sheep as she patiently tows a newborn lamb across the barn in an attempt to coax the lamb's mother to follow. On the other hand, he films short choppy shots to amplify confusion. When the sheep and the herders encounter a blocked path, getting through seems impossible and the risk of losing sheep is high. Here, Castaing-Taylor moves the camera in for fast close-up shots, often at the sheep's eye level. Another technique he employs is showing a wide-angle view of the vast landscape, then slowly zooming in to a range from which the viewers can notice details such as the "stream of sheep" descending the mountain. In this way, perhaps he is suggesting that the sheep are "part of a larger mineral ecology" (Sweetgrass, 2009).

With Visual Images

> ... I felt that *Sweetgrass*, in contrast to *I Am Not Your Negro* and *Number Our Days*, used film as a purely visual medium.
>
> —Garo Saraydarian

The aesthetic quality and artistic composition of the images were central to Barbash and Castaing-Taylor, as reflected in a voiceover conversation between them about the film as it unfolded (*Sweetgrass*, 2009). Castaing-Taylor analyzed the visual quality of images numerous times. For example, he was in awe of the interplay of triangles created by the tent and the fire in a scene of the herders settling into camp for the night and the teepee in the scene that immediately follows. In another scene, Castaing-Taylor admired the tactile richness of the hat, beard, scarf, and hands of the herder, which is shown as a close up, the viewer watching this herder eating his breakfast. However, Barbash and Castaing-Taylor went beyond merely presenting aesthetic and artistic visual images. They embedded visual cues to relay information and emotion in subtle ways, just as all narrative writers must do. For example, minutes into the film, we see the sheep in a group. As the camera moves closer, one sheep, first seen in profile, turns her head and looks directly at the camera and thus, the viewers. This close-up "shows the sheep as an individual" and "establishes a relationship between the sheep and the viewer" (Sweetgrass, 2009). As viewers, we may also begin to guess that *Sweetgrass* is a film about sheep. A rectangular green mark on the sheep's ear suggests that these sheep are not wild. This cue *foreshadows* a scene of docking the lambs right before they're herded up into the mountains. Implicit visual cues also suggest that a large number of people and animals (dogs, mules, and horses) work together to get the sheep up to the mountain basins. Since the herders work to spread their charges out and to move them fast so as not to lose any sheep, we cannot count the large number of people and animals involved in this effort. We only get a hunch. Only later, when they finally reach the mountain basin where the two herders would remain with the sheep for the remainder of the summer, we see everyone walk across the camera and we can actually count them.

With Sound (and Without):

Watching *Sweetgrass*, we are surrounded by sound. Unlike in many documentaries, sound encompasses us: the calls of the winds, birds, dogs, sheep, man-made machines, human voices, and moments of profound silence and solitude. Human dialogue is only a small part of the auditory experience of *Sweetgrass*. While filming, Castaing-Taylor used four microphones attached to different people. They even tried attaching microphones to the sheep, but that did not work so well (Barbash, personal communication, 2020). In collaboration with sound engineer Ernst Karel, Barbash and Castaing-Taylor experimented with sound mixing and didn't hesitate to break conventions. They clearly projected sounds that were actually produced far away from the camera and, as a result, viewers could not always see the sounds' source. When the sheep meandered off their designated area for grazing, for instance, we can hear the herder losing his patience and cursing even though the angry herder was away from the camera and can barely be seen. A radio cast up in the mountains reconnects us to the outside world.

With Human Voice:

The human voice is an integral part of the auditory experience in *Sweetgrass*, too. Interwoven with the sounds of nature, animals, and machines, we hear the herders joking, cursing, singing, talking to themselves, or communicating with their animals through gestures, conversation, or abstract sounds (for us). Human speech and conversations are presented as any of us would talk when not posing for an audience or camera: mundane topics at times, full sentences alongside incomplete ones; fragments of thoughts alongside longer monologues. Unlike in many other documentaries, the herders are shown sitting side by side in silent conversation, with each other or alone. Including this whole rainbow of communication was important to Barbash (personal communication, 2020). In particular she felt that "including the cursing was important to give context of who these people were" (Barbash, personal communication, 2020)—a context she could not fill in with narration or text tiles. Revealing the herders' moments of anger, vulnerability, tenderness, and humor through their own voices portrayed them not as idealized superheroes but as complex human beings, something that we talked about in our seminar in terms of the importance for all narrative writers to avoid the trap of portraying people simplistically, as heroes or villains (see Appendix C).

By Pushing the Boundaries:

Barbash and Castaing-Taylor approached the making of *Sweetgrass* "with a twist" on many levels. Experimenting with almost every aspect of the craft—sound, language, and visual imagery—they pushed the boundaries and broke conventions. As a result, "*Sweetgrass,*" as my classmate Rebecca Redlon so well described, "was not so much story (though of course, it was) as it was a kind of montage of sensory impressions" (personal communication, 2019).

In my interview with Barbash (2020), I learned that Barbash and Castaing-Taylor's commitment to creating a sensory experience and experimenting with the film medium lay the foundation for creating the Sensory Ethnography Lab at Harvard, which Castaing-Taylor directs, while Ilisa Barbash is curator of visual anthropology at Harvard's Peabody Museum.

Once told, Barbash invariably wonders (as I do about my own future qualitative research), will our readers hear, see, or feel our stories the way we hope they will?

Once a film or a piece of writing is released, the viewers or readers own the interpretation. The creators have little control of how it might be received. In addition, today, with DVD releases, filmmakers have little say about the context or the settings in which their films are viewed. Manola Dargis (January 5, 2010) of the *New York Times* wrote, "In *Sweetgrass*, a graceful and often moving meditation on a disappearing way of life, there is little here that is objective and much that is magnificent." However, two criticisms surprised Barbash: the critique that the viewers should have been informed up front that sheep are no longer herded for summer pasture on the Bear Mountains Basins and a complaint about the filmmakers' inclusion of the cursing. These critiques reflect the larger question about the limited control filmmakers (and all writers) have in terms of how their work will be received.

Reflecting with my peers on *Sweetgrass* several months after we had completed our narrative writing seminar revealed how differently we had experienced the film, even when watching it together through the shared lens of learning the craft of narrative writing. Watching the film we also wore our personal lenses—the places we came from, our professions, in short, our full lives. We felt differently about watching the film together, and, as my classmate Rebecca Redlon phrased it, our "thoughts about the film got tangled with our personal experiences" (Redlon, personal communication, 2019).

"Scenes are long enough to feel," classmate Denise Mytko noted. But, for others of us, sometimes the scenes felt too long, especially when coupled with stretches of silence. Classmate Krysta Betit "had a lot of trouble sitting in that level of silence with people I know, but did not know so well" (Betit, personal communication, 2019) but she could relate to the purpose and intent of the scenes with the sheep she knew so well from the family farm on which she grew up. Classmate Thelma Goldberg felt that emotional content can make it difficult to watch a film with others. But "*Sweetgrass* was not very sentimental, so I was fine watching with others" (Goldberg, personal communication, 2019).

Growing up in Israel, I saw many sheep on the hills of Jerusalem not far from the Muslim quarters of the city. So, at first when I saw the sheep in the film, I was expecting to hear the call of the *muezzin* (calling Muslims to pray five times a day). At first this was confusing because even though I recognized the lush green mountains of Montana on the screen, I was listening for the sounds of my homeland. My classmate Garo Saraydarian, on the other hand, was not looking for sound. He "appreciated the silence because sometimes film is too aurally stimulating for me and/or seems like it's manipulating me to feel a certain way. This way just seemed very honest" (Saraydarian, personal communication, 2019).

Watching *Sweetgrass* in class steered us to look "with enhanced attention" (Goldberg, personal communication, 2019) for the practices we were learning in our narrative writing seminar. Barbash's journey brought to life the complexity of taming the chaos and the patience it takes to find the story in what might seem like a pandemonium of data. As Thelma wondered, "How did they [Barbash and Castaing-Taylor] manage to have such patience in letting the rhythm of the animals guide the narrative?" We could hone in to better understand the difference between "narrative (the story) and narration (the way the story is told)" (Marsh, personal communication, 2019); we could "get a sense of what it means to really intimately portray a human subject" (Betit, personal communication, 2019). And we could see how "like everything we read thus far, like Michael Jackson's book and Wendy Luttrell's book, which we were to read for the following week (see Chapter 10), this film tries to understand humanity and our human condition by focusing on something very particular that might reveal something beyond the particular" (Heller, class notes, 2019).

"Film is another way of telling a story and thus a valuable technique and 'method' for us to consider" (Goldberg, personal communication, 2019). It can reveal something different than writing. In writing, "you can describe a person's mood and body language, but that information is mediated in your mind through the language. In film, you don't need the words, or as many words, and your mind can process these concepts without language—likely with different mysterious mechanisms" (Marsh, personal communication, 2019). When carefully made, film can create sensory experiences. Within its complexity of sound, visuals, and movement, it can also embed stillness and silence. I wonder if and how that could be achieved in our writing.

A film like *Sweetgrass* is an opportunity to look at our writing craft in a fresh way. On an essential level, we can identify many of the same craft elements we were learning to use as writers, see how they come into

Sweetgrass

play in ethnographic film, and sharpen our understanding of narrative writing for qualitative research. Beyond that, *Sweetgrass* teaches us to use our craft with intention, but at the same time to allow ourselves to push the boundaries. There are times and moments to break conventions. Above all, *Sweetgrass* is an invitation to put our notebooks (and laptops) aside, slip out of our academic mindset, and "inhabit the landscape"—be it in our research settings or on a mountain top—to look, listen, feel. This, I now fully believe, is where narrative writing begins.

QUESTIONS FOR FURTHER WRITERLY CONTEMPLATION

1. How would you prepare and set the stage for viewing the film?
    a. Is your classroom conducive to watching a film, particularly a relatively long film with expansive views like *Sweetgrass*? Do you have access to a large screen and a space that can be darkened?
2. Are you able to connect with the producer or anyone involved in making the documentary? If yes, and if they are able to visit your class in person or by Zoom, consider asking participants in your course to prepare and submit questions in advance. If the producer is not able to join, is there a short video you can share with the class about the filmmaking process?
3. Consider if the participants in your course watch the film on their own first, before watching or discussing it as a group?

Tips for Reflection on the Film

1. Inhabiting the landscape: Choose a place in your school or community and observe it for several hours. Immerse yourself in the surroundings, taking in the sounds, smells, textures, and any cues that you find that might suggest to you what happened or is going to happen next in this place. Experiment with positioning yourself in different places, such as sitting on the ground, on a bench, or on a high spot, or observe your landscape through a window perhaps from a higher floor. Look closely, focusing just on the few yards radius surrounding you and then zoom out and take in the whole view. Shut your eyes, or look up at the sky while listening. If you can, repeat this exploration on a different day and at a different time of the day.
2. Watch the film (or a part of it) with your eyes shut. What do you notice? What did you feel?
3. Watch the film (or a part of it) with a sketchbook and a pencil in your hand. Doodle, sketch, and take visual notes freely what comes to mind. Or you could try making marks following a guided prompt, such as responding just to the sounds, focusing on the different eye level

perspectives, or jotting down the verbal utterances and words, and sounds of the animals.
4. Compare *Sweetgrass* and other documentaries you have seen in class, like *I am Not Your Negro*, and *Number Our Days*. For example, one question you might consider is if and how is the participant researcher/film producer present?
5. Consider how all of the above explorations might shape your experience of watching the documentary film, and inform you of your writing?

SUGGESTIONS FOR FURTHER READING

Afron, C. (1982). *Cinema and sentiment*. The University of Chicago Press.
Arnheim, R. (1957). *Film as art*. University of California Press.
Corrigan, T. (2004). *A short guide to writing about film*. Pearson Longman.
McDonald, S. (2013). *American ethnographic film and personal documentary*. University of California Press.
Summerfield, E. (1993). *Cross cultures through film*. Intercultural Press.

REFERENCES

Barbash, I. (1997). Cross-cultural filmmaking: *A hand book for making ethnographic documentary film and videos*. Berkeley: University of California Press.
Dargis, M. (2010). Montana cowboys lead, coax and cajole their charges amid chorus of bleats. *New York Times,* https://www.nytimes.com/2010/01/06/movies/06sweet.html
Sweetgrass Reviews. (2022, July 15). http://sweetgrassthemovie.com/reviews/
Sweetgrass. (2009). Directed by Barbash, I. & Castaing-Taylor, L.: Grasshopper Films.

REVISIONS OF THIS CHAPTER

Climbing the mountain to write this chapter on *Sweetgrass,* I found that the path I had originally planned led me to a dead end, and I had to retrace my steps. When I started to formulate ideas for writing this chapter, I asked my classmates about their experiences watching *Sweetgrass* together and meeting the film producer. I was excited by the rich conversations that spontaneously emerged and was eager to write the chapter in the form of a dialogue. But after many tries and revisions, this approach simply was not clicking. Following Caroline's insight and guidance, I put my initial drafts aside. At first, it was unsettling to retrace my steps. But it was worth it. I discovered that revising was not only about the intricate word choices we make. It is also about being able to recognize when we reach a dead end, and it is time to start over and follow a different path to the top of the mountain.

My Hopes for Class Ten, by Caroline

I have always felt that I could use each of Wendy Luttrell's books and let them be the stuff of a whole seminar on beautiful narrative writing and sound humanistic research. Dr. Luttrell not only unpacks her research and writing processes, letting her decision-making become transparent, she succeeds in what we're all trying to accomplish—evoking the feeling in our readers that this is what it's like to be this particular human being at this particular moment; this is how it feels. In her book that I assigned for us to read, she not only shed light on the relationship of self-perception, pregnancy, and education, she looked at the process of data collection and analysis in ethnographic work. The story in Dr. Luttrell's (2003) book, *Pregnant Bodies, Fertile Minds*, is so clearly an embodiment of the findings, and she let us know how and why, tracing her interpretative journey and allowing her research participants to be the experts in telling their own stories.

CHAPTER 10

Envisioning and Embracing

Kat Marsh (followed by drafts of paper by Kat)

The beginning of any research study is a form of envisioning. Researchers like Wendy Luttrell (2003, 2010, 2020) form a vision of what stories might lie nestled under a veil of research fairness or hidden behind a façade of researcher neutrality. To lift the veil or peer behind the façade is to focus on the research participants, the true storytellers, and each storyteller's identity, patterns of telling, and positions in specific situations. Luttrell (2003) goes further, embracing the storyteller's representations and recognizing the tensions embedded between an experience and the telling of an experience, between a narrative (the story) and narrativizing (how the story is told). She offers up the vulnerabilities and strengths of the storyteller (participants in the research) along with the vulnerabilities and strengths of the researcher. With her strengths alone, a researcher can help readers meet the story behind the veil or façade. But with vulnerabilities, carefully rendered, a researcher can help readers make the leap to meet not only the story, but the storytellers themselves. When Wendy Luttrell visited our narrative writing class via Zoom, she shared her belief that relationships are central to research designs and continue to be central as an anchor for how research evolves (Luttrell, personal communication, April 15, 2019). Her research embraces the "links between psychodynamic processes and social structures of power and inequity," raising emotion-inflected relationships in subjective relief against the objective background of ethnographic curiosity (Luttrell, 2003, p. 167). Following a three-pronged process of doing, knowing, and telling in her book about pregnant high school students, Luttrell shares her view of ethnography as a social art form. She carries forward those crucial interdependencies between objectivity and "emotional participation and artful engagement" into a rethinking of education practices (p. 172). Luttrell's work echoes the permission we had given ourselves to be vulnerable with one another in class as narrative writers. Embracing such vulnerability is essential to releasing the inhibitions of the academy and offers readers a more candid and humble sense of what it means to be the researched as well as the researcher.

I consider Wendy Luttrell a courageous person from my own limited perspective on the subject. She was willing, despite barriers of racial and social distrust, to enter a world far distant from the one privileged White educators typically inhabit: the world of pregnant teens, in this instance, most of whom were young girls of color. Her aim was to gain understanding about the connection between sexuality and schooling, a frame of reference many might not consider worthy of deeper understanding. Certainly, this connection matters in terms of social science research and public policy decisions. Clarity about how we got here as a society would be well worth investigating. I can hear the most common question resonating through public high school staff and policy meetings: Did we do enough to provide these teens with education on safe sex and the benefits of a high school diploma as the path to a decent life? Luttrell bypasses that question in favor of recognizing that the girls (Luttrell called them girls, so I will, too) are but children themselves, yet they have made binding, adult-like choices, and she wonders how that came about. With its focus on achievement, the education community dodges underlying questions of social and racial justice for these young people and sets aside the factors outside of education that impact their lives and life-choices.

As an educator seeking ways of understanding the perspectives of middle school students, I wanted to know if these girls' stories reflected or differed from ideas I had been thinking about for my doctoral research. And I wanted to know how she did it. How did Wendy Luttrell enter the world of these young people, build rapport with them, come to understand something about them and then find a way to communicate all that to others in an engaging way? As Limerick (1993) points out in the parable of buzzards tied to a branch for a Hollywood movie (one of our first class readings), if we are repeatedly restricted from flying (i.e., writing with verve and voice), we might well give up. I was interested in ways Luttrell overcame the habit of academic writing (if she ever wrote in such a way) to find her narrative voice.

Before reading *Pregnant Bodies, Fertile Minds* for our 10th class meeting, I paused to critically examine my own knowledge. What did I know about pregnant teens of color? Not a thing. For that matter, what did I even know about schoolchildren of color, or lives of color in general? Pitiably little. I am a White suburban female of Scottish/Irish descent. Over the years, I have had (and still have) few students of color, and few colleagues of color. The grand sum of my experiences with persons of color would be near to nil. This alone informs me of the crucial relevance in reading Luttrell's book about these working-class, teenage mothers-to-be. Of course, this one book will not provide me with a comprehensive view of teenage mothers-to-be of color, but it may provide me with some ethical insights about how I can best reach and teach my students of color or any student coming from a background different from mine. I have some experience with family members (two nieces) who became mothers in their teens, so I had some basis to begin learning more.

Because many of the girls we meet in Luttrell's book are Black, I felt compelled to reexamine my initial encounter with a person of color, an event I have pondered from time to time, but not nearly deeply enough, and one I have never written about—until now. When a Black girl joined my 1st-grade class at the Catholic school that my three brothers, my sister, and I attended, I took no particular notice of her arrival, her introduction to the class, where she sat, or how she might have felt. She seemed quite like the rest of us, apart from her skin, and I, blissfully ignorant of the dominance of the White culture I was immersed in, didn't detect any unease in her or in the class.

Perhaps, as many Black children in predominantly White schools do, she had no choice but to appear comfortable with her all-White classmates. But I took no notice of her, nor any reactions from my peers, until we were out on the playground, a large, paved parking area beside the church. A group of more than a dozen of us were playing "The Farmer in the Dell," a game where we held hands to form a circle that moved clockwise while we sang a rhyme to select candidates to move from the circle into the middle to play the parts of the farmer, wife, child, dog, etc. When the Black girl approached to join us, smiling, singing the rhyme, holding both of her hands out, the dancing circle of children passed her by. No one broke their hand-clasp to gather her in. As I came around to her the second time, I broke my grasp to take her hand. She grinned, joined hands with me, and began moving with us. As we continued to move in a circle, I realized there was a gap in the circle. The person whose hand I had dropped to pick up the Black girl's hand, had not closed the gap by taking up the girl's other hand. Their arms were stretched out, reaching, but not touching. The circle was broken, and it puzzled me that we were able to keep moving, keep singing, continue our game with the connection broken.

Was I brave in that brief moment of reaching out? I hope you do not think so, since I do not. At that moment I was ignorant of the cloak of White privilege that surrounded and surrounds me, protected by it and simultaneously hampered by it in ways I have much more recently come to understand and acknowledge. It cannot count as bravery to invite someone to enter my world when mine is the dominant sociocultural world. That requires little to no bravery. What does require bravery is the reflective examination of ourselves and our precarious position as observer–participants, as fallible interpreters, and cautious, ethical narrators of the worlds we seek to understand. To do this we must be willing to look deeply into our own psyches, visit and revisit our most visceral reactions to things that puzzle, and disturb, and even frighten us. That is what Luttrell (2003) did. What that requires is iterative, reflexive thinking, cycling back to review and revise our thoughts and ideas when new information or new perspectives present themselves. Otherwise, we may continue circling and circling, looking on in wordless confusion for the reasons why the dance continues with improbable cadence while the connection between ourselves and those who would join us is broken.

Anticipating reading Wendy Luttrell's book had multiple meanings for me. The obvious ones such as enlightening myself about an important social justice topic (the lives of pregnant high school teenagers), expanding my educational range of knowledge, and fulfilling a course requirement. An important backburner meaning for me hovered over my shoulders as I read, throwing hints at me about how I, too, could write a compelling dissertation, perhaps ultimately a book, that might induce people to shift their perspective of a group of youngsters. One aspect I wondered about as I read was the process of writing such a book. Rarely are writings born whole cloth, emerging fully formed and ready for action like Athena from the head of Zeus. During her virtual visit to our class, Luttrell (Luttrell, personal communication, April 10, 2019) said that the purpose of her book came to her after she had written it all out. The act of writing isn't straightforward, just as qualitative research itself frequently is a nonlinear process (Luttrell, 2010).

In the book, Luttrell began with the *doing* step of the three-pronged process of *doing*, *knowing*, and *writing*. Because she recognized that there were adult ways of doing and of hearing that needed to be decoded and put aside in order to hear these girls, she was willing for the girls to take the lead in helping her consider how the research should unfold. Observing the girls' actions and interactions, Luttrell devised activities and provided materials to guide the girls' exploration of the intersectionality of their situation as teens, mothers-to-be, Black or Mexican-American or White, poor or working-class, and students at a public high school. Part of Luttrell's advocacy for these girls was to resuscitate play and "restore the artist," an idea she adapted from the work of psychologist Adam Phillips, taking an enquiring interest in their present situation with the perspectives of the girls themselves at the forefront. Restoring the artist doesn't refer to some sort of art therapy that can help restore the girls to their previous, unpregnant states so that they can do school. Restoring the artist means applying the girls' present, multiplicative states of being toward becoming educated. The power of Luttrell's narrative emanates from her observations, her reflections on her observations and her own reactions, and from the parts of themselves the girls were willing to share with each other and with Luttrell. During her visit to our class, Luttrell described this as "sharing what the participants were most public about" (Luttrell, personal communication, April 10, 2019).

Borrowing broadly from a type of action–research, Luttrell hoped to devise activities any teacher could use in a classroom to facilitate introspection and growth in students while furthering the up-close and personal interactions that could build mutual understanding between teachers and students. For her research, Luttrell was interested in the ways these activities could draw out the girls' perspectives on what it meant to them to be a pregnant teen. The activities involved both play in the form of creative activities (skits, collages, book-making), and work in the form of written texts and oral role plays. The girls created improvisational skits about aspects of their pregnancy stories, "Who am I?" self-portraits, and self-portrait collages with written descriptions. In all three activities, Luttrell's interest was in what the girls had to *say* about what they produced, rather than the product itself. The discussion around such creative products provides rich and detailed insights into the girls' ideas about their identities, including their changing bodies, sense of self-worth, and the contradictory emotions of growing up. On the verge of motherhood, these girls brought out family and cultural experiences in response to creating collages. From their artwork to their conversation about hair, Luttrell recognized the girls' struggles to create their own identities and style. The girls shared stories about their feelings of being cared for and being made aware of their beauty. On the other hand, the same topic (hair) brought forth stories of girls being criticized by their home community for either resisting or conforming to standards of beauty. In the book, Luttrell describes this as a theme in the girls' art and discussions, not—or not only—in the sense of superficial beauty, but in the sense of being female, a soon-to-be-mother, and a member of a minoritized group facing simultaneous pressures to fit in to that group while assimilating into the dominant group. Luttrell's interactions with the girls and analysis of their artwork and discussions highlight "insider" narratives of the difficulties of life as poor and working-class girls, ambivalent feelings toward their babies, and a confrontation with ways they are objectified and misunderstood by peers, school, and society. In discussion during her visit to our seminar, Luttrell described this as "opening the academy to new perspectives," closer to a coconstructed narrative than to the objective description by a researcher of a participant's world.

EMBLEMATIC EPISODES

Pregnant Bodies, Fertile Minds is full of what in our seminar we referred to as emblematic episodes—incidents or details that are symbolic or representative of a larger theme or concept. An image that sticks in my mind about the girls is the way their baby-developing bodies fit into the typical one-piece high school desks. While this is not an episode in the typical sense, it *is* emblematic. Luttrell mentions the ill-suited desks as a visual cue to the girls' physical states of pregnancy, but also as a hint of their prescribed status as misfits. The voluntary program the girls attended offered refuge but came with the stigma that implied the girls did not wish to be schooled with the regular population of students. Separated from their nonpregnant peers and schooled in a separate area with an academic program specifically designed for them, there is an implicit assumption that the girls have done something wrong in getting pregnant. Luttrell conveys this in her narrative as she shares bulletin boards and banners in the girls' classrooms proclaiming that safe sex and education are the only ways to "combat" teen pregnancy. Attempts to entrench the girls in a militant view of their bodies bring forth outbursts of resistance, and Luttrell records the girls graffiti-like responses, such as "It's a choice of one's own mind" and "Don't be ashamed of your kids cause you weren't ashamed of having sex!" (pp. xi-xii).

Like the melting red Popsicle in Boo's (2001) article about an economically depressed area of Washington, DC discussed in Chapter 2, the desks and the written messages echo the larger universe of meaning. That universe includes, and is perhaps dominated by, what Luttrell conveys about what most people think: these pregnancies are mistakes, unfortunate and perhaps tragic ones as far as the school and their families seemed to be concerned. The public school (and therefore society) must have failed them (i.e., failed to prevent them from ruining their lives), and to account for this failure, the school focuses on ways for them to gain their high school diplomas, so that "at least" they will have one accomplishment to balance against their poor decision-making. The girls' interactions with a strict teacher and with a librarian who glared at them with suspicion as if they were not to be trusted, further demonstrated the mismatch between what the school thinks it should be offering them and the ability of many of the school personnel to deal with the realities of the girls' pregnancies. Luttrell did not explicitly state this in her book or during our class discussion, but on later reflection in preparation for writing this chapter, I recognized that her work brought me to a place where I thought about the power of her research and writing craft to make me think this thought: a great deal of time and effort was put into the specialized program for these girls, but no effort was made to see them as pregnant, instead they were seen only through the lens of school expectations. In drawing attention to this small, but emblematic point, Luttrell asks us to examine aspects of its meaning. Does a student have to fit (physically, culturally, socially, economically) into a school in order to be taught there? Who fits and who doesn't in any given school? In what ways do fitting into a school and being fit for school differ?

Only a chapter into reading the book, I paused to ponder the individual stories of these girls. The stories of scores of students could address but never exhaust the topic of fitting in at school. It is disturbing for me to hear recent anecdotes from colleagues and parents about students who are denied participation in group activities such as field trips because their teachers feel they would be too disruptive or not benefit from the outing. In most cases, these were students of color, which is even more distressing. I have known a student with learning differences who was required to stay at school to clean desks while her peers went on a field trip to a science museum. She was not being punished for inappropriate behavior; it was simply assumed that she would not get anything out of the trip. Much education research, when it leans too heavily on objectivity, cannot adequately address the needs of students who deserve recognition, understanding, and compassionate advocacy. The narrative that emerged from Luttrell's research *with*—not *on*—these girls has the potential to fill this need, and emblematic episodes can heft up powerful meanings that individual people (teachers, parents, peers, administrators, policymakers) can connect with. Luttrell posed the girls' self-representations as emblematic of the ways that social research can be cocreated and the ways it can guide pedagogical changes. Luttrell was concerned with the dilemmas of representation, including claims of authority, the risk of reducing the girls' culture to only the parts presented, and the risk of appropriating the voices and experiences of the girls toward her own purpose. One way that Luttrell accepted the risk was to assert that her narrative of the girls brought forth an alternative, complex picture of a maligned group for the benefit of those who hold power and have influence over such groups. If Luttrell used the girls' self-representations, she used them to build an alternative vision of the girls because she felt she had a responsibility to take apart current "truths" and build or rebuild those truths more inclusively.

Luttrell chose emblematic episodes representing themes of respect for the individual and respectability in the sense of a social group. She described an incident in which one of the girls, Brandi, expressed interest in a book Luttrell had recommended. When Luttrell happened to find several used copies of the book, she offered them to all the girls. Brandi took offense at the idea that all the girls had been offered a copy of the book because such gifts crossed the boundary between an individual exchange and a cross-class exchange. Luttrell reflected on and examined her own feelings around these complex relationships and took a lesson from Brandi about the emotional politics of class, race, and gender differences that must be carefully and deeply examined to understand the positions of students and researchers. Luttrell recognized her ambiguous position of standing apart from the girls and yet, in their eyes and in her own, playing a role in their lives as a caregiver or mentor, a situation that clearly moved her from observer to participant. In a discussion about a class paper that I wrote about Luttrell's book, my classmate, Allison Horváth-Tucker, aptly described the situation as "a gift that was meant as neutral was unintentionally charged and powerful and had repercussions." What to do with such an unanticipated response like the one Brandi offered to Luttrell? Each time Luttrell experienced the raw edges of an emotional connection with the girls, she embraced (rather than set aside) her emotions, but she did it in a way that enhanced her position as a researcher. In writing up her field notes for the book, Luttrell described her reactions, which she realized upon writing them down, were often defensive ones. Writing about them gave her the opportunity to consider more deeply the reasons for her reactions as well as reasons for the girls' reactions (or sometimes seeming nonreactions), and to recognize that researcher–researched relationships must undergo ongoing close examination before we can understand them in their complex, emotion-laced contexts.

A key aspect of the theme of respect and respectability had to do with money. The collages the girls made to represent themselves included numerous references, both in words and in images, to money. Each collage was another artifact—an item that was not the girls', but something attached to them—that invited a reflexive accounting rather than serving as an "elicitation device" which Luttrell viewed as throwing the power dynamic askew (Luttrell, personal communication, April 15, 2019). The collages showed how Luttrell's themes materialized and became emblematic. In this way, for Luttrell and for the girls, the collages evoked a narrative worth investigating further.

At first glance, Luttrell figured the references to money were connected to consumer culture. Upon further reflection about the way the girls interacted with one another, she linked the strong awareness the girls have about the cost of material comforts with how out of reach those comforts were. She examined her own reactions to the girls' focus on money, recognizing in her reactions class-based differences of fiscal perception, which she described as middle-class insecurities about money compared with working class envy and fears for survival. Luttrell wrote about these episodes with a desire to shift the focus away from the assumption of over-consumerism to the candidness of class- and race-based conditions that persist in drawing young working-class people toward consumer goods.

Luttrell's goal was to move readers from judgment to interest (Luttrell, 2003). She recognized that humanity is prone to judgment and wanted her narrative to balance that judgment with curiosity. She accomplished this by adapting cultural anthropologist Robert LeVine's (1982) person-centered ethnography through the girls' subjective "cultural dramas" of themselves as "problems" (p. 7). Luttrell's analysis focused on identifying groups of emotions, both expressed and suppressed, the patterns of meanings within and across the girls' narratives, and the social divisions and cultural conflicts, including the ways those impact inner or more personal conflicts. In an effort toward honest disclosure, Luttrell shared her awareness that her own emotions and perceptions would shape what she heard and saw when interacting with the girls.

Emblematic episodes from the book highlighted the themes of difficulties and discomforts within qualitative research and writing that aims to represent research participants. Luttrell mentions an incident in which a girl's "showing" pregnancy precipitated discomfort on the part of an educator. The broader train of thought is this: the appearance, language, interactions, and the very cultures of students can cause unease in teachers. What do those of us who bear the heavy mantle of dominant representations do to move around this obstacle of ours? Luttrell recommends engaging in "activist ethnography," which promotes the ability of both researchers and the researched to "change how they see themselves and are seen by others" (p. 147). Emblematic episodes that demonstrate the impact of this change came in abundant form during the performances (short improvisational skits) the girls created about some aspect of their pregnancy stories that exemplified the complexities of their multiple positions. Luttrell devised a "freeze" element of the performances in part to invite multiple or contradictory perspectives from the girls. Playing with the format of the skit provided opportunities for the girls to pause the skit and interact with the players. This "freeze game" became a compelling addition to the improvisation and to Luttrell's research as the girls made it their own. Girls froze the skit when it wasn't going the way they thought it should, when they wanted to pause and ask one of the players to defend her actions, or when they wanted to add their own stories to the ongoing skit. As narrated in the book, the skits served to guide readers into the girls' personal story worlds, taking us to doctor's appointments at the moment of confirming pregnancy, or to an interaction with a parent just finding out that their daughter is pregnant. Aside from learning intimate details about the girls' lives, readers were immersed in the social and personal drama of the girls' experiences. Through these dramatic reenactments, readers shared the girls' experiences in the context of the larger public realm of discourse around teenage pregnancy. Playing with the girls' storytelling gave Luttrell a window into their thoughts, feelings, and interests. Luttrell underscored the value of being open to incorporating new elements as part of research methods and representational writing. Through these elements of play, Luttrell embedded the micronarratives of the girls within her narratives of them in the broader social contexts of their lives.

The complexities of who the girls are in the context of being a teenager and being pregnant huddle together within their dramas. They portray themselves in skits as vulnerable, strong, self-deprecating, and self-affirming with respect to their identities as sexual beings. Their skits also include sensitive or shaming nurses, passive or self-advocating girls, and understanding or frustrated mothers, incorporating a wide range of positive and negative feelings around self-esteem and responsibility.

For one of the skits, Luttrell played the part of a pregnant girl. During her interaction with a girl who played an aggressive nurse, Luttrell was pushed to tears. The girls thought she was playacting and applauded. When they realized her tears were genuine, they told her that she might feel like crying, but she should never let on. This playacting incident lets readers in on a painful, yet valuable, aspect of the process of ethnography. Because the girls are vulnerable as pregnant teens, their outward strength cannot be taken at face value. The play opens a raw space for the girls to air their disavowed feelings. In the process of reflecting on the incident, Luttrell leverages the positionality that catapults her away from her familiar ideas about her own identity. She exposed her vulnerability by being seen as emotionally wounded by the incident and was advised by the girls to tough it out. Through this play-incident, Luttrell guides readers to examine our own expectations of respect and how that might clash with similar feelings in those we research.

Throughout the ethnography, situations arise in which the girls "playfully engaged one another in dramas over goods and resources" (p. 157). At times, Luttrell is drawn into these dramas as if pulled by the current of the girls' approval. She feels she ought to be able to navigate these situations with reflexive aloofness, and wonders whether such interactions taint her interpretation or enhance her understanding of the girls. One example of this type of play illustrates what Luttrell found disturbing. Whenever one girl who had left the program visited, bringing her baby, one of the other girls would tease the baby, taking away its bottle or blanket and pretending to keep it or hide it. The other girls sometimes teased the baby to the point of the baby crying, which prompted Luttrell to intervene. She didn't understand why they would tease the baby in the ways they did. The girls returned the bottle or blanket, saying that they were just teasing, and it didn't mean anything. Still, Luttrell was disturbed by this type of teasing play with the babies. She was uncomfortable with the way the girls and mothers allowed the teasing to persist and examined her cultural bias over this type of play, prompting this reader, and perhaps others, to do the same.

Luttrell's description of the teasing play relates to the term "fussing," which Luttrell uses to describe interactions the girls had with teachers or with each other when they were self-advocating. Shirley Brice Heath (1983) discussed fussing among African American children, particularly girls, in her book about language differences in communities in the same area of North Carolina. Heath described fussing as a way for young Black girls to assert personal authority to bring out issues that needed to be aired in the social community. She observed that between the ages of 2 and 4, children were encouraged to challenge adults who tease them. Girls were especially encouraged to fuss at adults and other children. Heath ventured that fussing at someone allowed for a kind of practice at establishing the independent self via language while building a cohesive community that upholds a collective sense of right versus wrong. She emphasized that low-income Black children might need such training to stand up for their future employment or economic rights. Luttrell's work with the girls echoes this account and cites relevant references to unpack teasing situations in the broader social context. She concludes that such interactions are built on complex inner and outer factors, including how each girl may see herself individually as well as how class, culture, race, and gender identities play significant roles. As the girls prepare to cross the boundary into parenting, their opening bids for respect as responsible mothers can prove fragile, as can the sensibilities of experienced researchers, as they write about strong, yet highly vulnerable research participants.

These emblematic episodes or specific details within the episodes are bridges between the worlds of the researched and the larger universe of what it means to be human. As researchers and narrative writers, we can accept the challenges of writing about people in complex ways rather than portraying them in idealistic ways. At the same time, following Luttrell's lead, we can accept the challenges of knowing ourselves as writers, including our natural tendencies as storytellers. With feedback from peers and from Caroline on my optional writing piece for this class as well as from my writing piece for the scene assignment, which follows this chapter, I recognized elements of my writing that sought to right a wrong or to lead readers down a comparable path. Such portrayals feel overly narrativized to me now after reading and reflecting on Luttrell's work in light of the narrative topics we explored in class and during the collaborative process of writing this book. Narrativizing is the necessary process of shaping the raw material of research into narrative form, but in that process entire sets of biases deserve wary consideration, including, but not limited to: the bias of what the researched wish to say, the bias of what the researcher wishes to say, and the bias of what and how readers may interpret. As writers of our research, the warp of the data threads we collect are interwoven by the weft of the narrative, completing a fabric representation of a world apart from our own and yet of our own making. The work of Wendy Luttrell and my myriad interactions with it: reading and rereading it, discussing it with peers and professors and with the author herself, and now writing about it and receiving constructive feedback on that writing, provide an ample and effective practice for that weaving.

Drafts of Writing

Kat's SCENE Paper/First draft

"She's waiting." Rain's tone is biting as she yanks her hair back and binds it with a purple, tie-dyed kerchief. She's talking to the two boys, Arthur and Harrison, who are guffawing, heads bent over a page in a glossy, grayscale graphic novel.

Arthur glances up, meeting my gaze through sandy-colored bangs. Harrison jerks his head up, sweeping from Rain to me, his mouth open. I flash them my would-you-mind-terribly smile. Harrison closes the book and shifts it to his lap. Now, I have the complete attention of all seven children, five girls, two boys, combined 4th and 5th grades middle level reading group. Seated around the rectangular wooden table, they seem uneasy, lumpy and restless. My legs don't fit under the table, so my torso is facing them while my folded legs are bent sideways like some plastic, action-figure

Envisioning and Embracing

teacher commandeered on the spur of the moment and stiffly posed to fill in because a properly-fitting teacher couldn't be found.

"I want to give some instruction about our focus over the next few weeks," I say. "We're going to do things a bit differently. We are still working on reading fluency. We have modeled that and have our bookmarks with fluency tips. Now, we're going to work on measuring our fluency by timing how long it takes to read a certain number of words." I talk for about two minutes longer, showing them sets of non-fiction reading passages with line-by-line word counts, the two-minute sand timers, and the recording sheets where their partner will write the name of their reading passage and calculate their words-per-minute counts. They voice a few clarifying questions about exactly what they are expected to do for the next forty minutes. Their questions ebb. They seem eager to get started.

Rain abruptly asks, "Why are we in the bad group?"

"We are in the *reading fluency* group," I correct.

"But we're all bad readers." She pauses after the statement, but none of the others raise a challenge. "I'm the worst," she adds, not quite under her breath. Her head droops toward her neon pink folder. One thumb flips the readings in the folder over and over as if she's preparing to shuffle a deck of cards.

"Rain . . ." I start, but she interrupts.

"When will we be able to join the best reader group?" she pleads, making me feel like a wicked witch, tethering these students to the grubby ground of dusty reading fundamentals while their classmates fly to the lofty heights of advanced literary bliss.

'What if I say never?' The thought bursts out of my subconscious in a flash. Along with the thought comes a picture of Annette, the fifth-grade teacher, dark, bouncy curls draping her shoulders, her slim legs crossed, wiggling one ankle-booted foot. She's looking at the faculty administrator and saying, "I just think these children deserve a chance to soar. To not be held back for once." Annette means the best reader group. To Annette, the group of children sitting before me are undeserved fetters, unsightly carbuncles that hamper the progress of the Great Reading Ship to the Future.

"Rain, what we can best do with our time together," I say with mantra-like cadence, "is focus on what helps each of us become better readers."

Rain is hard on herself and quick to complain, but I've never seen her give in to despair.

"If you have no more clarifying questions," I say, "let's spread out to practice."

Arthur and Harrison push back from the table and head to one corner of the classroom. Olivia, Savina, and Elin open the folders and begin reading the titles of the passages. Malai and Rain slump at the table. Rain twirls a rectangular, pink pencil eraser. Malai, one fist propping up her chin, stares at a National Geographic book as if wishing herself into the wilderness scene.

The three fifth-grade children could be cast as ugly ducklings. Each reads at about grade level, but most struggle with multisyllable words, and all have quirks that make reading aloud a challenge. Rain gets anxious and hesitates, rereading words she has read correctly. "Did I read that right?" Malai pronounces every word with the careful precision of a bilingual Thai-English speaker. But if she reads too quickly, she'll have a limited idea of what she read. Harrison reads with an irregular staccato beat, as if the text is riddled with hiccup cues. But he can recall exacting detail without looking back at the text. As for the fourth-graders, they are all advanced for their grade level, but it would not serve Rain well if I point this out.

What salve could I apply to this unseen wound, this accurately imagined slight? Are they better off believing they are underperforming readers or confronting the knowledge that they are the odd birds in a flock of perfect readers who may rise best without them?

Olivia, Savina, and Elin have moved to the rug near the bookcase, continuing to look over the reading passage choices. "This one's about an Okapi?" Savina asks Elin. "Am I saying that right?" Elin shrugs, tossing back her blonde braid coming loose from a thin green ribbon. They look at me and I nod.

"Okapi? O-ka-pee?" shouts Arthur from across the room. "Haha . . . o-ka-peeeeee."

"It's a really weird animal," Olivia says, ignoring Arthur.

"Weirder than Harrison?" Arthur echoes back, evoking a snort from Harrison.

"Arthur, that will do," I say. "First, apologize to Harrison for the unkind remark, then to Olivia, Elin, and Savina for the rude interruption, and then focus on your own work please." He complies and the boys settle down to reading aloud to one another. As a group, they are well behaved, earnest with both mirth and discipline.

* * *

I set Rain to work with Malai, listening in and making notes about multisyllable words I can add to our on-going word study.

"Mrs. M.," says Harrison, coming over to me. "Um . . . Arthur read the whole . . . passage, but, but, the timer is . . . still going."

"The sand didn't run out yet," clarifies Arthur, holding up the slim hourglass as proof, just as the grey sand runs out. "What should we do?"

"Hmmm . . ." I say. Most of the readings I handed out were one or two grade levels low to give the students some initial success. I have higher level readings, but don't want to turn the practice into a competition. "What do you think you could do? Do you have any ideas?"

"Oh . . . oh . . . ah . . . we could . . ." Harrison's vocal hesitations often indicate deep thinking going on. "We could start . . . again at . . . the beginning."

Envisioning and Embracing

"But, how would we know how many words total?"

"Just add them up. I know what . . . to do." Harrison informs Arthur.

"Or, we could start on a second reading. Should we, Mrs. M.?" asks Arthur.

"Completely up to you. Your decision," I declare. They head back to their seats, tip the timer over and Arthur starts reading again as Harrison follows along with his own copy.

"Mrs. M., the sand's still running but Elin's done," calls Olivia from across the room.

"We just had . . . that happen," says Harrison, "We're going . . . to start on . . . a new reading at the . . . end and see how it works."

"Oh okay," says Savina. "We can try that."

"Yeah, or just start over again," he adds.

I like their support of and trust in one another. Malai calls time is up for Rain.

"There were words I didn't know," said Rain. "Can I read it again? I know them now."

"That's not fair. If you know the words, you'll get further," says Malai, tilting her head.

I remind them fluency isn't a race to read as quickly as you can. It's about pacing and smoothness. Rain and Malai agree to re-read if they want. Rain wants to keep practicing the same reading over and over, which is good for improving fluency, but perhaps not so good for her persistent anxiety. The students work steadily through a couple of readings. Before long, they figure out that the numbers in the lower right corner of each reading are a grade level. They ask if I have higher level readings. I open my accordion file and spread out readings from grades three through seven. Most take readings from each level.

"Grade seven is hard!" declares Savina. "I'm glad I'm just fourth grade."

"I can do 63 words per minute at grade six," says Olivia. "And I'm a fourth grader."

"I'm making my goal five hundred words per minute," declares Arthur.

I don't tell the fifth graders what Fountas and Pinnell recommend for oral reading fluency numbers for the beginning of grade five. They all have ability and interest enough to reach the goal I have in mind for them. I also don't tell them that if they can raise their reading fluency high enough, they might have a chance at joining their grade five classmates.

After twenty weeks of practice, all three fifth graders and two of the fourth graders are spot on or above grade level for reading fluency. However, the oral reading fluency assessments I hand to the fifth-grade teacher don't seem to please her. She measures their reading fluency for herself. We meet again with the faculty administrator.

"I don't know how else to say this," Annette intones, "they've all made significant gains in fluency. Their vocabulary is stronger. Even Malai has better comprehension."

The faculty administrator commends me. I nod, but am distracted by the realization of taint or disbelief, or is it fear, in Annette's voice. She leans forward, her flowered afternoon-tea dress and its numerous petticoats flounce over her knees as she crosses her legs. "The thing is, Harrison still hesitates if there's a word he's unsure of and his voice is just not as smooth as it could be. Malai and Rain both need to build their vocabulary. Their pronunciation of multisyllabic words is frequently awkward, and I'm not sure Malai's comprehension will continue to keep up. Rain still gets so anxious, too."

The faculty administrator asserts herself. "Annette, we were hoping the fifth graders could all be together for reading skills."

Annette leans forward even more, "Oh, I know. It's just that we're working on very advanced things like characterization, and having deep discussions about gender roles, and we're also doing a lot of writing about our own thoughts."

"And you think Harrison, Rain, and Malai could not benefit from that work?" I ask.

Her delicate hands cross, one over the other, the top one squeezing them together. "Well no, but as I said before. I just think these children deserve a chance to soar. To not be held back all the time. We started a new book last week. I couldn't possibly get those three caught up with it, and I don't want to make them read it for homework. It's a hard book. The class is together so much of the time and they are so considerate of their peers most of the time."

Considerate. Yes, of their *lesser* peers, apparently. Inclusion be disgraced. "Well, they're not ability grouped for math or any other subject, is that right?" A leading question.

"Exactly. I'm *so* glad you understand." Which led nowhere.

"I do understand," I say. "Here's what I suggest. Tell me what book your group is reading, I'll get them caught up with chapter summaries, and then they can join you."

"Oh, that would be difficult. We're already halfway through the book."

My mind leaps into the abyss of derision. Fortunately, my mouth is only teetering at the edge of that sarcastic cliff. Halfway through a book they just started last week? There are more holes in this Great Reading Ship to the Future than a block of Swiss cheese.

Annette's ankle begins a miniature jitterbug. Her gaze displays openness, her brows raise up. Is this true villainy or fear of dealing with children who are unusual? Or a bit of both? In any case, what benefit would the children draw from being wedged in where they're not wanted?

"Okay, so I'll continue to work with these three fifth graders," I say. "I would like to have them read the same books as your group is reading, except we'll read key excerpts only and focus on vocabulary development."

"That sounds great," Annette replies, leaning back with a cheery smile.

"I'm going to have them take key scenes and vocabulary from the end of the book and write a five-to-ten-minute play. My group can perform for your group after we finish the book."

"Oh my, how will you be able to do all that? That's a lot of memorizing."

"No memorizing. They'll be reading, demonstrating their excellent reading fluency."

Annette sinks back into her chair, eyes fluttering in slow beats. "Oh."

Kat's Scene Paper/revised draft

27 Feb 2019—Revised 8 May 2019

"She's waiting." Rain's tone is biting as she yanks her hair back and binds it with a purple, tie-dyed kerchief. She's talking to the two boys, Arthur and Harrison, who are guffawing, heads bent over a page in a glossy, grayscale graphic novel.

Arthur glances up, meeting my gaze through sandy-colored bangs. Harrison jerks his head up, sweeping from Rain to me, his mouth open. I flash them my would-you-mind-terribly smile. Harrison closes the book and shifts it to his lap. Now, I have the complete attention of all seven children, five girls, two boys, combined 4th and 5th grades middle level reading group. Seated around the rectangular wooden table, they seem uneasy, lopsided and restless. My legs don't fit under the table, so my torso faces them while my legs are bent sideways, folded like some plastic, action-figure teacher commandeered on the spur of the moment and stiffly posed to fill in because a properly-fitting teacher couldn't be found.

"I want to give some instruction about our focus over the next few weeks," I say. "We're going to do our reading fluency differently." I explain that we are going to measure fluency by timing how long it takes to read a certain number of words. I show them sets of non-fiction reading passages with line-by-line word counts, two-minute sand timers, and recording sheets. They voice a few clarifying questions about exactly what they are expected to do for the next forty minutes. Their questions ebb. They seem eager to get started.

Rain abruptly asks, "Why are we in the bad group?"

"We are in the *reading fluency* group," I correct.

"But we're all bad readers." She pauses after the statement, but none of the others raise a challenge. "I'm the worst," she adds, not quite under her breath. Her head droops toward her neon pink folder. One thumb flips the readings in the folder over and over as if she's preparing to shuffle a deck of cards.

"Rain . . ." I start, but she interrupts.

"When will we be able to join the best reader group?" she pleads, making me feel like a wicked witch, tethering these students to the grubby ground of dusty reading fundamentals while their classmates fly to the lofty heights of advanced literary bliss.

'What if I say never?' The thought bursts out of my subconscious in a flash. Along with the thought comes a picture of Annette, their fifth-grade teacher, dark, springy curls draping her shoulders, her slim legs crossed, wiggling one ankle-booted foot. She's looking at the faculty administrator and saying, "I just think these children deserve a chance to soar. To not be held back for once." Annette means the best reader group. She makes a good point, but it leaves behind the mixed feelings my group is struggling with.

"Rain, what we can best do with our time together," I say with mantra-like cadence, "is focus on what helps each of us become better readers."

Rain is hard on herself and quick to complain, but I've never seen her give in to despair. Arthur and Harrison push back from the table and head to one corner of the classroom. Olivia, Savina, and Elin open the folders and browse the passage titles. Malai and Rain slump at the table. Rain twirls a rectangular, pink pencil eraser. Malai, one fist propping up her chin, stares at the wilderness scene on the cover of a National Geographic book. I stifle the temptation to imagine myself away from the work ahead. I consider each child and ask myself if I have demanded too much of them.

How would most teachers cast these three fifth-grade children? Each reads at about grade level, but most struggle with multisyllable words, and all have quirks that make reading aloud a challenge. Rain gets anxious and hesitates, rereading words she has read correctly. Malai pronounces every word with the careful precision of the bilingual Thai-English speaker she is. But if she reads too quickly, she'll have a limited idea of what she read. Harrison reads with an irregular staccato beat, as if the text is riddled with hiccup cues. But he can recall exacting detail without looking back at the text. As for the fourth-graders, they are all advanced for their grade level, but I'm not sure it would serve Rain well if I point this out. What salve can I apply to this unseen wound, this accurately imagined slight? Are they better off believing they are underperforming readers, or should I work harder to help them understand that a range of skill is present in any group of readers?

Olivia, Savina, and Elin have moved to the rug near the bookcase, continuing to look over the reading passage choices.

"This one's about an Okapi?" Savina asks Elin. "Am I saying that right?"

Elin shrugs, tossing back her blonde braid coming loose from a thin green ribbon. They look at me and I nod. I set Rain to work with Malai, listening in and making notes about multisyllable words I can add to our on-going word study.

"Mrs. M.," says Harrison, coming over to me. "Um . . . Arthur read the whole . . . passage, but, but, the timer is . . . still going."

"The sand didn't run out yet," clarifies Arthur, holding up the slim hourglass as proof, just as the grey sand runs out. "What should we do?"

"Hmmm . . ." I say. Most of the readings I handed out were one or two grade levels low to give the students some initial success. I have higher level readings, but don't want to turn the practice into a competition. "What do you think you could do? Do you have any ideas?"

"Oh . . . oh . . . ah . . . we could . . ." My observations of Harrison indicate his vocal hesitations are due to deep thinking going on. "We could start . . . again at . . . the beginning."

"But, how would we know how many words total?"

"Just add them up. I know what . . . to do." Harrison informs Arthur.

"Or, we could start on a second reading. Should we, Mrs. M.?" asks Arthur.

"Completely up to you. Your decision," I say. They head back to their seats, tip the timer over and Arthur starts reading again as Harrison follows along with his own copy.

"Mrs. M., the sand's still running but Elin's done," calls Olivia from across the room.

"We just had . . . that happen," says Harrison, "We're going . . . to start on . . . a new reading at the . . . end and see how it works."

"Oh okay," says Savina. "We can try that."

"Yeah, or just start over again," he adds.

I like their support of and trust in one another. Malai calls time is up for Rain.

"There were words I didn't know," said Rain. "Can I read it again? I know them now."

"That's not fair. If you know the words, you'll get further," says Malai, tilting her head.

I remind them fluency isn't a race to read as quickly as you can. It's about pacing and smoothness. Rain and Malai agree to reread. Rain wants to keep practicing the same reading over and over, which I know is good for improving fluency, but perhaps not so good for her persistent anxiety. The students work steadily through a couple of readings. Before long, they figure out that the numbers in the lower right corner of each reading are a grade level. They ask if I have higher level readings. I open my accordion file and spread out readings from grades three through seven. Most take readings from each level.

"Grade seven is hard!" declares Savina. "I'm glad I'm just fourth grade."

"I can do 63 words per minute at grade six," says Olivia. "And I'm a fourth grader."

"I'm making my goal five hundred words per minute," declares Arthur.

The students all have ability and interest enough to reach the goal I have in mind for them. I also don't tell them that if they can raise their reading fluency high enough, they might have a chance at joining their grade five classmates.

After twenty weeks of practice, all three fifth graders and two of the fourth graders are spot on or above grade level for reading fluency. However, the oral reading fluency assessments I hand to Annette, their fifth-grade teacher, don't seem to please her. She measures their reading fluency for herself. We meet again with the faculty administrator.

"I don't know how else to say this," Annette says, "they've all made significant gains in fluency. Their vocabulary is stronger. Even Malai has better comprehension."

The faculty administrator commends me. I nod, but am distracted by the realization of taint or disbelief, or is it fear, in Annette's voice. She leans forward, her flowered afternoon-tea dress and its numerous petticoats flounce over her knees as she crosses her legs. "The thing is, Harrison still hesitates if there's a word he's unsure of and his voice is just not as smooth as it could be. Malai and Rain both need to build their vocabulary. Their pronunciation of multisyllable words is frequently awkward, and I'm not sure Malai's comprehension will continue to keep up. Rain still gets so anxious, too."

The faculty administrator asserts herself. "Annette, we were hoping the fifth graders could all be together for reading skills."

Annette leans forward even more, "Oh, I know. It's just that we're working on very advanced things like characterization, and having deep discussions about gender roles, and we're also doing a lot of writing about our own thoughts."

"And you think Harrison, Rain, and Malai could not benefit from that work?" I ask.

Her delicate hands cross, one over the other, the top one squeezing them together. "Well, no, but as I said before. I just think these children deserve a chance to soar. To not be held back all the time. We started a new book last week. I couldn't possibly get those three caught up with it, and I don't want to make them read it for homework. It's a hard book. The class is together so much of the time and they are so considerate of their peers most of the time."

Considerate. Yes, of their *lesser* peers, apparently. Inclusion be disgraced. "Well, they're not ability grouped for math or any other subject, is that right?" A leading question.

"Exactly. I'm *so* glad you understand." Which led nowhere.

"I do understand," I say. "Here's what I suggest. Tell me what book your group is reading, I'll get them caught up with chapter summaries, and then they can join you."

"Oh, that would be difficult. We're already halfway through the book."

My mind leaps into the abyss of derision. Fortunately, my mouth is only teetering at the edge of that sarcastic cliff. Halfway through a book they just started last week?

Annette's ankle begins a miniature jitterbug. Her gaze displays openness, and her brows raise up. I know there is no villainy here. Annette is an excellent teacher who cares for the children in her class. I sense her unease about working with these children. Perhaps she feels less capable of helping struggling readers, or that she is responsible for their struggles to progress?

After all, she's been their teacher since first grade. In any case, what benefit would the children draw from being wedged in where they're not wanted?

"Okay, so I'll continue to work with these three fifth graders," I say. "I would like to have them read the same books as your group is reading, except we'll read key excerpts only and focus on vocabulary development."

"That sounds great," Annette replies, leaning back with a cheery smile.

"I'm going to have them take key scenes and vocabulary from the end of the book and write a five-to-ten-minute play. My group can perform for your group after we finish the book."

"Oh my, how will you be able to do all that? That's a lot of memorizing."

"No memorizing. They'll be reading, demonstrating their excellent reading fluency."

Annette sinks back into her chair, eyes fluttering in slow beats. "Oh."

Revision Notes

My intention in revising is threefold: to make my own interpretive statements more overt, to temper any sense of villainy of the 5th-grade teacher, and to convert some dialogue to prose. In addition, I have taken up several grammatical and construction suggestions from all reviewers. Overall, the goal is to make the piece flow more smoothly, allowing the reader to seep into the moment of the scene without overburdening overt cognition and imaginative memory.

QUESTIONS FOR FURTHER WRITERLY CONTEMPLATION

1. Consider re-examining moments in your life where you recognized one of your vulnerabilities, particularly those that touch upon distinctions in your positionality or identity. How could writing about one of these moments help you reflect on how to approach narration?
2. Choose a piece of writing about an underrepresented group of people and examine its claims of authority. What parts are presented and what parts may have been left out? How might you revise the piece to minimize the possibility of the misappropriation of the voices of the people in the group?
3. Why might it be difficult to distinguish between curiosity and judgment? How could an emblematic episode work to separate them?

My Hopes for Class Eleven, by Caroline

We had a great online conversation about the "Wrong Answer" by Rachel Aviv (*The New Yorker*, July 21, 2014), focusing a lot on the power of implicit analysis and other narrative craft topics. Her piece focused on the cheating crisis that brought a Georgia school superintendent down, but Aviv gives each character in the story so much complexity that it became a wonderful illustration of narrative description that eschews the constructs of heroes and villains. We worked online so that we could devote our seminar meeting time to the third writing assignment: the interview. I hoped to spend the entire evening with students reading aloud and sharing their thoughts on the interview process itself and the writerly challenges of representing the interview to an audience.

SUGGESTIONS FOR FURTHER READING

Behar, R. (1996). *The vulnerable observer: Anthropology that breaks your heart.* Beacon Press.

Lawrence-Lightfoot, S., & Hoffman-Davis, J. (1997). *The art and science of portraiture.* Jossey-Bass.

REFERENCES

Boo, K. (2001). After welfare. *The New Yorker,* 93–107.

Heath, S. B. (1983). *Ways with words: Language, life, and work in communities and classrooms.* Cambridge University.

Limerick, P. (1993). Dancing with professors: The trouble with academic prose. *The New York Times.*

Luttrell, W. (2003). *Pregnant bodies, fertile minds: Gender, race, and the schooling of pregnant teens.* Routledge.

Luttrell, W. (2010). Reflexive writing exercises. In W. Luttrell (Ed.), *Qualitative educational research: Readings in reflexive methodology and transformative practice.* Routledge.

Luttrell, W. (Ed.). (2010). *Qualitative educational research: Readings in reflexive methodology and transformative practice.* Routledge.

Luttrell, W. (2020). *Children framing childhoods: Working-class kids' visions of care.* Policy Press.

Levine, R. (1982). *Culture, behavior, and personality: An introduction to the comparative study of psychosocial adaptation.* Routledge.

CHAPTER 11

Wrong Question and Finding and Writing the Angle of an Interview

Kat Marsh (followed by drafts of paper by Kat)

At a national education conference that I attended 2 years ago, a large group of researchers and educators listened to a panel discuss what was presented as the five most challenging issues in education. One topic, the persistent opportunity gap between Whites and people of color, prompted a White male educator from Ohio to say, "I have poor White students in rural areas whose test scores always lag behind the state average. Are we even asking the right questions about this opportunity gap?" Immediate and loud responses came from people of color sitting at a nearby table. Their reply: "Do not start us back at the 'it's all due to poverty' stage. We've come too far in identifying the elements of systemic racism." Most thoughtful educators realize that the opportunity gap is surely influenced by economics, but even if it were possible to provide sufficient funding, solving the economic problem would be but a partial solution, not a sustainable answer to the larger question of why those rural people, and many more people of color, are poor to begin with. About 11% of White people in the Ohio gentleman's state are poor, whereas nearly 30% of Black people and more than 25% of Latinx people are poor (Larrick, 2019).

Indeed, you *will* get the wrong answer if you ask the wrong question. Yet, asking the right questions isn't an easy task, especially if you're a White person with little experience working with children of color or other marginalized groups. That is where an article such as Rachel Aviv's "Wrong Answer" (2014) provides invaluable insights, not only by presenting crucial information for those who are less knowledgeable about educational challenges and educational equity, but also by her narrative approach to offering data. As Caroline outlined in the syllabus for our seminar, narrative journalism mirrors ethnographic methods of inquiry, telling stories in order to better understand other human beings, other settings, and to translate (i.e., represent) that complex understanding to an audience.

Aviv used implicit analysis to guide readers to come away with an understanding of why moral boundaries might be crossed by teachers who want to give their struggling students a chance at success. Implicit analysis trusts the reader and works toward presenting or representing elements of a situation from which readers draw their own interpretations. Since we decided to devote our seminar time to sharing our interview papers, we had our discussion of the Aviv article on our online discussion board. My classmates did a superb job with their posts and with their permission I'm sharing their thoughts and words to examine some of the narrative craft topics Aviv employs in her article.

My classmates pointed out that while Aviv provided facts about educators in an Atlanta suburb who changed student answers on state standardized tests, she avoided explicit analysis and characterization, allowing readers to gather for themselves a more complete picture of the situation. My classmate Rebecca Redlon pointed out an example of implicit analysis when Aviv wrote that Governor Sonny Perdue's panel investigating the erasures "concluded that there had been no coordinated effort to manipulate test scores, a finding that Perdue called 'woefully inadequate'" (p. 62). Rebecca wrote, "Here she [Aviv] provides the panel's conclusion and another person's analysis of the conclusion." Aviv does not need to draw her own conclusion, or even to point out whether the panel or the governor is right or wrong. Aviv trusts readers to draw their own conclusions. My classmate Jeanne Lima asserted that although Aviv provides explicit information, she also provides the individual lenses of the people in the story. For example, Jeanne pointed out that Aviv shares that "Half of the homes in the neighborhood are now vacant" (p. 57), followed by the nicknames (e.g., Jack City) the students had for the neighborhood because of all the armed robberies. Jeanne wrote, "We view the armed robberies through the eyes of the middle school students . . . at the same time we are horrified by their environment because we see it as they do." Because I don't believe there is a single neat truth guiding readers to develop their own interpretations, using implicit analysis is more valuable than insisting that readers agree with one version of truth. When we'd discussed implicit analysis in an early seminar meeting, Caroline commented that it's powerful quite because it "lets people's words speak for themselves."

Aviv also uses small moments as a bridge to the larger universe of meaning, another narrative craft topic that previous chapters have focused on. In another discussion post, Allison pointed out that the educators in the article start out photocopying test questions to reassure themselves that their students are prepared for the test. As time progresses, the educators become a team, erasing answers to ensure modest improvement in order to avoid having the state shut down their school and to give the body of students some sense of success. Allison Horváth-Tucker wrote, "What started as a small and tentative moment, captured through Aviv's use of descriptive imagery, completely morphed into a huge scandal." In response to Allison's post, Caroline agreed that escalation was a theme that came through and that Aviv "rendered the escalation in a way that felt so true to human nature." What

Aviv does so well with her rich and vivid representation of all the people involved is to shed nonjudgmental light on the moral players within education. As Boo (2007) points out, narrative reporting can "engage the public, almost against its will, in crucial questions of meritocracy and social justice" (p. 14), bringing tough issues into a space where situations and people can be described with the richness and uncertainties of all their multiple facets.

Writing about people with such attention to complexity avoids what in our seminar we called the "heroes and villains trap," something we were encouraged to work against as we wrote about our interviews with a stranger. Aviv does this particularly well, as another classmate, Thelma Goldberg, pointed out in an online post. "I experienced many highs and lows when reading this article," she wrote, "and [Principal] Waller is just one of the many complex characters in this story. Aviv managed to paint him as constantly evolving from good guy to bad and, in the end, she frees him from the villain trap and we see him as yet another victim of a greatly-flawed system." My classmate Garo responded to Thelma with agreement and added that one of the middle school teachers, Damany Lewis, could have also fallen into the villain trap, except, Garo Saraydarian wrote that Aviv included Lewis's difficult "childhood in Oakland and his gifts as a teacher and his dedication to his students," providing "a more nuanced . . . representation of a very human situation." In a later response, Caroline agreed that through avoidance of the heroes and villains trap, Aviv helps readers to see "the ways that the macro works to diminish the moral agency within the micro context . . . to see the sociological factors of our lives more clearly."

Aviv presents in a humanistic way the bigger picture of the pressures these teachers experienced, maintaining a level of sentiment without sinking into sentimentality. Garo suggests that in Aviv's conclusion that follows the postscandal life of teacher Lewis, "the reader is not forced to feel sad and hopeless over Lewis's struggle to find a job and meaning." Garo quotes Lewis' commentary that, "Education let me go" (Aviv, 2014, p. 64). In reply to Garo's post, Rebecca summed up Aviv's conclusion of the postscandal life of teacher Lewis in her online discussion post as effective "because it traced the outer edges of the ripples effected by the pressures on teachers to cheat. The ending is poignant and eloquent without dipping into sappiness." Aviv simultaneously provides some closure to the narrative of the situation and the people involved and leaves readers with multiple thoughts to consider rather than a precanned and definitive conclusion.

INTERVIEWING

The online discussion of Aviv's article allowed our 11th class meeting to be devoted to discussing our writing assignment, "Portrait of a Stranger." The assignment elicited various reactions from classmates, since it contained the provision that the interviewee must be a stranger, preferably someone from a different walk of life. Caroline's goal for the assignment was for us to interview and report that interview so that a reader would feel as if they, too, had met and had a chat with the interviewee. I am fairly certain that many of my classmates shared my own trepidation at this assignment, perhaps echoing sociologist Wendy Simonds' (2001) thoughts in an essay Caroline had given us the week before: "I talk to strangers, and then I write about what they tell me. And it still frightens me" (p. B14). For many of us, the first obstacle would be to figure out how to locate a stranger. Avigail Shimshoni expressed this conundrum well in a postclass reflection, where she wondered, "Is a stranger simply somebody I have never met before, someone I might have met but do not know too well, or someone who is totally different from myself?" I, like most of my classmates, counted on connections I had with people I already knew to locate my stranger. I secured an interview with a woman, disabled for several years after a car accident, who had asked my husband, a volunteer at Spaulding Hospital, if he would be able to repair an exercise machine in her home. Other classmates relied on chance encounters, former acquaintances, connections developed from previous writing assignments, or ongoing research connections. For some, arrangements fell into place without difficulty, while others had a hard time finding and connecting with their stranger.

In preparation for the interview assignment, we'd read a number of essays and articles about interviewing. I wrote down some open-ended questions. I'd done practice interviews for my foundational qualitative research courses the year before, but for those assignments I'd interviewed fellow teachers, people I had worked with and knew fairly well. For this interview, I had only the briefest bits of information: a woman in her 90s—a former "Rosie the Riveter" during World War II—who lived with and helped care for her daughter, who had been seriously injured in a car accident several years ago. I was worried about encountering sensitive topics such as those that might be related to the car accident. The interviewing chapter that Caroline provided from Michael Patton's (1982) book provided advice about good follow-up questions. His example of follow-ups to open-ended questions got at the subtleties of the art of interviewing. Consider the difference between "How satisfied are you with . . ." and "How do you feel about . . ." (p. 169). The former narrowly focuses the interviewee onto the concept of satisfaction, while the latter raises the more general concept of feelings. I found Patton's explication of that distinction hugely helpful.

I can admit it was a challenge to describe the two people—mother and daughter—present when I conducted my interview. I had set up the interview by email with the daughter, who used a wheelchair after being in a car accident several years prior. She had lost her husband in that car accident, and I was initially interested in how she had handled such a dramatic change in her life. In the confirming email, she didn't consider her own life that interesting and suggested I interview her mother instead. I could not realistically plan out time to interview each of them, so I chose to take the daughter up on her suggestion. The daughter was present and openly involved during the interview, a situation which may have led her mother to remain at a surface level when telling her story. Additionally, when I arrived, the daughter had neglected to tell her mother that I was coming. The mother, caught unaware and put on the spot, did not seem uncomfortable, just surprised and thus, felt unprepared. Because her daughter was present, I sensed that the mother was telling what she thought her daughter wanted me to hear rather than what I might have heard had we been alone. I feared that I would not find a way to get at the "information that is locked inside people's heads" (p. 66) that Zinsser (1994) had discussed in another handout we'd studied for this assignment. Despite my worry about being overborne by the daughter, I did capture the essence of the mother's remarkable story of becoming a welder during World War II instead of going to business school as her parents had wanted. She also told many small, fascinating details about her childhood—what it was like to grow up in her isolated rural neighborhood with neighbors depending on one another, her experiences in a one-room school, and much about the local people (iceman, farmer, baker, peddlers of a variety of wares) in her life in a small town in central Massachusetts.

The challenge of this assignment came in writing up the interview, which entailed not only what journalist John McPhee (2014) (another handout) describes succinctly as "selection," but also the tentativeness of wondering, as Simonds (2001) does, whether the interviewer is no "more than an intruder, a voyeur, a manipulator" (p. B15). Caroline provided guidelines for discussing our interview processes during class. She suggested we describe who we interviewed and why, what challenges we had, how we went about finding an angle in representing our interviewee's story, writing challenges we encountered, and how we solved them.

Figure 11.1. Interview Guidelines

Give the context of the interview.

Who did we interview and why?

What challenges did we face in setting up and conducting the interview and how did we resolve them?

How did we go about finding an angle in representing our interviewee's story?

What challenges did we encounter in writing up the interview and how did we resolve them?

Learning from my classmates about their interview experiences, I echo Avigail's postcourse reflection that "we had a lot to talk about the process and experience of the interview as well as the writing itself." Rebecca's postcourse recollection was of impressions, but her words capture the essence of the challenges we faced: "How Garo threaded the needle of hero-worship; how Allison tried to temper her own bias against what her interviewee stood for . . . how Krysta exposed her own feelings of awkwardness . . . how you [Kat] handled the insistent presence of an intrusive second . . . Thelma's struggle to find someone to interview . . . Avigail's images of the interview setting, where she was surrounded by art the interviewee used to teach." I would add Garo's sharing of a recorded clip of his interview so that we could hear the colloquial language and unique tones of his interviewee, things that would not have come across as well in written text alone.

Our challenge was finding an "angle" or "slant" to frame what we had heard and experienced during the interview and, for most of us, finding it was more challenging than we'd anticipated. I had in mind what McPhee (2014) wrote about a writer's "responsibility to be fair to the subject, who trustingly and perhaps unwittingly delivers words and story into the writer's control" (p. 53). I did feel as if I had succeeded in making "it possible for the person being interviewed to bring the interviewer into their world" (Patton, 1982, p. 161). Yet, I did not want to simply recount what my interviewee had said because I worried that the result might feel mundane to readers. I had captured nothing that was not already familiar to me and did not know how to make the interview write-up feel "strange" or "real" so that it would be optimally interesting to a reader. I also wanted to write in a way that if my interviewee were to read my write-up, she would feel seen and understood with regard to what she had shared with me. As Simonds (2001) asked about writing up interview data, "how does one guarantee a nonexploitive, beneficial experience?" (p. B14). I valued this woman's life and stories and wanted my reader to value them, too. I owed my interviewee, who had given me her time and trust, a vivid and compelling representation of who she is.

I had recorded the interview and transcribed it, listening to it several times to ensure that my transcription had captured all the words, tones, hesitations, as well as the silence of pauses. It was then that I dealt with the ache of what on earth to write. What was the intriguing angle here? As journalist McPhee (2014) put it, "Once captured, words have to be dealt with. You have to trim and straighten them to make them transliterate from the fuzziness of speech to the clarity of print" (p. 53). McPhee's article contained solid recommendations about how to use pronouns, how to handle a speaker's repeated words, and the benefits of including indirect discourse, a paraphrasing that remains true to the speakers' words. It was less of a struggle for me to decide to trim out the small nonwords that indicated their pauses, perhaps to stop and think. I understood that in some cases these little "ums," "hmms" or "ahs" could be valuable additions to help readers understand places where the interviewee may have paused to collect her thoughts, recall events, or indicate reticence to speak. However, I also recalled an incident from my high school days in which I was one of eight graduating seniors selected for a group interview by the local newspaper as a graduating high school senior. I had no specific understanding of why I was selected to participate. The newspaper reporter asked us basic questions such as what our plans were postgraduation, what our aspirations were, and how well prepared to achieve our goals we thought we were. When the article appeared in the newspaper, I was dismayed to see that the reporter had left in all of our "ums" and similar hesitations. Though I don't recall any quote specifically attributed to me, I felt that the overall impression in reading our quotes made us appear lost, uncertain, and incapable of securing the futures we so hopefully, if hesitantly, expressed. I was determined not to allow that impression to creep into my own interview work. Initially, I wrote up every story my 94-year-old interviewee had told, hoping that themes and an "angle" would emerge, but the writing fell as flat as I had feared it might. In the end, I prefaced my interviewee's stories with parts of the story of my own interview process. As I look back, I recognize the high degree of writing craft needed to bring to life the woman with whom I'd sat down one afternoon in the spring of 2019.

Bringing out the most compelling parts of people's narratives takes not only strong interviewing techniques, but a keen sense of the message coming across from the interviewee. Vivid visual description is a crucial starting point because it helps create a picture in the reader's mind. I used details of what the women were wearing blended with how they were moving rather than simply listing how they looked. I hoped to convey not just a picture, but a small movie in the reader's mind. Upon revision following Caroline's comments, I added phrases such as "seeming to" or "as if" to make places where I interpreted more evident, while at other times I passed my interviewee's own words directly to readers for their own interpretations. Because I was not alone with my interviewee, I was uneasy whenever the interviewee's daughter prompted her mother to tell certain stories. I shared my vulnerability about this dynamic in my write-up, my narrative because my own uneasiness seemed to serve as an objective correlative, highlighting the multiple tensions I felt in the presence of two people instead of one. Sharing this vulnerability about the presence of my "interview helper" suddenly provided me a possible explanation for the interviewee's initial reticence to speak to me. In my write-up of the interview, I wanted to offer readers an opportunity to consider the interviewee's relationship with her daughter as the context for the stories she chose to tell about her life. Without even quite looking for it, I had found my angle.

Drafts of Kat's Interview Assignment

Reminiscence of Community

Long silence greeted my bare-knuckled knock on the blue wooden door. I chose a more resonant spot and rapped again, glancing about for a doorbell. I worried they wouldn't hear me. Clara is ninety-four years old, and lives with her daughter, Laurie, who has been wheelchair-bound after a paralyzing accident some dozen years ago. I twisted the smooth, brass knob and called out a robust hello through the partly-open door. A voice asked "yes?", so I entered and turned a corner, spotting Laurie in a u-shaped alcove, her electric wheelchair just turning to face me. I gave her my name again and reminded her that we'd set up an interview a week ago. With her memory refreshed, she zoomed off down a hallway, telling me to follow.

"Mom, I forgot to tell you that I invited this woman to interview you," called Laurie as she zipped around to the right into a small space.

A petite woman with feathery white hair was bent over a rectangular table, sorting church flyers, newsletters, and envelopes. Clara looked up. "Interview? Oh my. What, now?"

Laurie explained our connection through a volunteer at Spaulding Hospital and repeated that I was here to do an interview. She declared we should go back up the hallway and sit in the living room. Clara looked over her work as if trying to memorize where she left off before accepting this interruption. I scurried back up the hallway because the motor on Laurie's wheelchair sounded close at my heels, but paused in the square living room, not knowing where best to sit in this neat and tidy space. Clara passed me in slow, graceful strides like a cruising swan. She sat on the couch and clasped one bronzed, wrinkle-weathered hand over the other. Laurie navigated her wheelchair around to face us. I settled into a chair halfway between mother and daughter. Laurie told her mother more about me, and then I chimed in to explain my purpose to Clara, who seemed caught off guard, not knowing what would be expected of her. When I had emailed Laurie to request an interview, she insisted I interview her mother instead. Balancing the awareness of imposing on Clara with the confusion of two potential interviewees, I took out my pen, notepad, and digital recorder and asked permission to audio record. Both women agreed. To work past the initial awkwardness, I tried out a conversational style, telling them about my own schooling history before I asked Clara if she liked school when she was a child.

"I can't think back that far!" Clara declared, smiling for the first time, the tint in her rectangular glasses too faint to hide the sparkle in her brown eyes. "Where did I go to school? In a very small town, South Hadley, Massachusetts. The high school is now the town hall." She crossed one leg over the other, canting forward in a relaxed hunch and adjusting the hem of her pullover sweater. Its bright blue stood out against the white turtleneck beneath and a small gold cross draped the two.

"How many kids were in your high school class?" Laurie asked, prompting her mother to add details, but shifting us into a more journalistic interview format.

"I think we started off with twenty. By the time we graduated the war was on and the boys were all off, drafted, or off to war. There weren't many left." She looked down at her hands, rubbing prominent knuckles exposed over thinning skin. An awkward hesitation followed, but I didn't interrupt her recall, and hoped Laurie wouldn't either. I knew from caring for older people in nursing assistant jobs when I was younger, that it could take time to get started with telling stories from long past. With her head still crouched, Clara slowly lifted her gaze and squinted at me. "Instead of going to business school like I was supposed to do, I signed up to be a welder in defense. I thought, my brothers were all off and I wanted to do my part. So, I signed up to weld."

Clara probably wasn't used to talking about herself, but her iron voice held a note of pride about making the choice to learn welding. I asked her to tell more about how signing up for welding came about. Still reticent to share with ease, Clara recounted the basics: an announcement at the school, requesting people to work in defense, mostly girls were left at the school, Clara and two girlfriends signed up. Laurie asked where they learned the welding and how long it took. Clara said they left school for a month and learned welding at a shop down in Holyoke. I asked Clara to describe the kinds of welding they did. She told me they did all kinds of welding, stick welding, overhead welding, but didn't add any description of the process, or the work. I didn't know enough about welding to ask a deeper question, so I paused again to see if she would add details. "I passed with flying colors," said Clara in a tone that held a note of surprise at her own skill. Following her lead, I asked if she had expected welding to be hard. She said she never expected to be good at something so intense and difficult, and the experience changed her view of herself. The welding company wanted her to move to Quincy, to work in the shipyards there, but her father said no. He wanted her to stay near home, worried that his only daughter (she had two older brothers), barely eighteen and just graduated from high school, would need supervision in the rough, man's world of a city shipyard.

Unwilling to defy her father, she stayed in the Holyoke area where there was plenty of war work for her to do with the other women, and a few men, who worked on anti-aircraft guns for the army, and then pontoon boats, which the navy used to support bridges as the troops deployed across Europe. Clara hardly fit the look of a Rosie the Riveter as Laurie called her mother. Her slight build and barely five-foot frame did not look capable of doing overhead stick welding. I asked her how hard the work was. "It was difficult to do and not everyone could do it," she said. She developed skills around having the right length of the welding stick material, how close to get to the sheets of metal when welding, and how much pressure to apply to make the most efficient welds. Of course, she had to be strong enough to hold everything up over her head for long hours. "It was interesting to me. I was good at it. I really liked doing it," she said, and then laughed suddenly, warming to a memory. "Smoke from the welding process got all over me. I'd come home and my mother would look at me and say, 'Couldn't you have done something else?' But I found it interesting." Her laughter faded to a light chuckle, followed by a long pause, as if the memory was all too fleeting. "As soon as the war was over and the boys came back, we got our pink slips," Clara said with a tone that failed to hide disappointment. Clara glanced over at Laurie, who was beaming at her mother's accomplishment. Later in a follow up email from Laurie, I learned that when the war ended Clara didn't want to go to business school, a choice that was being pushed by her parents who wanted her to have options to fall back on in case she didn't marry. She went to Western Union school near Washington, New Jersey and worked there at Western Union where she met her husband and later married.

Now that Clara seemed a bit more comfortable, I asked her to tell me about her childhood, describing what it was like for her growing up. "It was the best of times, before the war started. I really loved my childhood," she said, the war still framing her thoughts. Clara was born about midway between World War I and World War II. She described a small-town community where the neighbors were all close and she felt safe as a child walking around town alone. She'd head down to the empty lot to play baseball, or go to a neighbor's house and help them clean their house or do their hair. "Neighbors took care of one another," she said. She recalled a time when her mother was quite ill, and Clara came home from school to discover that her mother had been taken to the hospital. A neighbor was there waiting for her. The neighbor said, "Don't think you're not going to school because your mother is sick. Your father will be home to get you to bed. When you get up in the morning, you come over to my house and I'll have breakfast for you and your school lunch, and when you get home, I'll have your dinner."

Clara lamented that people don't "do for each other" like that anymore. Her childhood was a time when you could expect all types of people passing by or arriving at your home on a regular basis. "We had a milkman, and a ragman, and the iceman. We had an iceman that used to whistle and every time he came, we'd tease our mother that he was whistling to her and she'd tell us, 'You kids keep quiet!'" The milkman would come and leave the milk in glass bottles on the porch. In winter time the cream would freeze, leaving lumps floating on the top that the children scooped out with their fingers and ate. The baker would come along in his truck every few days, say what he had available, and her mother would buy his wares to carve out extra time in her busy day. The baker was a "very nice man" who let the children come into the truck to pick out something to snack on at no charge. Clara commented several times that she grew up in a world very different from today with so little direct experience with human interdependency. Her family had an old-fashioned icebox, the kind that you put ice in at the top, but because there wasn't room next to the ice, you couldn't freeze much food. For most of the growing season there was a local farmer who would come around almost every day. Her mother would go out and buy food right off the truck: tomatoes, cucumbers, beans, corn on the cob, lettuce, apples. The farmer had "everything you could want." Toward the Fall they would buy extra, and Clara's mother would can jar after jar of vegetables to carry the family through the winter.

"When we were kids, we sometimes tried to steal something. An apple maybe." She chuckled, recalling innocent childhood mischief.

"Would they let you get away with that?" I asked.

"My mother wouldn't. She'd say, 'He has to make his living, too. And maybe he'd lose his living if we took something from him without paying.' That's when you were really reprimanded. You felt ashamed at it. And you hoped that your Dad didn't hear about it." If Clara's Dad heard one of his children had done wrong, he'd go behind the stove where he kept a leather strap, a razor strap. I asked if all kids were kept in line that way back then. In line, yes, she answered, but it was more the awareness of their place and what was expected. "People just don't do what's expected these days," she said. Clara recalled the Works Projects Administration (WPA) that was active during the Great Depression. "Men didn't just not work," she declared. "The WPA put in a wading pool in our town, and did all the sidewalks in town. It wasn't just a job. You were hired to do projects everyone could be proud of." Clara wondered why we don't have something like that now. She lamented that some people just collect money from the government, which she is not opposed to, but there are projects that need to be done and people who need more than money. "The WPA helped people feel good about the work they did for the community." The pool is still there and still in use, something Clara saw as indicative of what's missing in today's American society: the idea of helping one another for the sake of community. I enjoyed hearing about Clara views, and agree with her that if we are willing to work past our awkwardness and get to know people individually, we might learn what the past has to offer us to create a better future for everyone.

Reminiscence of Community (revised)

(To reader: See if you can locate changes in text and determine why Kat made these changes.)

Long silence greeted my knock on the blue wooden door. I chose a more resonant spot and rapped again, glancing about for a doorbell. I worried they wouldn't hear me. Clara is ninety-four years old, and lives with her daughter, Laurie, a wheelchair driver after a paralyzing accident some years ago. I twisted the smooth, brass knob and called out a robust hello through the partly opened door. A voice asked, "yes?", so I entered and turned a corner, spotting Laurie in an office-like alcove, just turning to face me in her electric wheelchair. I gave her my name again and reminded her that we'd set up an interview a week ago. With her memory refreshed, she zoomed off down a hallway, telling me to follow.

"Mom, I forgot to tell you that I invited this woman to interview you," called Laurie as she zipped around to the right into a larger room.

An older woman with soft white hair was bent over a rectangular table, sorting what looked like flyers and envelopes. Clara looked up. "Interview? Oh my. What, now?"

Laurie explained our connection through a volunteer at Spaulding Hospital. She declared we should go back up the hallway and sit in the living room. Clara looked over her work as if trying to memorize where she left off before accepting this interruption. I scurried back up the hallway because the motor on Laurie's wheelchair sounded close at my heels, but paused in the living room, not knowing where best to sit in this neat and tidy space.

Clara passed me in slow, graceful strides. She sat on the couch and clasped one work-weathered hand over the other. Laurie navigated her wheelchair around to face us. I settled into a chair halfway between mother and daughter. Laurie told her mother more about me, and then I chimed in to explain my purpose to Clara, who seemed caught off guard, not knowing what would be expected of her. When I had emailed Laurie to request an interview, she insisted I interview her mother instead. Balancing the awareness of imposing on Clara with the confusion of two potential interviewees, I took out my pen, notepad, and digital recorder and asked permission to audio-record. Both women agreed. To work past the initial awkwardness, I tried out a conversational style, telling them about my own schooling history before I asked Clara if she liked school when she was a child.

"I can't think back that far!" Clara declared, smiling for the first time, the tint in her rectangular glasses too faint to hide the sparkle in her eyes. "Where did I go to school? In a very small town, South Hadley Falls, Massachusetts. The high school is now the town hall." She crossed one leg over the other, canting forward in a relaxed hunch and adjusting the hem of her pullover sweater. Its bright blue stood out against the white turtleneck beneath and a small gold cross draped the two.

"How many kids were in your high school class?" Laurie asked, prompting her mother to add details.

"I think we started off with twenty. By the time we graduated the war was on and the boys were all off, drafted, or off to war. There weren't many left." She looked down at her hands, rubbing her knuckles. An awkward hesitation followed, but I didn't interrupt her recall. I knew from caring for older people in nursing assistant jobs when I was younger, that it could take time to get started with telling stories from long past. With her head still crouched, Clara slowly lifted her gaze and squinted at me. "Instead of going to business school like I was supposed to do, I signed up to be a welder in defense. I thought, my brothers were all off and I wanted to do my part. So, I signed up to weld."

Clara probably wasn't used to talking about herself, but her voice held a note of pride about making the choice to learn welding. I asked her to tell more about how signing up for welding came about. Still seeming reticent to share with ease, Clara recounted the basics: an announcement at the school, requesting people to work in defense, mostly girls were left at the school, Clara and two girlfriends signed up. Laurie asked where they learned the welding and how long it took. Clara said they left school for a month and learned welding at a shop down in Holyoke. I asked Clara to describe the kinds of welding they did. She told me they did all kinds, including stick welding and overhead welding, but didn't add any description of the learning process or the work. I didn't know enough about welding to ask a deeper question, so I paused again to see if she would add details. "I passed with flying colors," said Clara in a tone that held a note of surprise at her own skill. Following her lead, I asked if she had expected welding to be hard. She said she never expected to be good at something so intense and difficult, and the experience changed her view of herself. The welding company wanted her to move to Quincy to work in the shipyards there, but her father said no. He wanted her to stay near home, worried that his daughter would need supervision in the rough man's world of a city shipyard.

Unwilling to defy her father, she stayed in the Holyoke area where there was plenty of war work for her to do with the other women and a few men who worked on anti-aircraft guns for the army, and then pontoon boats, which the navy used to support bridges as the troops deployed across Europe.

In my own mind Clara hardly fit the look of a Rosie the Riveter as Laurie called her mother. Her slight build and medium frame did not look capable of doing overhead stick welding. I asked her how hard the work was. "It was difficult to do and not everyone could do it," she said. She developed her skills and of course, she had to be strong enough to hold everything up over her head for long hours. "It was interesting to me. I was good at it. I really liked doing it," she said, and then laughed suddenly, seeming to warm to a memory. "Smoke from the welding process got all over me. I'd come home and my mother would look at me and say, 'Couldn't you have done something else?' But I found it interesting."

Her laughter faded to a light chuckle, followed by a long pause, as if the memory was all too fleeting. "As soon as the war was over and the boys came back, we got our pink slips," Clara said with a tone that failed to hide disappointment. Clara glanced over at Laurie, who was beaming at her mother's accomplishment. When the war ended Clara didn't want to go to business school, a choice that was being pushed by her parents who probably wanted her to have good options to fall back on in case she didn't marry. Instead, she went to Western Union school near Washington, New Jersey and worked there at Western Union until she married.

Now that Clara seemed a bit more comfortable, I asked her to tell me about her childhood, describing what it was like for her growing up. "It was the best of times, before the war started. I really loved my childhood," she said, the war still framing her thoughts. She described a small-town community where the neighbors were all close and as a child she felt safe walking around town alone. She'd head down to the empty lot to play baseball or go to a neighbor's house and help them clean their house or do their hair. "Neighbors took care of one another," she said. She recalled a time when her mother was quite ill, and Clara came home from school to discover that her mother had been taken to the hospital. A neighbor was there waiting for her. The neighbor said, "Don't think you're not going to school because your mother is sick." The neighbors pitched in to take care of her family and Clara thought nothing of it, as it wasn't unusual at all.

Clara lamented that people don't "do for each other" like that anymore. Her childhood was a time when you could expect all types of people passing by or arriving at your home on a regular basis. "We had a milkman and a ragman and the iceman. We had an iceman that used to whistle and every time he came, we'd tease our mother that he was whistling to her and she'd tell us, 'You kids keep quiet!'" The milkman would leave the milk in glass bottles on the porch. In winter time the cream would freeze. The baker would come along in his truck every few days, say what he had available, and her mother could buy what she needed. The baker was a "very nice man" who let the children come into the truck to pick out something at no charge. Clara commented several times that she grew up in a world very different from today where people have so little knowledge of their neighbors.

Her family had an old-fashioned icebox, the kind that you put ice in at the top, but because there wasn't room next to the ice, you couldn't freeze much food. For most of the growing season there was a local farmer who would come around almost every day. Her mother would go out and buy food right off the truck: tomatoes, cucumbers, beans, corn on the cob, lettuce, apples. The farmer had "everything you could want."

"When we were kids, we sometimes tried to steal something. An apple maybe." She chuckled, recalling childhood mischief.

"Would they let you get away with that?" I asked.

"My mother wouldn't. She'd say, 'He has to make his living, too. And maybe he'd lose his living if we took something from him without paying.' That's when you were really reprimanded. You felt ashamed at it. And you hoped that your Dad didn't hear about it." If Clara's Dad heard one of his children had done wrong, he'd go behind the stove where he kept a leather strap, a razor strap. The children had a clear awareness of their place and of what was expected of them. Clara recalled the Works Projects Administration (WPA) that was active during the Great Depression. "Men didn't just not work," she declared. "The WPA put in a wading pool in our town, and did all the sidewalks in town. It wasn't just a job. You were hired to do projects everyone could be proud of." Clara wondered why we don't have something like that now. "The WPA helped people feel good about the work they did for the community." The pool is still there and still in use, something Clara saw as indicative of what's missing in today's American society: the idea of helping one another for the sake of community. I enjoyed hearing about Clara views, and agree with her that if we are willing to work past our awkwardness and get to know people individually, we might learn what the past has to offer us to create a better future for everyone.

QUESTIONS FOR FURTHER WRITERLY CONTEMPLATION

1. In what ways are narrative journalism and ethnography similar? Different? Setting aside differences in potential audiences, is one superior to another in representing the complexity of human beings in particular settings?
2. Consider a piece of writing that has a clear hero or villain (or both). What could be added to that narrative to avoid the "hero or villain" trap? Would that addition rescue or ruin the piece? Why?

SUGGESTIONS FOR FURTHER READING

Josselson, R. (2013). *Interviewing for qualitative inquiry: A relational approach*. Guilford Press.

Mishler, E. (1986). *Research interviewing: Context and narrative*. Harvard University Press.

O'Reilly, M., & Dogra, N. (2017). *Interviewing children and young people for research*. SAGE Publications.

REFERENCES

Aviv, R. (2014). Wrong answer. *The New Yorker*, July 21(20), 54–65.

Boo, K. (2007). Difficult journalism that's slap-up fun. In M. Kramer & W. Call (Eds.), *Telling true stories* (pp. 14–16). NY: A Plume Book, Penguin.

Larrick, D. (2019). The Ohio poverty report.

McPhee, J. (2014). Elicitation. (7).

Patton, M. Q. (1982). *Practical evaluation*. SAGE Publications.

Simonds, W. (2001). Talking with Strangers: A Researcher's Tale. *Chronicle of Higher Education, 48*(14), B14.

Zinsser, W. (1994). *On writing well: An informal guide to writing nonfiction* (5th ed.). HarperPerennial.

CHAPTER 12

Circle of Trust
Vulnerabilities Carefully Rendered

Rebecca Redlon and Garo Saraydarian

As we enter this final chapter of the book, we can't help but look back along the stream of our experience to see how we got here. Though perhaps clichéd, each of us is like a pebble tossed into the same narrative stream, causing ripples that lap the banks and even the edges of each other's ripples. We have moved away from each other and back again so many times—from the Narrative Writing for Qualitative Research classroom, to the tiny seminar room where the ripple of this book began to take shape, to the meetings on Zoom during the pandemic—and we toss ourselves into the stream anew each time, layering new ripples atop the old. Our individual lives have changed so much since we first gathered in that University Hall classroom at Lesley University, in Cambridge, MA, and yet we continue to share the impact that class experience had upon us. In this chapter, we reflect on the powers that limned the overall shape of the class and its collective and profound effect on a group of individuals whose lives and educational and professional experiences are so varied.

As it is with writing, the best instruction looks effortless. The truth of the matter is that good instruction takes as much thoughtful planning and tinkering as the strongest piece of writing. The care that Caroline brought to her construction of the scope and sequence of the class may not be apparent to any but those who participated, but we will attempt to share the value of her instructional leadership here, beginning with her text selection and sequence of assignments.

One of the subtle but powerful ways in which Caroline conveyed what she wished us to pay attention to was in her careful and strategic choice of a diverse set of texts. We learned about the craft of representing an interview or a scene through exemplars of qualitative researchers such as Barbara Myerhoff (1980), Wendy Luttrell (2003), and Anne Haas Dyson (1995). These texts would prepare us, by example, to practice particular narrative choices, especially as they relate to the deeply human aspect of rendering lives and lived experience in qualitative research. Yet the selections were not confined to those written solely by qualitative researchers; instead, they included works by historians, investigative journalists (Katherine Boo's pieces were class favorites), anthropologists, and documentary filmmakers, all of whom are "inquiring into the human condition, plumbing the same depths of insight and humanity that qualitative researchers within academia explore" (Heller, 2019, p.1). In spite of the differences in modality (from case study to documentary to journalism) and subject matter (Australia's aboriginal people, Wyoming cowboys, a community of elderly Jews in California, a family in Washington, DC), all of the texts offered complex representations of our shared humanity. These curated texts exemplified researchers who—avoiding the academic "cult of obscurity" (Limerick, 1993)—place an ethical importance on how their words represent their participants, people who all too often have been *mis*represented.

In addition to assigning texts to engage our hearts and minds, Caroline made an effort to vary the classroom experience by inviting guest speakers such as Michael Jackson and Wendy Luttrell; we watched films together and were able to have a postviewing conversation with Ilisa Barbash; and (though we didn't devote a chapter to our visit) we met at the Harvard Archives with an archivist who shared materials with us, giving us a taste for how archival research gets done.

Class readings dovetailed with writing assignments and were sequenced in a way that helped us build from one skill to the next. The first assignment was of a personal nature, and though it was listed on the syllabus as optional, we all completed it. Writing about a personal experience allowed us to dip our toes into the narrative stream; writing about something about which we were already expert gave us the chance to probe personal experience for meaning, and because we read these pieces aloud during class, we began to open up and learn about one another. Even those of us who were acquainted from taking previous classes together learned new—and sometimes surprising—details. Thus, this opening assignment bound us in a circle of trust and brought us together as a nascent community.

Each writing assignment, coupled with its weekly reading assignment, built upon the previous one, ensuring that we simultaneously deepened and broadened the complexity of our knowledge and our writing (see Chapter 4 for an example of how this worked). Writing assignments were not graded until we submitted a final portfolio and reflection on our work, which served to shift the focus of assessment away from *product* so that we could invest ourselves more fully in the *process* of writing. Each week, the iterative nature of writing and revising was underscored by the feedback we gave to one another in class and then online in our collaborative documents, and issues of craft were punctuated in "minilessons" delivered during class or in a handout.

All teachers have a particular "style" that, in part, marks their success—it is a slippery thing to pin down. And while Caroline certainly does have a signature way of conducting her classes (one of us describes her as "an approachable juggernaut"), her approach is deeply rooted in an understanding of adult learners. Eschewing the title of Instructor with a capital I, she made it clear that we were writers together, that she was sharing with us—in a collegial way—the tips and tricks she picked up on her own learning journey. This is a powerful stance and immediately resets the power dynamic in the classroom. While we were all eager for Caroline's feedback on our work and placed a high value on it, we also knew that in the end we were the authors of our work and had complete sovereignty over content and voice.

Genuinely caring about one's students is another mark of the strong classroom leader; that caring sets the tone for all. Though never stated outright, we knew we were meant to take care of/with one another. This is especially crucial in a class focused on writing, which is so personal to each of us. Caroline modeled rather than preached how to give and respond to feedback, how to be a helpful peer editor, how to open one's self up, and how to listen. Caroline's willingness to be vulnerable, to humanize herself as a fellow writer, not only engendered our trust in her but also in each other. A course such as this one depends on an environment in which students feel comfortable taking the risks of reading out loud as well as receiving *and* giving feedback. Not every course modeled on the one presented in this book will have the advantage of being taught by someone with Caroline's seemingly inherent sense of writing pedagogy. However, we hope the choices described here might help anyone establish the nurturing and trusting environment that writers need.

How does a close-knit community come to be? In the writing classroom, there are several things the leader can do to facilitate a sense of togetherness: insist on moving the furniture into a circular formation; ask people to step up to bring snacks; model caring in both deed and word; be welcoming; and be clear about what helpful feedback looks and sounds like. Caroline did all of these things, and we followed her lead.

Once set in motion, growing a community becomes a self-feeding circle. Because we engaged in seemingly mundane acts of collaboration—moving the furniture when we got to class, snacking together during a break—we came to know each other as people whose lives embraced worlds larger than the one we shared as doctoral students at Lesley. This interest burgeoned into a bona fide investment in each other's stories; when one of us was brave enough to read a personal narrative aloud, the rest of us listened intently. The act of listening then helped feed the growing sense of community and collegiality even further. In the listening, we came to know sacred things about our personal lives and experiences; we came to know one another as writers, to hear each distinctive writing voice, to feel each unique presence.

And so we came to write for one another; in essence, our sense of audience shifted from writing solely for an instructor for a grade to writing for our little community of writers. This is part of the elusive magic of writing groups: seeing the commitment and effort of a single classmate had the effect of making us all want to dedicate our whole selves to our writing as a way of honoring that person's hard work. In this way, we constructed a circle within a circle: the outer circle was the community that bound us together, and the inner circle was our own path toward improvement. These hoops that bound us were strong and brooked no entry to petty concerns like envy or one-upmanship. We viewed writing as the serious business of us all—we might be writing separately, but we were learning and improving together.

Who was this assembled class? Though we shared the same experience as doctoral students, we also brought other attributes to the group. We were dancers, actors, musicians, community organizers, wranglers, architects, educators all, and yes, some of us even identified as writers. Our lived experiences, our cultural experiences, and our expertise enriched the community that seemed to grow effortlessly around us and through us. These bonds were essential in our learning to respond to both our own and each other's writing, and it is a goal that we would recommend to anyone hoping to organize such a course. Through such a community we responded not only to the work of the writers, but to the writers themselves, focusing on what they meant to say and what the writing meant to them. And we only knew this because we knew each person. We learned intimate backstories that our classmates felt comfortable sharing with us and that informed their approach to writing and self-expression. We knew about Jeanne's love of horses, Rebecca's love of the woods and rivers of her home in Maine, Thelma's passion for tap dancing. And this knowledge gave us a deeper sense of how to help a colleague in the quest to meet their *own* standards of expression, not those of an impersonal, standardized rubric. Being in the writing circle elicited our most generous spirits and a willingness to suspend our own egos for the benefit of others, which then led to a desire not only to help one another produce the best work we could, but also to produce the best work we could for our audience.

One of the greatest impacts this course had on our writing was the change in our attitudes toward revision. What was before, at best, a task we were better at preaching to our own students than following ourselves, at worst, an excuse for procrastination that blocked further growth, became an act of re*visioning*. As opposed to being overwhelmed with how to begin revising, losing ourselves in seeming minutiae, we gained as a lodestone the aim of calibrating our writing so as to present a more honest picture to the reader. All drafts converged on whether our writing was a truer vision of a person, a scene, our own selves. And the writing craft we learned fit perfectly into this schema. Revision became for us as writers a way of caring for the people and scenes we represented.

We each experienced this new-found clarity in different ways. For some, specific technical suggestions stand out—sentences are too long, avoid comma-splicing, too many semicolons, don't overuse the passive voice, use more verbs and fewer adverbs. For others revising meant excising material; Thelma recalled being told to take out her entire introduction and to start *in medias res* because the story was not in the set-up but in the action. She learned that instead of spending time describing a scene she needs to describe what is actively going on *in* the scene. Her original introduction provided the scaffolding to get to that space in the story, but was now no longer needed. In the past Jeanne thought of herself as a "lone wolf" when it came to writing and revising. But here we moved from what Krysta described as an "I am listening but not really hearing" attitude of receiving feedback to one in which we actually heard other people's advice. Those of us with degrees in writing were used to writing classes in which the environment was much more competitive, making it difficult to trust the feedback of others or the revision process. Yet in this class, we learned to depend on each other, finding ourselves by losing ourselves in a supportive environment. We uncovered a uniqueness within ourselves that, ironically, we would not have found in a more competitive classroom culture.

A course such as this is helpful on many levels, as represented by the diverse ages, careers, backgrounds, countries of origin, and doctoral stages, from first-year to dissertation phase, that we were in. For those reaching the end of our coursework, the writing undertaken in this class had a direct impact on keeping the momentum going for qualifying papers and dissertations. On the other hand, first-year doctoral students benefited from the opportunity to cultivate their writing craft going forward in their studies. As a whole, seeing each other's dedicated work on revising made the process more transparent and hence doable; we saw the results that careful attention to feedback and constant revision produced in our classmates' writing.

All of us entered this class with previous writing experience, some from advanced academic coursework, others as graduate writing majors, and some from various professional genres. Thelma had for 10 years written for a dance magazine and remembers her experience with revision as being told by the editor to trim her writing to meet a specific word count. Denise was adept from her job at writing training manuals and curricula. Allison, an actor and stage manager, was immersed in scripts. However, through this class our previous writing experiences were transformed into a greater confidence and understanding of why and how we write. Because of the collaborative nature of the course, the audience for our writing assignments changed from teacher-centered to peer-centered.

We also realized quickly that turning in an assignment that was not quite up to the mark did not receive a low grade from Caroline, but was returned for revision. The expectation was clearly communicated that we were going to learn to write and that we were going to revise until we met a certain standard as opposed to simply checking off on a poor grade and moving on to the next assignment. This prepared us to be judicious recipients of feedback not only before a dissertation committee, but for our future life as published scholars. Responding to another is a form of relating to another, and through reading aloud to our peers and receiving immediate verbal feedback, or through peer-reviewing a specific classmate's paper, we received practice in both giving and receiving feedback. We gained the ability to discern what feedback we agreed with and what we could set aside, understanding that in our writing, though we may feel unprepared in opening up our drafts to critique, we will never be found lacking.

Now, Thelma's practice in this class with responding to other students' writing has placed her in a position where she is currently a reviewer of article submissions for a peer-reviewed journal. She has the confidence to be the person giving feedback and asking the right questions to improve the writing of others in her professional field. Denise has expressed the shift in her own writing through the metaphor of being a waitress taking orders. Before this class, she was in a situation of having to bring food to a table without knowing what was on the menu, and hence not knowing whether the customers were happy with what she brought out to them. Now, Denise feels she can approach writing reasonably informed of what is on the menu; she has gone from "trying to write for an audience when they know what I should be doing but *I* didn't know what I should be doing" to a skilled awareness of how she can better reach the reader of her research.

Writing and sharing about ourselves, along with the critical experience of offering and receiving feedback from our classmates, made us aware of the hidden complexities of human lives and the circumstances in which humans live those lives. In this class, we discovered where our voices belong in qualitative research and "academic" writing. As mentioned before regarding the optional assignments, writing one's own story down and then reading it aloud is more risky than simply talking about it. It requires more intention and consideration of how our words are transferred to another person, and how that person would receive, would *get* what one is trying to say. Especially because we were trying not to hide behind the armor of academic opaqueness, this caused us all at times to feel vulnerable, to face those previously listed fears of inadequacy as writers. Many of us believe we have become more honest writers, a difficult but necessary accomplishment. As researchers, we are now more willing to expose our own vulnerabilities to better convey the reality of those we are studying. Indeed, honesty often requires one to visit places in one's life that one would prefer to avoid. But if we wanted to be effective writers we knew we had to become reacquainted with these places. We were able to negotiate these tricky inner journeys through the concrete writing techniques we learned in this class and by reading researchers who exhibited this type of honesty, scholars whose writings, as Kat so eloquently expressed, are models of vulnerability carefully rendered.

For instance, the readings by Luttrell (2003) and Jackson (1995) presented us with writers who wrote about others from a place of privilege. What characterized these writers' research is a way of being vulnerable that is not whining for attention. Instead, it allows readers to see *themselves* in that vulnerability. Looking at the years that have passed since this class, some of us now in our dissertation phase or even newly minted PhDs, we see more than ever the importance of how to represent with integrity human beings who are not necessarily like us. We saw this with Luttrell's (2003) transparency in narrating the many times that her socioeconomic and White privilege came jarringly to the fore in her research with young pregnant high school students. Jackson (1995), a White man from New Zealand who has done extensive research in Sierra Leone and among Australian aboriginal communities, managed to locate himself in the wider conversation matter-of-factly as "born of privilege." For those of us concerned specifically with how we sit in various discourses as mostly White-presenting people, the class readings by these researchers helped us work through questions of how to think about representation and whether we have the right to tell the stories of other people. This was intimately tied to the type of writing we practiced. Upon watching the film *I Am Not Your Negro* (2016), Krysta could not *unsee* the potential to make writing more approachable and to open up academic thought to young people who might otherwise not have an entree.

The strategic pairing of readings and assignments drove home some very important—and often tricky—aspects of writing about other people's lives and experiences. The participants in our research are anything but passive; they are living, breathing, sovereign beings. We would argue that we are duty-bound to present them as more than one-dimensional, that they deserve our best attempts to portray them and their circumstances in all their shaggy messiness. Rebecca found this to be true in trying to capture the rich and complicated life of the hospice nurse she interviewed for our seminar assignment. Even in the interview, Rebecca felt the nurse's life pressing against the unnatural confines of the interview situation; the nurse's life was so much *more*, and the boundless energy of it could hardly be contained in the square box of the interview format. For Rebecca, such a life and work, prescribed as they were by such unknowable mysteries as death, deserve more than the "censorious hold of science writing" (Richardson, 2000, p. 960).

Some of us even changed our research topic as a result of this class, questioning "whose story needs to be out there?" "whose story isn't out there?" and, "what impact will [my research] have directly on the people I am writing about?" The focus here shifted from "what can I do for my project?" to "what can I do for the people?" Thelma observed that our writing assignments (especially the scene paper) helped many of us to realize that we were putting too much of ourselves into the scene—our jobs as qualitative researchers is to put those we are researching out there. At the same time, Avigail pointed out that researchers like Myerhoff did put themselves into their research. It was refreshing for us that there could be a place in research writing for care in highlighting a human story and that we could allow ourselves to become comfortable with the feelings we have toward the people we are researching. One loves the participants and that is why one writes about them.

Writing is a deeply personal act; to dig into one's mind and imagination for something novel and then to offer it up on the page with the goal of making it public is risky. We open ourselves up to possible criticism and ridicule. Most of us guard our thoughts, and PhD students are no exception—in fact, we might be more guarded than most, the stakes feeling high. After all, we are here because we *have an idea*; if that idea is laughable, then what does that mean for our purpose, our identity? Add the potential for criticism of our writing—the medium by which we communicate our ideas to others and the very thing that PhD students *do* more than anything else—and we build those bulwarks higher and higher. The proposition of sharing our work—our ideas and our writing—with others, can make a writing class feel daunting, if not downright dreadful. We all entered this class with at least a slight frisson of anxiety. We looked around and saw a roomful of capable, accomplished people, not counting ourselves among them. We certainly couldn't imagine how close we might become, how we would evolve into a caring circle of writing friends.

As has been emphasized throughout this book, our aim—Caroline's aim—was to respond to the beauty in each other's writing, focusing on the methods by which we could bring a situation or an idea as fully as possible in all its complexity to the reader. And just as our aim was to present the manifold of reality through our writing, our response to each other and ourselves as writers was predicated on the vision of each of us as complex human beings, with our own prior backstories, front stories, talismanic details, and experiences. These personal and writerly transformations unfolded gradually and subtly over the course of the semester. However, once felt, they became a common experience that drew our classroom community even closer. It was as if every week we shared a small flower that each of us had discovered blooming inside of us. Cupping our hands, we carefully passed our flowers around, enjoying their delicate scent, marveling anew at our own fertility, feeling the soft slip of each petal. "Here" we would say to each other in wonder. "Look what I found."

"Look what I found!" This conjures up for us the emotions Caroline described feeling while defending her own dissertation. The ripples of this personal discovery have moved ever outward, touching and transforming further shores. As an echo of Caroline's first encounter with the Tenderloin Women Writers Workshop, we too grew together into a community of writers. Caroline became our Mary TallMountain, whose wisdom and compassionate insight guided us as we became conscious of the wonder of the telling. Our hope is that this book will be a link in that lineage that began with the advertisement that caught Caroline's eye so many years ago in San Francisco. And so the story continues.

REFERENCES

Barbash, I., & Castaignh-Taylor, L. (Directors). (2009). *Sweetgrass* (film). The Cinema Guild.

Boo, K. (2001, April 2). After welfare. *The New Yorker*, 93–107.

Dyson, A. H. (1995). Children out of bounds: The power of case studies in expanding visions of literacy development. *National Center for the Study of Writing and Literacy*.

Heller, C. (2019). *Narrative writing for qualitative research* (course syllabus). Lesley University.

Eliot, T. S. (1920). *The sacred wood*. London: Methuen & Co. L.T.D.

Jackson, M. (1995). *At home in the world*. Duke University Press.

Limerick, P. (1993, October 31). Dancing with professors: The trouble with academic prose. *The New York Times*, Section 7, p. 3.

Luttrell, W. (2003). *Pregnant bodies, fertile minds: Gender, race, and the schooling of pregnant teens*. Routledge.

Myerhoff, B. (1978). *Number our days*. Simon & Schuster.

Richardson, L. (2005). Writing: A method of inquiry. In N. K. Denzin & Y. S. Lincoln (Eds.), *The SAGE handbook of qualitative research* (pp. 959–978). SAGE Publications.

APPENDIXES OF SEMINAR HANDOUTS

APPENDIX A

Revision Worksheet

Each writer needs to look at different things as she reads and revises her writing. Here are some questions to ask yourself. But a big key beyond these questions IS TO KNOW WHAT YOUR TENDENCIES ARE AND TO KEEP AN EYE ON THEM.

1. In a few words, what is the piece telling us? Is the meaning clear to you? Will it be clear to a reader?
2. Does the piece have a structure? If not, what sort of structure does the material suggest? Is it chronological, thematic, or something else? Do the beginning and ending share some link?
3. What images and metaphors do you use? Do they "hold water"? Are they related to the content? Are they woven into the piece in different ways?
4. Do you tend to say the same thing in three different ways? Choose one. Condense.
5. Strengthen your verbs. Verbs like *is, are, went, did, saw* are too general in many cases. Use clearer, more powerful verbs. Instead of "I went" did you actually *walk, sprint, hurry, stroll, or drive you aunt's car*?
6. Check your adjectives with a critical eye. Read the sentence with and then without the adjectives. If they don't add to the meaning, take them out.
7. Does the piece sound like you? Is it written in your own words? Are there phrases that sound familiar, that are clichés? If so, can you state what you mean in your own way? Can you find a truly unique description of something that happened, something that perhaps you alone can offer?
8. Read the paper aloud. Does the rhythm please you? Does the rhythm speed up at important moments? Does it slow down when you want to create a feeling of calm?
9. Look at the sentences. Read problematic sentences out loud one at a time. Do they make sense when read alone? Is each one smooth and coherent?

10. Now, how could you vary them? Start them differently. Try to avoid using the same construction too often. Switch clauses around for variety.
11. Vary the lengths of the sentences. If you tend to use long, even ones, throw in some short spicy ones.
12. Do certain words stand out as you read to yourself? If so, give those words careful thought. Is the word the closest one to your meaning? Look it up. Look up and consider other possibilities.
13. Check your punctuation. Do commas and periods give clues to the reader how to imitate your natural rhythm, when to pause, when to stop, whether thoughts are separate or continuous? Use quotation marks, bold print, underlining, italics, etc. only if the meaning is not clear without them.
14. As you wrote, did you think, "I'm thinking of trying this in my writing, but . . ." If you thought about it and liked the idea, you owe it to yourself to try it!
15. Last of all, what didn't you tell us? What did you leave out that really matters?

APPENDIX B

Taming the Chaos of Your Data

Choosing what to leave out and what to put in is a central task for a writer/researcher. Researchers give "form" to their data, by analyzing and interpreting it—i.e., examining it again and again to discover common themes and threads. Then, when writing up the study, we must be wise "communicators" of those threads, those moments that illuminate the meaning we have painstakingly analyzed and interpreted.

The following "hypothetical journey" is offered as a framework for thinking about this process, what one might describe as "taming the chaos." Annie Dillard, whose essay "To Fashion a Text" you'll have read for February 6, illustrates her own clarity about this difficult process in a very straight-forward way on p. 68 of her text: "I leave out many things that were important to my life but of no concern for the present book. Like the summer I spent in Wyoming when I was fifteen. I keep the action in Pittsburgh; I see no reason to drag everybody off to Wyoming just because I want to tell them about my summer vacation."

Ah, but Dillard makes this decision sound so easy! Let me warn you: It's not!

Let's look at it from the point of view of imaging how Katherine Boo might have made these sorts of choices. But you can do this exercise in the future for the work of Michael Jackson, Wendy Luttrell, Barbara Myerhoff, the documentary filmmakers we'll watch, and ultimately most important, your own (future) work.

The Imagined Journey of Katherine Boo that led her to know what to leave out and what to put in for "After Welfare":

PART I

- Ms. Boo has grown concerned with how welfare reform has affected the lives of families in which the head of the family (usually a mom) enters the work force. She is looking for families in this situation who can help her to better understand what this transition involves.
- She is troubled by the tendency of people creating welfare policy to overlook the daily lives of families going off of welfare and

to overlook important aspects of the general well-being of such families. She is concerned that policy treats the meaning of their well-being too simplistically. She wonders if having a job is truly enough for families who have been poor and on welfare to "enter the mainstream" with hope and safety. Do their lives become better?
- She is particularly interested in/drawn to the lives of families where the mother (single) has actually found successful employment and has entered the workforce fully. She is interested in understanding how the family manages under those circumstances.
- She is concerned that while she is a deeply thoughtful researcher, there is an inherent distance between her own rather privileged life and the lives of the people she wants to better understand. She is concerned with how to bridge her world and theirs—how to enter their lives as a researcher, and at the same time not commit to the page too much "self-consciousness" about "self" in the process of building this bridge between her life and theirs.

These, she considers her preresearch concerns or "preliminary questions/topics" of interest. Prior to any plans to go forth with more formal research, she is drawn to these questions and topics. She wonders. She questions. She cares. How might she proceed?

Important things for Katherine Boo to consider at this stage of her research process:

- Examine her commitment to these concerns, including her preconceptions about welfare-to-work families, poverty, etc. Is her interest part of a matrix of questions about the nature of women going off of welfare? Do one or more questions about the lives of families and welfare reform's impact on them intrigue her more than other questions? Does she feel guilt over her comparative well-to-doness? What is driving her and what assumptions does she carry? She should never stop thinking about these matters, and might consider keeping a running notebook of her preconceptions and how they change, how they are challenged or confirmed by what she learns once out in the field.
- Begin reading about welfare reform and its history so that she can paint a broad context for her reader and infuse her research with that knowledge. If she were writing a dissertation instead of a *New Yorker* article, she could include what she learns here in her literature review. It could be Chapter 1 of Boo's dissertation.
- Figure out circumstances that will allow her, in a thoughtful and useful way (to her research participants and to the world) to come to a clearer understanding of her concerns and questions.

Appendix B

PART II

With written and oral permission from family members, in which she lets them know exactly how the "data" will be used, and perhaps, too, offers to show them early drafts of her article, she might become participant/observer in the lives of a family or of several families that has/have gone from welfare to work. The research design/mode of her participation will be determined by what is feasible, do-able, with full consideration given to the family whose life world she enters *and* to herself. She may decide to live close to the pulse of their lives for a month or so, arriving in the morning and leaving at night; going on the bus with the children; going to school, to the mother's place of work; hanging out with the family and people close to the family on different occasions, interviewing the children, the mother, teachers, friends, etc.; taping some sessions; finding times during the day to take careful field notes. She may wish to create a rich portrait of this family. She should figure out a way to give back to the family for their time and energy: tutoring the children? Giving rides when needed? Doing legwork for them?

PART III

Katherine Boo now has 10 binders of notes and 50 audiotapes!
She feels like her research is not research at all. IT IS CHAOS!

If Ms. Boo keeps in mind that she is approaching this work because of her concern that little is known about the transition from welfare to work in the lives of families;
if she guides her initial "data analysis" around her questions/topics and the themes that emerge through examining her data;
if she maintains careful records, with rich description to offer context (i.e., she will not necessarily keep accounts of *everything*, but rather that which is pertinent to what she hopes to better understand);
if she analyzes her field notes and interviews based on these concerns, highlighting sections that seem to shed light on them, giving consideration that her notes may bring forth other themes, other concerns as time goes forward, and she may need to change and reorganize her earlier themes based on her discoveries;
as she analyzes her field notes and interviews and writes preliminary stories from them, she must renew her commitment to themes and stay true to them as she begins to write up the study. Perhaps they are the themes she began with; more likely they are somewhat altered, perhaps in a substantive way.

When she organizes and writes, the chaos can be controlled by keeping in mind these themes. She'll keep these at the forefront of her writing, building bridges between particular incidents/statements she writes about that illuminate these themes and their bigger significance (the wider universe of meanings).

AND HERE'S THE RUDDER, A DIFFICULT ONE, OF KEEPING HER SENSE OF CHAOS AT A MINIMUM: Perhaps during her time with the family, there was a dinner conversation about a baseball game that Dernard saw on television. She had the best time participating in this conversation, but ultimately, through discovering the deeper themes from the data, she knows that nothing about the conversation has to do with the themes. She must savor the conversation (just as Annie Dillard savored her trip to Wyoming!), and perhaps one day write a short story about it. But, she mustn't include it for this research study. At the writing stage of things, this is one major way to tame the chaos. She's going to love a lot that she sees and hears. She'll care a lot about moments and people that don't really connect to the themes of what her data is telling her, the story she's attempting to render for the reader. She must stay true to the concerns she wishes to illuminate! Little by little, the chaos will dissipate.

And she will create, from what she decides she must leave out and what she decides she must leave in, a readable and meaningful account true to the lives of Cookie, Dernard, Drenika, and Wayne, and the themes of their "After Welfare" lives that she has come to better understand.

Pictorial Version of "Taming of Chaos" will be presented in class (see Denise's pictorial version in Chapter 3).

APPENDIX C

Thoughts on Characterization

After reading Samuel Freedman's wise words about human complexity, you may want to look at a chapter in E.M. Forster's classic book, *Aspects of the Novel* quite simply called "People." (This gives away its applicability to qualitative research writing, doesn't it?)

While, of course, most "studies" of characterization involve thinking about character vis-à-vis fiction, they offer applicability to writing about the people we wish to characterize accurately and clearly in our research studies.

One of the greatest failures in characterization—one most all of us struggle with, but a particular trap for those involved in "Educational Studies," for we sometimes believe (and often rightly so!) that we see clearly how to make educational institutions work better—is forgetting, as Freedman points out, that all people are complex human beings. George Orwell had a wonderful phrase in his essay called "Reflections on Gandhi": *Saints should always be judged guilty until they are proved innocent.* Orwell's words, meant a bit tongue-in-cheek, I'm guessing, are a useful reminder that the interesting aspect of any human being is not saintliness or villainy, but, as Freedman reminds us, complexity.

The question that arises then is how to approach this complexity.

Here's one central hint that works in dual missions: Complicate people who do things that are not altogether commendable through sympathy. Complicate people who are always doing perfectly wonderful things through finding one or two of their flaws.

Impossibly good characters and impossibly not good characters don't lead the reader to the stuff of life and this is what we all want to know more about, in fiction, in poetry, in movies, in plays, in journalism, *and* in qualitative research in education.

Sympathy doesn't imply that everyone should be likeable; only that, as Freedman suggests, we must find out what motivates them—this depth will invariably bring forth a sympathetic feel. The Oxford Dictionary defines "sympathy" as the "fact or capacity of entering into or sharing the feelings of another." The writer/researcher must (to the extent possible, which, of course, is limited) try to feel the pain and pleasure and everything in between of a human being she tries to render on paper. This is an essence of characterization and an essence of thoughtful, humane research that endeavors to affect the reader.

In my own piece, *Optilenz*, for instance, I try to let you know that my father is a difficult man. But I don't leave it at that. By getting into the nature of his struggle to read and by invoking his "former self," full of promise and vitality, as well as his fortitude to overcome the limitations of his near blindness, I attempt to paint him as more than a crabby father, but rather, as a complex man, worthy of sympathy and regard, as well as a bit of impatience. For each of the people we aim to render, we have a different "referential totality" (remember the Dyson article about the boundaries she had to consider, and possibly expand, in order to understand how young children learn to write) to which to refer—decisions about how much context, history, etc. to offer so that the reader sees the person in his/her complexity, affected, as Freedman discusses, by "the macro" (backstory, wide lens), whatever that may be.

In the next week look at Cristina Rathbone's book with that in mind. Did she complicate her "people?" How? How will you choose to complicate the people who inhabit your scene paper due in a couple of weeks? And as you approach your own "interview a stranger" paper, how will you "complicate" your interviewee?

APPENDIX D

Sentiment and Sentimentality

SENTIMENT: does not soothe or comfort, does not prescribe, does not simply divert attention from intellect to emotion. Writing of merit involves both our emotions and our intellect.

SENTIMENTALITY is by nature simplistic, inviting readers to surrender the intellectual, the mindful, aspect of their makeups. For don't we soothe or comfort someone by saying, in effect, There, there, don't think about it? To do this, the narrative volume is raised and made artificially lush: our attention is asked to turn from the action itself to the sound and stridency of the prose and second, the location of the feeling, the source of the sentiment would have resided not inside the character, but outside, in the author imposing a heightened mood by turning up the dials. A trigger for sentimentality is lots of adjectives and adverbs.

Sentimentality is also the attempt to get some effect without providing due cause . . . it is emotion or feeling that rings false, usually because it is achieved by some form of cheating or exaggeration.

Rathbone, I think, is a master of sentiment and, working with a subject that is so hard NOT to sentimentalize, avoids it (I think) successfully. Study how she does this. Let's talk about it with her next week.

Objective Correlative: T. S. Eliot

The only way of expressing emotion in the form of "art" is by finding an "objective correlative"; in other words a set of objects, a situation, a chain of events which shall be the formula of that particular emotion; such that when the external facts, which must terminate in sensory experience, are given, the emotion is immediately evoked.

Note: How does the author make this happen? Through giving us the emotional richness of details rather than giving us the emotion itself. In his piece about storytelling in his family, Garo, for instance, gave us an amazing description of his throat swelling rather than saying "I hate imaginative play."

Index

The Adventures of Huckleberry Finn (Twain), 81, 86
An American Childhood (Dillard), 52
Assignments, 15–17
 optional prompts, 25
 "Portrait of a Stranger," 147–159
At Home in the World (Jackson), 56, 65–76
Authority, voice of, 65–66
Aviv, R., 145–159

Backstory, 30
Baldwin, J., 89, 92, 93
Barbash, I., 112–122
Behar, R., 47
Berger, J., 1, 2, 5, 26, 28, 31–32
Betit, K., 119
Boo, K., 28, 29–30, 40, 41, 42, 55, 96, 129

Cappetti, C., 79, 81
Carroll, L., 20
Castaing-Taylor, L., 113–114, 117, 118, 119
Cather, W., 85
Chaos, taming, 40–42, 173–176
 responsibility to reporting, 42–44
Characterization, 177–178
Chicago School of Sociology, 4
Chicago sociology, 81
Children Out of Bounds: The Power of Case Studies in Expanding Visions of Literacy Development (Dyson), 52
Circle of trust, 160–167
Cohen, L. H., 8

Community, 44–48, 55–60
 reminiscence of, 152–159
 study of, 95–110
Craft, reality through, 27–31

Data collection, 40
Death Comes for the Archbishop (Cather), 85
Dialogues, 83
"Difficult Journalism That's Slap-Up Fun," 40
Dillard, A., 42, 43, 52, 53, 55, 61, 96
Drafts of writing, 33–36, 45–48, 56–60, 71–76, 134–143
Dyson, A. H., 43, 52–54, 55, 96, 160

E.B. White: A Biography (Elledge), 21
Eliot, T. S., 55, 79, 181
Elledge, S., 21
Emblematic episodes (Pregnant Bodies, Fertile Minds), 128–143
Embracing, 124–143
Envisioning, 124–143
Ethan Frome (Wharton), 81, 86
Explicit analysis, implicit analysis vs., 83–84

Farrell, J. T., 81
Films, narrative gifts in, 89–93
Front story, 30

Geertz, C., 4
Goldberg, T., 41, 44, 47
Graduation-Siyum scene (Number Our Days), 102–109
Grammar, 31

Hardy, T., 86
Havel, V., 62–63
Heath, S. B., 133
Hemingway, E., 85
Hermeneutic Axis, 52

I Am Not Your Negro (file), 89, 92–93, 96, 166
Implicit analysis *vs.* explicit analysis, 83–84
Industrialization, 81
Information-gathering process, 40
In Her Own Time (film), 102
Interview, 147–159
  guidelines, 149

Jackson, M., 56, 65–76, 95, 99, 165

Lewis, D., 147
Limerick, P., 20, 125
Littman, L., 95–110
Lover Come Back (film), 91
Luttrell, W., 99, 124–127, 160, 165

McClintock, B., 8
McPhee, J., 149, 150–151
Memory, 47
Mencken, H. L., 81
Micro-process writing, 79–81
Myerhoff, B., 95–110, 160
Mytko, Denise, 45, 51, 53, 79, 119

Narrative gifts in film, 89–93
Narrative puzzles, 26
Narrative writing, 27
  reality through craft, 27–31
Narrative Writing for Qualitative Researchers (seminar)
  assignments, 15–17
  description, 7–8
  invitations and permissions, 19–22
  overview of, 8
  participation requirements, 10
  revision worksheet, 171–172
  schedule, 10–15
  topics, 9
Number Our Days (film), 95–110

Objective correlative, 55, 79, 87
Opportunity gap, 145
Optilenz (Heller), 30, 96

Park, R. E., 6
Parks, R., 81
Participants, research, 43
Patton, M., 148
Peck, R., 89, 90, 92
"Portrait of a Stranger" (assignment), 147–159
Pregnant Bodies, Fertile Minds (Luttrell), 125–143
  drafts of writing, 134–143
  emblematic episodes, 128–143

Qualitative inquiry, 56
Qualitative narrative study, 5

Rashida, S., 2
Reality through craft, 27–31
Redfield, R., 81
Referential Totality, 52
Remember This House (Baldwin), 89–91
Representational adequacy, 78–87
The Return of the Native (Hardy), 86
Revision, 31–32, 34–36
Richardson, L., 79–80, 81
Rilke, R. M., 20

Saco River, 51
Saraydarian, G., 53, 147
Scene consideration, 78–84
Sentimentality, writers, 54–55, 85, 179
Sentiments, 179
Shimshoni, A., 148
Shulman, L., 92
Simonds W., 149, 150
Sinclair, U., 81
Story, finishing, 33–34
Storytellers, ourselves as, 25
Sweetgrass (film), 112–122
  composition of images, 117–118
  human voice, 118
  story of, 113–116
  storytelling, 116–121
  with/without sound, 118

Index

TallMountain, M., 2
Taming chaos, 40–42, 173–176
   responsibility to reporting, 42–44
Taylor, D., 85
Tenderloin Women Writers Workshop, 1, 3
Thomas, W. I., 81
Threshold, 56–60
   writing process analysis of, 60–63
"To Fashion a Text," 43
To the Castle and Back (Havel), 62–63
Tuchman, B., 4, 20
Twain, M., 81, 86

Urbanization, 81

Visual description, 151
Voice of authority, 65–66

Wharton, E., 81, 86
Writers community, 44–48

Writing about ourselves, 25–26
Writing: A Method of Inquiry (Richardson), 79
Writing process analysis of threshold, 60–63
"Wrong Answer" (Aviv), 145–159

Zinsser, W., 149

About the Contributors

Krysta Betit has taught high school English and history in multiple states and districts for the last 15 years. Her PhD scholarship is centered on student experience and student input. She hopes to tell the stories both *of* the students and *for* them to reveal the depth and breadth of their lives through the voices they gravitate toward in literature and the choices they make in their own modes of expression. Her mother tells her that she wrote her first short story when she was 6. It was about a miserable young girl who found herself suddenly with a younger sibling and desperate to be rid of it—a thinly veiled autobiography.

Thelma Goldberg is an adjunct professor of tap dance and artistic director of the Dance Inn, a tap dance school in Lexington, MA. She writes and develops resources for tap dance education. Thelma started her doctoral studies with little confidence in her writing and now enjoys sharing her thoughts and observations through words. She feels that finding the right word or writing the perfect sentence is as satisfying as choreographing a great dance step.

Caroline Heller is the director of the individually designed specialization of the PhD program in educational studies at Lesley University and a professor in Lesley's Graduate School of Education. She is the author of *Reading Claudius: A Memoir in Two Parts* (Dial Press, Random House, 2015), which was recently reissued in paperback (2021) by Leapfrog Press in the United States and Can of Worms Enterprises in the United Kingdom.

Jeanne Lima is a computer programmer turned educator. She focuses her teaching and research on students who are challenged by school systems because of language and/or learning differences, illnesses, or perceived behavioral issues. She offers tutoring in a wide variety of subjects and disciplines to pre-K–college students. Her commitment is not only to students, but to their caregivers who may struggle to find a voice in the educational establishments in their communities. Jeanne's dissertation research focuses on linguistic theories to support English language learners in building disciplinary knowledge. She is an avid horseback rider, and this activity forms the background of some of her stories. She is earning certification in teaching others to ride in such a manner that they come to know the bond that the rider can develop with the horse. She is an avid reader of the classics.

Katherine (Kat) Marsh is a special educator who enjoys working to adapt supportive strategies to individual human beings. It's also important for her to adapt her approach to each of her students, meeting them where they are and helping them to grow as students and young humans. Kat lives her life so that she will always be a student, not only of academic topics, but of humanity out in the world. Kat sees writing not only as a way to understand her own thoughts, but to help others understand her thoughts and interpretations of the thoughts of others.

Denise Mytko works as a community college career coach and workforce development project manager and serves as adjunct faculty at Northeastern University. She aims to make career pathway planning better suited to all students as they explore and reach their life goals. Denise has been supporting students and professionals for more than 15 years. Her work has focused on professional environments, early childhood education, higher education, business, and nonprofit management. Denise is a first-generation college student and has seen herself as a nontraditional student since graduating high school. She knows the passion, hard work, leadership and impressive skill sets that nontraditional students bring to the labor market and is conducting research on the *personal, economic, and social impacts of nontraditional college students*.

Rebecca Redlon is a child of Maine and strives to reflect some of her state's finer qualities: independence, creativity, and fair-mindedness. She was raised by a family of teachers and in the company of older adults, all of whom were grand storytellers. She has been in the classroom—as student, as teacher—since she was 5 years old, and has been writing for nearly that long. Teaching writing has been the cornerstone of her career. Most currently she teaches college writing, and it is her greatest hope that her students learn to write to discover what they think. She is a leader of the Southern Maine Writing Project (SMWP), a satellite site of the National Writing Project, which seeks to nurture teacher writers and leaders. Her work with the SMWP has remained her anchor and buoy for over a decade. Working with the fine educators who pass through the SMWP institutes has led her to pursue an understanding of how writing can transform teaching practice and inspire teacher-leader identity.

Garo Saraydarian is a lecturer at MIT, where he teaches musicianship and aural skills. Garo also teaches in the master of music in music education program and the composition and theory department at the Longy School of Music of Bard College. His research interests include marginalized pedagogical practices, descriptive inquiry, critical theory, digital humanities, pedagogies of place, and philosophy of education. Garo enjoys studying Carnatic music and al-'ud. He is currently working on several projects, including computational analysis of makams in late-Ottoman printed music, an archive of Armenian folk music printed in post-genocide Beirut and Soviet Armenia, a solfege-based web application for dictation skills, and the application of descriptive review to music composition.

Avigail Shimshoni is a licensed architect in Israel and the United States, an adjunct professor at Lesley and an urban planner. Growing up in Israel, she fell in love with the richness and complexities that the intermingling of cultures and religions brought to every aspect of her life. As an adult she went from studying chemistry and East Asian studies (Japanese) in Jerusalem to architecture and city planning in Cambridge, MA, and eventually to Lesley University's PhD program in educational studies. Avigail has collaborated with colleagues in practice, teaching, and research in Japan, Korea, Israel, and the United States. In all she does, she infuses her joy of bringing together multitudinous ways of looking at our world. A poet and visual artist, Avigail always wanted to know how to paint with words.

Allison Horváth-Tucker is a theater artist who most recently taught at Nazarene College in Quincy, MA. She studied theater at Emerson College and has acted in and directed countless plays in the Boston area. She is focusing her PhD studies on the intersection of theater work and social justice activism.